Leone's Italian Cookbook

A. Laviosa

MOTHER LEONE

LEONE'S

Italian

COOKBOOK

by Gene Leone

HARPER & ROW, PUBLISHERS

New York, Evanston, and London

TO THE MEMORY
OF MY
BELOVED MOTHER

Contents

Illustrations follow page 116

Foreword

My friend Gene Leone, who is the only Honorary Member of the West Point Class of 1915, to which I also belong, has for years been noted as an outstanding cook. Now I learn that the recipes he has used so long and so successfully in pleasing the public have stemmed primarily from his mother's ability in producing delectable Italian dishes.

He has assembled all her instructions in the culinary art into this volume, publishing it as an "Italian" cookbook.

I am quite sure that his classmates, all of whom have so often enjoyed his 1915 picnic dinners, and anyone who has ever been a guest at the famous Leone's Restaurant in New York will be eagerly awaiting the book's appearance on the bookstands. All others, once they have discovered this treasure trove of Italian recipes, will enthusiastically join his present admirers in acclaiming him as "Master cook" and his book as a real service to the public.

Dwight D. Eisenhower

Gettysburg, Pennsylvania
June, 1966

ix

Introduction

In this book I've tried to present, in a form easily followed by the creative home cook, all the recipes that were most popular at my mother's restaurant through the years. And each recipe was tested by my wife, May, and me.

Since I was accustomed to cooking for from four thousand to six thousand people every day, reducing these restaurant recipes to quantities suitable for four to six servings presented quite a chore. Although difficult, I assure you it was a great pleasure, especially with May at my side still helping me after thirty-nine years of marriage.

It is always a joy to recommend the food and the wine that I have found most enjoyable and delicious throughout my many years in the restaurant. However I would like to point out that there is one and only one reason for my recommendations, and that is merit—merit based on taste, quality and enjoyment.

Salute e Pace.
GENE LEONE

1 🌺

About Mother Leone's Restaurant— and Your Kitchen

MOTHER Leone's restaurant was born on Mother's thirty-second birthday.

It opened with only twenty seats, grew to 1,500 seats and wound up a multi-million-dollar business.

Enrico Caruso, the great tenor and a close friend of the family, was among the guests at Mother's birthday party. He was the man most responsible for getting Mother to open her little Italian restaurant. *"Un piccolo posticino,"* as he called it.

Mother first heard of her party on the morning of her birthday, November 2, 1905. As Father was leaving the house he turned and said, "Oh, by the way, Luisa, for your birthday I've invited a few of our friends from the Metropolitan Opera House back here for dinner tonight after their rehearsal."

"Good," Mother said. *"Quanti saranno?"* (How many will there be?)

"Oh, there'll be a few," he answered. *"Una cinquantina."* (About fifty.)

This news might have floored the average housewife, but not Mother. She just smiled and said, "Fine. I'll get busy right away. I'll prepare a magnificent dinner for you."

The fact that she would be tied up all day in the kitchen didn't bother her a bit. There is nothing in this world that Mother enjoyed more than making her friends happy with her fabulous cooking.

She took my older brother Joe and me to Paddy's Market on the West Side to buy all the necessary foods. We borrowed the meatman's pushcart and returned with a load of fine foods.

1

Soon, Mother was cooking and singing away to her heart's content. It wasn't long before she had her sauces simmering and the cacciatora on the fire. The whole stuffed chickens, sprinkled with rosemary and covered with slices of salted pork and with some olive oil poured over them, were roasting slowly in the oven.

The kitchen and the wine cellar, where the party was going to be held, were filled with the grand fragrance and aroma of Mother's mouth-watering cooking. She was busy but happy.

She set to work preparing the many varieties of antipasto that only she could dream up. She made a sauce for her shrimps that was so delicious that I couldn't stop until I had dunked more than half a loaf of bread into it.

Sixty guests showed up. The walls of the big room were lined with barrels with wooden spigots to draw the wine. There were also thousands and thousands of bottles of the choicest wines on the racks against the wall, Papa being an outstanding vintner of his day.

A long table, the full length of the wine cellar, was loaded with many of Mother's antipasto dishes, ravioli, bowls of cacciatora, trays of whole roast chicken, platters of bugie, loaves of good-crusted Italian bread, Parmesan and Swiss cheeses and lots of luscious fresh fruits. My brother Joe and I were kept hopping, helping Mother take care of the guests. Joe was nine years old and I was seven.

Maestro Clemente de Macchi, a dear friend, a fine musician and an excellent vocal coach, took a glass of wine and a chicken leg over to the piano. Papa filled the wineglasses, and this was what everyone was waiting for. They knew that as soon as the maestro began playing, the room would be filled with music and singing. Sure enough, as soon as he went into an aria, the first to sing was the great Caruso.

As Caruso lifted his glorious voice in song, so did the thirty members of the Met's singing chorus. He sang an aria from *Lucia di Lammermoor* and his clear notes made the glasses on the table tinkle. The chorus, a fine collection of beautiful voices, had such power that the walls seemed to vibrate and I thought sure the streets were trembling. Any one of these chorus singers might have been a star in his own right had he had the opportunity and the funds to study under the great voice teachers of the time. Listening to the music was like having a private opera, sung by the world's greatest company, right in our own home.

This, to Father, was living. He was never happier than when he was surrounded by his friends, music, singing, Mother's delicious food and his own good wine. Papa, believing that he could sing, especially when the party was in his own cellar, often sang duets with Caruso. The way I remember it, half of the duet sounded wonderful.

The glorious singing continued and there was plenty of good food and good wine being consumed, too. Caruso, seated with Arturo Vigna, Giacomo Puccini, Pasquale Amato, Antonio Scotti, Giulio Gatti-Casazza and Nellie Melba, was enjoying a dish of Mother's ravioli. Delight was written all over his face.

"Luisa," he said in his booming voice, "like fine wine you improve with age. Tonight you have outdone yourself with this magnificent feast. I am convinced that you are the greatest cook in the world."

Then, for about the hundredth time, he asked when she was going to open that *piccolo posticino, solamenta per noi* (little restaurant, just for us).

Looking around, Mother visualized this as her own little restaurant. The wine was flowing, the food was delicious, the piano was playing, Puccini and Arturo Vigna were conducting the Anvil Chorus from *Il Trovatore*, and no one in the room seemed to have a care in the world.

This had to be a great moment in anyone's life, and Mother, who had a marvelous sense of timing, knew this was the chance to get what she wanted. To open a restaurant had been her dream for a long, long time. But Father, like most Italian husbands, didn't like the idea of his wife working. Whenever she spoke of opening a restaurant, which she did frequently, he said no. And Papa was *il padrone* (the boss).

When asked why he objected to her opening a restaurant Papa would reply, "Can you imagine my wife being in business for herself? *Sicuramente, no!* I certainly cannot."

But Mother now was really convinced and more determined than ever that this was to be her life and that this night, her birthday, might be the right time to have her dream come true.

She turned to Caruso. "Enrico," she asked, "do you really believe that I could run a good restaurant?"

"Certainly," he practically shouted, "with food like this?"

"Well then," she added, "let's ask Gerome right now."

Caruso took Mother by the hand and went over to Papa, who was singing the quartet from *Rigoletto* with Amato, Scotti and Melba. Father was singing the tenor's part and Caruso joined in "to help out."

When the serenade ended, Caruso threw his arm around Papa's shoulder, gave him a little squeeze and said, "Gerolamo, will you allow Luisa to open our little restaurant?"

Papa looked straight into Mama's eyes and asked, "Luisa, are you serious? Do you really want a restaurant?"

Mother never blinked an eye.

"Yes," she said, "do you think I've been joking all these years? There is nothing I want more."

Father hesitated and then continued, "Do you know what it means, how hard you'll have to work?"

Mother laughed. "Who's afraid of hard work? I love it!"

So, Papa gave his permission and Mother went on to follow his good advice. He told her, "Luisa, I will not have anything to do with your restaurant, but please remember, decorate the plate, not the place."

I always felt that he was on the spot and couldn't say no in front of all his friends. I also think that he never imagined Mother would go through with it and be so successful.

How wrong he was!

Caruso, as happy as anyone in the room, except perhaps Mother, took a large knife from the table and tapped it against a barrelhead. "Quiet, everyone. Fill your glasses," he said. "I have an announcement to make."

Raising his glass toward Father he boomed, "Leone has just given permission to Luisa to open our little restaurant."

Shouts of *"Bravo," "Bravo"* and *"Viva Leone"* echoed through the room.

Again Caruso signaled for silence. This time he raised his glass toward Mother and said, "Tonight is our dear Luisa's birthday and she has given us an evening never to be forgotten. I do not know what the future holds, but I pray that her restaurant will be filled to overflowing to match the kindness and generosity overflowing from her heart."

Everyone in the room drank to that. Maestro de Macchi struck up the famous drink song from *La Traviata*, "Beviamo, Beviamo, Beviamo," and again the walls shook. The party was in full swing

ɔma and, with a sweeping motion of his arm, said to his guests,
aradiso."

ile Papa was pouring Caruso's wine, the great singer patted
the backside and handed me a dime. I didn't know whether
ept it or not, but I did. This was the first money I ever earned.
ıgh the years, I got to see more and more of Caruso. Never did
e across anyone who enjoyed good food as much as he did. He
tremendous chest and stomach, and a great big heart, always
to help everyone.

en the opening night was over, Mother was really pleased. She
ıat everyone had enjoyed his dinner. We were all tired but it
een well worth it. When we went to bed that night I'm sure no
isualized that Leone's would eventually grow to the point that
ɔuld serve over 6,000 dinners on our busiest nights.

en Father died in 1914, Mother faced a critical time. She was
vith four healthy sons, the remnants of a good wine business,
-two rooms and her restaurant. The restaurant, which Papa had
sed in the beginning and never did like, was now going to keep
amily together. The restaurant, that is, and Mother's cooking
ıs.

ɔther Joe, being the oldest son, took over as head of the house-
I asked Mother what she wanted me to do and she said, "You
ɔome into the kitchen with me." I did and I loved it. Under her
ing hand I learned the difficult art of good cooking. I learned
a master. When it came to cooking, I always felt I had talent.
Mother was an absolute genius.

ır old friends from the Metropolitan Opera and new friends
the theatrical world continued to jam Mother's place. Then,
ld War I broke out in Europe and Joe enlisted in the Italian
Force long before America entered the war in 1917.

'hile Joe was in Italy we moved to larger quarters just down the
k from where we had been located. We more than doubled our
ng capacity, but had no trouble filling the place.

ɔe returned from the war with his bride, Antoinette, and again
. over as head of the family. We soon decided to move to our
ent location on West 48th Street, right in the heart of the
.trical district. The seating capacity was about the same.

lother was never too interested in expansion. All she wanted was
ace to cook and to take care of her friends. But before making the

and everyone settled down to relaxing and h:

That was how Mother started in the resta

For the next few months Mother was busie
room, on the first floor over the wine cellar,
restaurant. Behind the living room she set up
would spend so many days and nights doing
cooking.

Mother spent many hours making the prett
lovely draperies that decorated her restaurant.
linens in an effort to create a homey atmosp
customers to feel they were eating in their h
not in an impersonal restaurant.

Finally, on April 27, 1906, she opened fo
twenty seats—and they weren't nearly enoug
came in with a huge party and took over the
I had to run to the cellar and get some benche
extra guests. Some were seated on wine cases a
Her *piccolo posticino* was already too small.

Mother had no printed menu for opening n
first dinner:

Antipasto Supremo

Minestrone

Spaghetti or Ravioli con Ragout di

Roast Chicken or Scaloppine Pic

Green Salad

Cheese

Spumoni, Fat' in Casa (homema

Caffè Nero (black coffee)

Also on the dinner was a half-bottle of Papa':
with the meat course. The price of the meal? .
was the prevailing price at Ganfaroni's, one of the
rants of that time.

Mother, Joe and I waited on the tables. First we
ful antipasto; then Mother handed me a large hot
my first customer, Caruso. I carried the dish in bo
a big grin on my face placed the dish in front of h

move she asked the advice of a few of her old friends. One of these was Victor Herbert. He was enjoying one of her fine dinners when she said to him, "My sons want to move to a better location but I like it here. Would you come all the way uptown to 48th Street if I go there?"

He looked at her and said, "Mother, for you and your wonderful cooking I'd follow you to the ends of the earth!"

We moved to 239 West 48th Street and, sure enough, all our old friends showed up. Mother and her fabulous cooking made many new friends. It wasn't unusual to have W. C. Fields, William S. Hart, James Montgomery Flagg, Victor Herbert and George M. Cohan all dining at the same time.

Nor was it unusual for Victor Herbert to go to the upright piano against the wall and play his popular music. This never failed to start everyone singing. He always wound up playing "Kiss Me Again" over and over. This was Herbert's particular favorite.

It was on West 48th Street that I started my collection of art for the restaurant. My first purchase was eight life-size plaster model statues from Alexander Pelli, a marble dealer on Long Island. These had been the models for pieces sculpted in marble for the wealthy Donahue family of Woolworth fame. By the time I sold the restaurant, the art displayed there was valued at a quarter of a million dollars.

From 1920 to 1934, with the curse of prohibition and the terrible depression, there wasn't any reason to expand the business. But this certainly wasn't an idle period for me. Late in August of 1926 I met a very sweet, lovely Irish girl of twenty, Mary Sullivan. She came into the restaurant with friends and, here, too, the restaurant was responsible for another of the many wonderful things that happened to me. I fell for her right away. After a courtship of six months, we were married on February 22, 1927, in St. Brendan's Church in Brooklyn, my bride's parish. May, as I always call Mary, and I set up house in Dobbs Ferry, New York, where our two daughters, Luisa and Eileen, were born.

By 1935 the restaurant was doing well. We bought three adjoining buildings and tore them down to give us more room. Two years later, Joe decided to retire and live in California. He soon tired of the inactivity and learned something that all restaurateurs find out sooner or later—you miss the restaurant business. So, Joe decided to open a very smart, intimate place on The Strip in Beverly Hills and Mother flew to California to assist at the opening. She stayed on the coast with Joe for six months.

By 1942, Luisa was fourteen and Eileen was twelve and both were growing into fine young ladies. They would come into the dining room for an early dinner, around four, with May and my mother. I'd join them for coffee just before the rush because I didn't get a chance to spend too much time with them.

When Luisa and Eileen went upstairs to do their homework, May took her place at the door. She developed into a terrific asset. It wasn't easy handling a crowd of impatient, hungry diners night after night, but this lovely lady commanded the respect of everyone. Her warm smile, sweet manner and charming personality won her the love of our customers and all the employees in Leone's.

Mother left us on May 4, 1944. She had made many, many friends and had done lots of good on this earth. She left us with a smile on her lips. I am happy that she lived to see and enjoy the fruits of her work, which she loved so much. With Mother gone, May took over as a very gracious lady who made customers feel welcome. We were fortunate that there was still a grand lady in Leone's.

Joe was in California and Frank was living in Italy so my third brother Celestine, May and I carried on until I bought Celestine out in 1952 and became the sole owner of Leone's.

Around this time my son-in-law Tom Mesereau resigned his commission as a lieutenant colonel in the Army to work with me in the restaurant. Ned Bowen, who later became my second son-in-law, had majored in accounting at Fordham, but he too entered into the restaurant business with me.

The strength of these two stalwart young men, their intelligence, personality and willingness to work, gave me new incentive. They came right into the kitchen with me and I taught them everything I could. In the evenings they were perfect hosts. With the assistance of May, Tom, Ned and May's brother Bill Sullivan, we went on to the best years Leone's ever had.

The crowds kept on getting bigger and bigger. I solved the need for more room by buying the President Theater right next door. The best night we ever had was on a Saturday following an Army–Notre Dame game at Yankee Stadium. We served over 6,000 dinners and had to turn away many, many others because we still didn't have enough room. I think the entire Cadet Corps showed up for dinner that night.

By 1958, the restaurant had gotten so big and the crowds so huge that even Tom and Ned began to tire. Sure, it required long hours of preparation, overseeing the help, the cooking, the serving and the catering, to keep the tremendous business going. My sons-in-law began dreaming of a smaller, more intimate place. "A nice little spot across the river," as they put it.

Finally, they bought some property on Route 9W in Englewood Cliffs, New Jersey, and on March 5th, 1959, they left me and opened their dream place, The Opera.

This move insured Tom and Ned of a better home life, and I can't underestimate how important that is. They could now spend more time with my daughters and their lovely children, something that I missed during my early married life.

After Tom and Ned left, and the crowds didn't lessen, I found myself getting tired. It was a tremendous organization for one man to run. I had twenty-five women assistants working with me in the morning preparation of soups, sauces, roasts and other dishes that must be cooked in advance.

At night I had about one hundred people in the kitchen. Many of these assistants were specialists. There were always three people working at the steak broiler, two cooking roasts, three preparing cacciatora, scaloppine and other specialties, three on spaghetti, two on the fishes, two for vegetables and potatoes, five at antipasto and hors d'oeuvre, two butchers, two opening oysters and clams, and one preparing only baked hot clams on the shell. The food came out fast and delicious and hot.

My lady assistants all knew cooking and they loved it. This was the secret of keeping Mother's high standard of quality in the kitchen. I always felt that women were for cooking and men for lifting.

I listened to my doctor and to my friends, who I'm sure meant well, and they told me I was killing myself. They said I looked like hell and began working on May to get me to quit. All this started to have an effect on me. It was sort of a light brainwash. I began to listen to them. I really felt that I could see and feel myself getting tired . . . and with good reason.

On a typical night we served over a ton of shrimps, and comparable quantities of pasta, bread, and wine. We served it to Marlene

Dietrich, Rudy Vallee, Bernard Gimbel, Rocky Marciano, Ed Sullivan, and thousands of other wonderful people—New Yorkers and tourists alike.

There were times, when I looked at the crowds jammed into Leone's and the long lines of people standing outside waiting to get in, that I marveled at the fact that no one got trampled. But on many occasions I was really worried.

Mrs. Eleanor Roosevelt came in for dinner shortly after her return from touring the Pacific area on behalf of the Red Cross during World War II. She was a very gracious lady who signed autographs and answered questions for many of our customers who gathered around her table.

However, the big commotion occurred outside. We already had our usual throng waiting to get in and when word got around that Mrs. Roosevelt was in Leone's, an even bigger crush developed. The crowd was so tremendous that our customers couldn't get in, or out, of the restaurant. We finally had to call the police to restore order.

Another commotion took place late in 1956, inside Leone's, and the cause of it all was Liberace. Someone in his party had requested a reservation for six and I had picked a spot in the wine cellar where he would be able to eat without too many interruptions. But Liberace showed up with a party of fourteen and it was impossible to squeeze him into the wine cellar. All I could do was set up a table for him in a corner of the main dining room, in full view of everyone.

There he sat, with his dazzling smile, wavy blond hair, frilly shirt front and a kind word for everyone who came near. Someone discovered that you could get a better view of the dimpled pianist by going up the balcony stairs leading to the art room. This led to a constant procession through the dining room and to the balcony where one woman, about forty, blew Liberace a kiss. That did it! He blew kisses back to the balcony with both hands and for the next fifteen minutes all you could hear or see was the sound of kissing and arms waving. All this, mind you, on a Saturday, the busiest night of the week.

Finally, so many customers jammed around him that he could barely lift his fork. I had to use a dozen of my men to form a ring around his table so that he could eat in peace at a time when I needed all the help I could get, and more, to handle our usual big crowds. I could have crowned him with a bottle of Chianti. He disrupted my entire organization all the time he was in the restaurant and he topped it all by enjoying a very leisurely dinner. Although I didn't appreciate it that night, I was watching a great showman in action. He really gave me, and my customers, a night to remember.

President Harry Truman didn't create a panic but he did give us a laugh. On September 13, 1957, he attended a reunion luncheon with members of the Truman Committee which had conducted a Senate investigation of war contracts in 1941.

Mr. Truman was served Steak à la Eisenhower, prepared exactly as Mr. Eisenhower had showed me on my farm in 1950. Naturally, we didn't tell Mr. Truman that, and unless he reads it here, he'll probably never know. I instructed one of my good waiters, Benito, to show and serve the former president a bottle of 1929 Château Mouton-Rothschild. I prompted Benito to tell Mr. Truman what a great year this was. As Benito mentioned 1929 and the word "great" Mr. Truman interrupted, "What year?" Benito repeated 1929 and Truman snapped, "Like hell it was. It was the worst year of our depression."

This was part of the pleasant side of the business, but there were constant headaches, too. One of the biggest worries of any restaurateur is the danger of food spoiling and food poisoning. I always personally saw to it that the help put away the food at the end of a busy day. Storing it properly is important. For example, hot food cannot be stored in a refrigerator immediately. It must be allowed to cool first. Fortunately, and I say this with pride, we never had a single case of food poisoning among the millions of people we fed in more than fifty years in the business.

Another problem was pickpockets. Where there are big crowds there are pickpockets and where did you get bigger crowds than at Leone's? We had members of the Pickpocket Squad of the New York City Police Department milling among our guests. They knew the pickpockets by sight, and vice versa, so this helped keep this danger to a minimum.

Thievery on the premises was another matter that required lots of attention. The great majority of employees are honest but those who aren't can hurt you. In the space of two years I had over $100,-000 worth of olive oil and shrimps stolen. A porter allowed two or three men who posed as our garbage men to steal from fifty to one hundred pounds of shrimps and five to twenty-five gallons of olive oil a night until we caught them in the act. Liquor, meats, and other prime expensive foods are high on the list of items that disappear. This kind of thing can put you out of business as quickly as bad food.

The time had come to make a decision. I weighed all the pros and cons with May. Should I continue in the business I loved so much knowing how hard I would have to keep working or should I sell out and retire?

I decided to send out a feeler. I let the word get around that I *might* sell. Within a few days, I had offers from eight of the top restaurateurs in New York.

I weighed each one carefully. I was determined not to sell to the highest bidder necessarily. I wanted to make sure that the new owners would carry on the fine tradition of Leone's, established by my mother and continued by me to the best of my ability.

On June 9, 1959, I sold to Restaurant Associates for two and a half million dollars. That figure included the restaurant, the property, my art collection and the food on hand, among which was $125,000 worth of shrimps.

The main purpose of this book is to acquaint you with the wonderful recipes that made Leone's so famous and so successful. If they enable you to serve delicious meals at home then I have achieved my goal.

However, there are times, such as a birthday, an anniversary or some other special occasion, that you will be going out for dinner. Perhaps your job calls on you to entertain clients, prospective customers or business associates at dinner. Here then are answers to questions pertaining to dining out that I have been asked most frequently during my many years as a restaurateur and since my retirement.

Do I have to tip the person at the door to get a table?

No, not if the place is properly supervised and well managed. You are doing them a favor by spending your money for dinner in their place, you should not have to *buy* a table, too.

What about the captain? Does the waiter split his tips with the captain?

No, he does not. You may tip the captain if he has given you especially good service or has recommended certain items on the menu for your dining pleasure. One or two dollars or 5 percent of your bill is sufficient.

Do I tip the busboy?

No. The waiter gives the busboy a percentage of his tips.

Should I tip the wine steward?

This depends on the size of the party, the quality of the wines and the amount consumed. The sommelier, a good one, can add considerably to the festivity of the occasion by performing his chores with a flourish and with the artistry associated with rare, vintage wines. Should you be celebrating a birthday or an anniversary in a group of six to ten people and the sommelier puts on a good show, five dollars would be appropriate.

If you are only two people and he opens one or two bottles for you, one dollar is sufficient.

Do I tip the strolling musicians?

The rules that apply for the wine steward are pretty much the same for the musicians. If you are in a group and members of the party make specific requests for certain favorite songs, you should tip from three to five dollars.

If it is just two of you and the musicians play a medley at your table, one dollar is sufficient.

What about hatcheck girls, cigarette girls and washroom attendants?

Twenty-five cents is standard, but the amount is doubled if an extra service, such as minding valuable papers or removing a spot from a jacket or dress, is performed.

I have left the most important tip, that given the waiter, for last. The waiter can make or break your dinner. You never see the chef and you rarely see the owner, so the waiter is the person you must depend on.

A waiter's job is not an easy one, particularly in a busy restaurant. I spent most of my life working with waiters and found nearly all of them to be honest, kind, hardworking, and decent family men, putting in long hours to send their children to college.

It distressed me to hear a customer screaming at one of my good waiters. Often it wasn't the waiter's fault because he found it necessary to be serving a couple of extra tables and there is a limit to how many customers any waiter can handle efficiently. I would like to suggest that you be considerate of this hard-working man. You can get more with sugar than with vinegar and getting irritated while eating is not good for the digestion.

Now, for the tipping. Some people, very few, I must admit, tip the waiter as soon as they are seated. They hope that this gratuity will entitle them to a few extras (more shrimps and clams) but it doesn't work out that way. This pre-tipping is wrong.

When the waiter presents the check, 15 percent is the usual tip. If you have been given exceptionally good service you may want to give 20 percent. If the service was horrible and the waiter insolent, you might want to leave 10 percent or less. However, this is not recommended. It's best to leave the 15 percent but tell the waiter that you were very dissatisfied and tell him that you are going to report him to the manager.

If you are disappointed in the food, don't take it out on the waiter. He doesn't buy it nor does he cook it.

One more thing. Should the group of six, eight or ten all be women dining out, the same rules for tipping apply to them, too. A dish of ravioli and a bottle of Chianti weigh the same whether you are serving them to a man or to a woman.

On the following pages is a varied collection of recipes that should enable you to put outstanding meals on your table. I say *should,* because good cooks are NOT born, they are made. Any person who wants to cook, can cook. All you need is a desire to learn and the proper ingredients and instruction. You furnish the desire and we'll take care of the rest.

Mother, whom I consider the greatest cook who ever lived, always said that the basis for good Italian cooking is pure olive oil, butter, and salt pork for that extra flavor. Use the freshest and the best foods available, for the better the ingredients, the better the dinner.

Never cut corners in cooking inasmuch as every little detail helps toward perfection. Too much good food is spoiled by cooking too fast. Cook slowly. Observe what is happening. Perfect one recipe at a time.

Seasoning is an art which goes with good cooking. Spices are necessary, but even more important is knowing what seasoning goes best with a certain food. This comes only with experience.

Even the best food can be made to seem better if it is presented properly. When people sit down to dinner at your table, make sure that you have a platter filled with celery, tomatoes, radishes, scallions, raw carrots, green peppers, green and black olives and a wedge of aged Swiss cheese. A loaf of well-crusted Italian bread and a nicely arranged basket of fresh fruits complete a beautiful picture that is a delight to the eye as well as the palate.

Many years ago Mother and I established this fine tradition of setting a colorful, tempting table filled with delicious foods, and it is still carried on today. In fact, it is well worth a trip to Leone's just to see it and enjoy it.

I know that everyone cannot go to the famed Cordon Bleu in Paris to learn the fine art of cooking. But what I am trying to do here is to call on all my years of experience in the kitchen, as well as those of my mother, and make good cooking as easy for you as boiling water.

Here is a list of ingredients and equipment I recommend for your kitchen.

SEASONINGS AND HERBS TO KEEP IN THE HOUSE

Whole black pepper
Whole white pepper
Crushed red pepper
Cayenne pepper
Paprika
Caraway seeds
Ground allspice
Salted capers
Unseasoned and seasoned bread crumbs
Virgin olive oil (made from the first pressing of the olive; if not available, use the next best, but always use olive oil. There are excellent Spanish, French, Greek, Turkish, Italian and State of California olive oils. In our salad dressings and mayonnaise we use a light virgin olive oil from the Tuscany Region of Italy, but in our soups and sauces we use a heavier Sicilian oil. If for some reason you must use a substitute for olive oil, use corn, cottonseed or peanut oil)
Red- or white-wine vinegar

Cinnamon sticks
Whole cloves
Orégano
Whole nutmeg
Bay leaves
Whole marjoram
Saffron
Tarragon and cider vinegar
Powdered and prepared mustard
Hot cherry peppers
Tabasco, Lea & Perrins Worcestershire sauce, chili sauce and catsup

I prefer these fresh:
Basil
Rosemary
Chives
Shallots
Sage leaves
Parsley
Garlic
Scallions
Onions (Bermuda, California or Italian sweet red onions for salads)
Thyme

BASIC INGREDIENTS YOU WILL NEED

Fillets of anchovies in olive oil
Italian tuna in olive oil (*ventresca*)
Imported sardines, in olive oil preferred
Italian, French or American mushrooms
Dried mushrooms
Small hearts of artichokes
Small jars of small artichoke hearts in olive oil to be served on the
   antipasto
Small jars of Italian or French mushrooms in olive oil, for antipasto
Italian or California tomato paste
Italian or California peeled plum tomatoes
Chicken or beef broth
Cheese (two kinds for the table): Bel Paese, Camembert, Brie, Roque-
   fort, Gorgonzola. Keep wrapped in the refrigerator, but take out
   two hours before serving. (If you have Swiss cheese that has hard-
   ened you can grate it and use it in your cooking.)
Parmesan or Romano cheese for grating
Salt pork
Prosciutto
Genoa-style salami
Cans of Italian white truffles

PASTA TO HAVE ON HAND

Pasta	*Cooking time*
Vermicelli	About 6 minutes
Spaghettini	10 minutes
Spaghetti	12 minutes
Ziti, farfalle (butterflies), penne lisce mostaccioli	18 minutes
Fettucini noodles, white or green	15 minutes
Linguini	15 minutes
Rice	25 minutes
Polenta (cornmeal)	15 minutes
Shells or elbows	15 minutes
The heavier pastas	25 minutes

COOKING UTENSILS

1 large kettle for soup, 5 quarts or more
1 medium-sized saucepan for pasta, etc.
2 saucepans with lids
1 deep fryer
2 strainers, tea and gravy
1 large strainer spoon
2 colanders, 1 medium-sized and 1 larger
1 large frying pan
1 medium-sized frying pan with lid
1 small frying pan for crêpes, etc.
1 double boiler
An electric blender, or mixer
1 specially made spaghetti fork
1 set of mixing bowls
Several glass measuring cups
Measuring spoons
2 or more wooden spoons
1 large fork
Flour sifter
1 large chopping knife

1 half-moon chopper
2 chopping boards, 1 small and 1 large heavy board
Several ladles
Egg beater
Pastry bag
Pastry roller cutter for ravioli and pastry
Bread knife
Large sharp knife for slicing
Set of regular, large, and heavy kitchen knives, including heavy cleaver
Kitchen shears
Large salt shaker
Pepper grinder
2 graters, 1 small and 1 large
2 larding skewers, 1 large and 1 small
Roasting pan with rack
Covered casserole dishes
1 large pastry board (about 20 by 30 inches)
1 24-inch rolling pin

WINES OF ITALY

Nothing goes better with food than wine. When traveling from the tip of the Adriatic down through Sicily, it is evident to even the most casual observer that all of Italy is great grape country. Here are just a few of the many Italian wines that May and I have enjoyed and would like to recommend to you.

Barbaresco, Barbera, Freisa secco, Barolo, Gattinara (all still dry reds)
Chianti (a husky dry ruby red wine)
Valpolicella (light dry red wine)
Casteller Gran Rubino (dry ruby red wine)

Bardolino (dry ruby red wine)
Recioto (heavy dry red wine)
Recioto Amarone (heavy dry red wine)
Dolcetto spumante (semisweet sparkling red wine)
Lambrusco (semisweet sparkling red)
Prosecco Brut (very dry white)
Orvieto secco (dry white wine)
Soave bianco secco (dry white wine)
Prosecco bianco secco (still dry white wine)
Portofino Massucco (dry white wine)
Cinque-terre secco (dry white wine)
Freccia Rossa bianco secco (dry white wine)
Termeno (dry white wine)
Verdicchio (fruity dry white wine)
Prosecco Carpene (semidry sparkling white wine)
Orvieto abboccato (semisweet white wine)
Prosecco Valbona (semisweet sparkling white wine)
Grignolino, Freisa amabile, Brachetto, Nebbiolo spumante (semi-
    sweet wines)
Asti Spumante (sweet white wine)
Gran Cavit Brut (sparkling white wine)
Moscato San Vigilio (sweet muscat dessert wine)
Moscato passito (sweet still amber dessert wine)
Chiaretto del Garda (dry rosé)
Rosato di Trento (light dry rosé)

And now that you have the necessary ingredients, equipment, and appetite, choose the recipe that teases your palate, follow the instructions I've tried to keep simple, add a creative touch of your own if that's your inclination, and—*Buon Appetito!*

2

Mother Leone's Antipasto Supreme

CREATED by her in her modest little kitchen in her own home, while dreaming of *un bel di* (one beautiful day) when she would open her own little restaurant, Mother's antipasto with her shrimps and her special sauce became the toast of connoisseurs, world-famed celebrities and literally millions of friends and diners who graced Leone's Restaurant during the past half century.

Roy Howard, the Hon. Herbert Hoover, Gene Tunney were among the frequent visitors to Leone's. They enjoyed a few of our special antipasto dishes, especially our baked clams and our savory pâté of fresh chicken livers with Italian white truffles. Many of these antipasto dishes are suitable for luncheons, after-theater dinners, buffet suppers, etc. Choose a few that appeal to you, set them out attractively, and wait for the compliments that are sure to follow.

Hot Chopped Clams on Toast

36 medium-sized cherrystone clams
2 large garlic cloves, mashed
14 fresh parsley sprigs, leaves only
4 fresh sage leaves or 8 dried sage leaves
2 tablespoons olive oil
1/4 cup fresh creamery butter
1 medium-sized green or red pepper, sliced very thin
Pinch of flour
Pinch of crushed red pepper
Pinch of black pepper
1 medium-sized ripe tomato, sliced very thin
1 loaf of Italian bread

Open the clams, saving any juice, and chop the meat coarsely. Set aside all the juices. Chop the garlic and parsley together. If using dried sage, soak the leaves in lukewarm water for a few minutes.

Combine oil and butter in a skillet and heat. Add pepper slices and cook for 5 minutes. Add drained chopped clams, cook for 4 minutes, then stir in the flour. Add garlic and parsley, red and black pepper, and sage leaves. Cook for 3 minutes. Add tomato slices and 2 tablespoons of the clam juice. Bring to a boil and simmer for 10 minutes. Serve on toasted slices of Italian bread. Serves 4 to 6.

Note: To make a refreshing and invigorating drink using the rest of the clam juice, boil clam juice slightly, then chill; add the juice of ½ fresh lemon and a glass of Champagne.

Mother's Baked Clams

One of the most delicious specialties on Mother's antipasto

36 medium-sized fresh cherry-stone clams, plus 8 extra shells
24 raw jumbo shrimps
1 live lobster (2 to 2½ pounds)
4 cups milk
½ pound fresh Maryland crab-meat
1½ cups fresh creamery butter
1½ cups sifted all-purpose flour
1 cup heavy cream
2 cups freshly grated Parmesan or Swiss cheese
½ teaspoon black pepper
½ teaspoon crushed red pepper
Salt

Open the clams, saving the natural juice and the shells. You will have 72 empty shells. Ask your fish dealer for the 8 extra shells. Shell and devein the shrimps. Wash shrimps and shells well and save these shells also. Split lobster down the center. Take out head sac and intestinal vein and discard. Cut lobster into pieces. Crack and mash all claws, carcass of lobster, and shrimp shells. (Your fish dealer can do this for you.)

Place the milk in a large pot with half of the saved natural clam juice. Add lobster pieces and carcass and all shrimp shells. Bring to a boil and cook slowly for 30 minutes. Cool for 10 minutes. Strain, reserving the liquid.

Take lobster meat out of shells. Place lobster shells and carcass and shrimp shells on a French sieve and pound extra well through the sieve to get all the juices and flavor out of them. Discard all shells. Put raw shrimps and clams and the cooked lobster meat through a food chopper or grinder. Then place back in the strained liquid all the juices, including the rest of the clam juice, the ground lobster, shrimps and clams, and the crabmeat. Bring to a boil slowly over low heat. In a saucepan melt the butter and add the flour. Stir well and do not allow to scorch. Add the cream and all but ½ cup of the cheese. Stir and blend the flour and cheese mixture into the milk and shellfish mixture. Again bring the mixture slowly to a boil and cook over low heat for 30 minutes. Add black and red pepper. Taste for salt and add a little if necessary. If mixture is too liquid, blend in a little more flour. Stir well.

Fill as many clam shells as you plan to serve immediately. Sprinkle cheese lightly over them, and place under a preheated broiler for a few minutes, until bubbling. Serve 2 or 3 to each person as an antipasto; or you may serve 6 to a person as a main course.

Fill the remaining shells and place in aluminum oven pans holding 6 or 12 shells. Cover, wrap twice, and freeze them. I recommend making a large quantity so you have a reserve in the freezer. Baked clams freeze very well. Serves 12 to 18 as an antipasto or 6 as a main course.

Cozze alla Romana

(baked mussels)

6 dozen large fresh mussels	1 cup toasted bread crumbs, sifted
¼ cup olive oil	½ teaspoon black pepper
2 tablespoons butter, melted	½ teaspoon crushed red pepper
3 garlic cloves	Salt
10 fresh parsley sprigs, leaves only	

Place mussels under cold running water and scrub well with a brush. Pick out open ones and discard. Put mussels on the bottom of a shallow baking pan. Pour olive oil and butter over them. Chop the garlic and parsley together and sprinkle over the mussels; then add the bread crumbs, black and red pepper, and very little salt. Cover tightly with aluminum foil. Bake in a moderate oven (375° F.) for 30 minutes. Serve hot on warmed plates, with toasted garlic Italian bread. Pour pan juices over mussels. You may dunk your Italian toast into the juice. Serve 12 or more mussels to each person. Serves 4 to 6.

Note: If mussels are not available, substitute littleneck clams. Cook the same amount in the same way. They are delicious, too.

Shrimp Salad

6 slices of Italian salami ¼ inch thick
1 large green, red or yellow pepper
20 jumbo shrimps, boiled
2 celery stalks with leaves, diced
6 whole fresh green scallions, diced
3 hard-cooked eggs, quartered
3 medium-sized hard tomatoes, quartered
Pinch of salt
Pinch of freshly ground black pepper
6 heaping tablespoons Mother Leone's Shrimp Sauce (below)

Cut the salami into strips 1¼ inches long, and slice the peppers into long thin strips. Place in a large bowl with shrimps, diced celery and scallions; refrigerate. Refrigerate eggs and tomatoes separately. When ready to serve, add salt and pepper and toss. Arrange eggs and tomatoes over top. Spoon shrimp sauce over all. Serve on the antipasto or as a main course. Serves 4 or 5.

Mother Leone's Shrimp Sauce

A simple but delicious sauce, known the world over

2 whole green scallions or 1 tablespoon grated sweet onion
6 tablespoons finely chopped fresh green or red pepper
2 tablespoons Spanish capers, chopped fine
2 tablespoons prepared horse-radish
1 cup mayonnaise, preferably homemade with virgin olive oil
½ cup chili sauce
½ teaspoon crushed red pepper
½ teaspoon freshly ground black pepper
½ teaspoon salt
1 garlic clove, mashed

Slice scallions lengthwise and chop fine, or grate the sweet onion. Place scallions or onion, green or red pepper, capers and horseradish in a strainer and drain for 15 minutes. Combine mayonnaise and chili sauce in a bowl. Add red and black pepper, salt and garlic. Whip well together with a whisk. Add drained ingredients and beat or mix well. Taste for salt. Refrigerate. Use over shrimps, crabmeat, or cold chicken lobster. Makes about 2 cups.

Boiled Jumbo Shrimps

25 raw jumbo shrimps
12 fresh parsley sprigs, leaves only
2 large garlic cloves, mashed
6 tablespoons fresh creamery butter, melted
Pinch of black pepper
Pinch of crushed red pepper
Pinch of salt

Boil the shrimps in their shells for 20 minutes. Remove from water and drain. Cut back of shells with a scissors and devein, but do not peel the shrimps. Chop parsley and garlic together and combine with remaining ingredients in a small saucepan. Heat, but do not cook. Stir and pour over shrimps. Serve shrimps in their shells, garnished with lemon wedges. Serves 5.

Avocado Salad

2 ripe avocados
Boston lettuce
2 fresh sage leaves or 4 dried sage leaves
2 tablespoons wine vinegar
6 tablespoons olive oil
Pinch each of salt and black pepper
Juice of ½ lemon
1 garlic clove, mashed
1 teaspoon Worcestershire sauce

When selecting avocados, be sure they are a little underripe. Peel and cut lengthwise into halves. Remove pits. Arrange on several leaves of crisp Boston lettuce. If using dried sage, soak the leaves in the vinegar for about 15 minutes before using. Combine the sauce ingredients and blend well. Discard bits of garlic and pour the sauce over avocados. Serves 4.

Avocado with Fresh Crabmeat I

1 avocado
Boston lettuce
2 heaping tablespoons fresh lump crabmeat
3 tablespoons Mother Leone's Shrimp Sauce (page 22)
3 tablespoons Leone's Master Salad Dressing (page 50)

Peel avocado and halve lengthwise; remove pit. Arrange on lettuce leaves. Spoon crabmeat into avocado halves. Make a dressing of the shrimp sauce and salad dressing. Spoon over crabmeat. Serves 2.

Crabmeat and Smoked Nova Scotia Salmon

1 pound fresh Maryland lump crabmeat

4 slices of Nova Scotia smoked salmon, cut into squares

6 fresh parsley sprigs, leaves only, chopped coarsely

2 whole fresh green scallions, diced

1 Bermuda, Italian or any sweet onion, sliced thin

Dressing (see below)

Arrange crabmeat nicely on a good-sized platter. Sprinkle the pieces of smoked salmon over crabmeat. Sprinkle parsley and scallions over the salmon. Separate sweet onion slices into rings and place over top. Refrigerate. Serve with a loaf of Italian bread and a bottle of white Frascati or Orvieto. Serve as an antipasto or luncheon dish. Serves 4 to 6.

DRESSING

¼ cup olive oil

2 tablespoons wine vinegar

Juice of ½ lemon

1 tablespoon Worcestershire sauce

½ teaspoon freshly ground black pepper

½ teaspoon powdered mustard

Salt

Mix all ingredients in a bowl and beat well. Salt lightly and carefully because the smoked salmon is salty. Spoon over crabmeat salad.

Fresh Crabmeat Sautéed in Cream Sherry

6 tablespoons sweet butter

1 pound fresh Maryland lump crabmeat

6 tablespoons good cream sherry

10 fresh parsley sprigs, leaves only, chopped fine

Pinch of crushed red pepper

Pinch of freshly ground black pepper

Salt

Place butter in a skillet and heat. Add crabmeat and sherry and sauté slowly for about 5 minutes. Add parsley, red and black pepper and a sprinkle of salt. Cover and simmer for 10 minutes. Serve over toast. This also makes a delicious main course. Serves 4 or 5.

Chilled Maryland Crabmeat

1 garlic clove, mashed
6 tablespoons olive oil
3 tablespoons wine vinegar
Juice of ½ lemon
1 teaspoon Worcestershire sauce
Pinch of salt
Pinch of crushed red pepper
Pinch of freshly ground black pepper
½ teaspoon powdered mustard
6 fresh parsley sprigs, leaves only, minced
1 pound fresh lump crabmeat
Boston lettuce leaves

Mix garlic into the oil with a fork. Add vinegar to garlic and oil; then add lemon juice, Worcestershire sauce, salt, red and black pepper, mustard and parsley. Mix well together. Discard bits of garlic. Arrange crabmeat on chilled lettuce leaves. Spoon the dressing over. Serves 4 to 6.

Avocado with Fresh Crabmeat II

Peel 1 ripe avocado. Cut into halves, remove pit, and cut into quarters. Place quarters on chilled Boston lettuce leaves and cover with fresh lump crabmeat. Spoon the light salad dressing (see above) over it; or dress with Mother Leone's Shrimp Sauce (page 22). Serve 1 avocado quarter on the antipasto to each person. Serves 4.

Broiled Fresh Oysters

10 fresh parsley sprigs, leaves only
6 leaves of fresh or dried basil
1 garlic clove, mashed
2 shallots, chopped very fine
¼ cup olive oil
½ cup fresh creamery butter, melted
½ cup sifted bread crumbs
¼ cup grated Parmesan cheese
Pinch of black pepper
Pinch of crushed red pepper
Pinch of salt
36 large juicy oysters on half shell, freshly opened

Chop together the parsley, basil and garlic. Mix with shallots, oil and butter. Then add all the other ingredients except oysters and mix well. Place oysters in their half shells on an open pan and cover each oyster with some of the dressing. Cover tightly with aluminum foil. Place pan in preheated slow oven (300° F.) and bake for 15 minutes. Uncover and place pan under preheated medium broiler for 5 minutes. Serves 6.

Italian Tuna Salad

1 can (8 to 10 ounces) Italian *ventresca* tuna, or the best available
½ pound Italian red sweet onions, sliced very thin
5 fresh basil leaves, chopped, or pinch of dried basil

10 fresh parsley sprigs, leaves only, chopped coarsely
2 medium-sized firm tomatoes, sliced extra thin
Salt and black pepper
Dressing (see below)

Remove tuna from can and mix with onions, basil and parsley. Place on a platter and lay very thin slices of tomato on top. Sprinkle with salt and pepper. Refrigerate. Just before time to serve, pour dressing over the salad and toss well. Serves 4.

DRESSING

1 garlic clove, mashed
¼ cup wine vinegar
1 teaspoon Worcestershire sauce

Juice of ½ lemon
Pinch of salt
Pinch of black pepper

Mix all ingredients together in a bowl. Pour over tuna salad and toss.

Anguilla Fresca Carpionata
(*pickled fresh eel*)

2½ pounds fresh eel
½ teaspoon freshly ground black pepper
Pinch of crushed red pepper
3 bay leaves, crumbled
Salt

½ cup olive oil
¼ cup wine vinegar
3 garlic cloves, mashed
4 fresh sage leaves or 1 teaspoon crumbled dried sage
Black pepper

Have a fishman skin the eel and prepare for cooking. Cut into 2-inch pieces, wash, and dry well. Preheat broiler, arrange eel in broiler pan, and set the pan 8 inches below the source of heat. Cook slowly for 3 minutes. Turn, and cook for 3 minutes longer. Sprinkle black and red pepper, bay leaves and salt over top. Cook slowly for 15 minutes and turn. Cook for about 15 minutes longer, until golden brown. Remove from the broiler and place in a bowl.

Combine in a skillet the oil, vinegar, garlic and sage. (If using dried sage leaves, soak them in the wine vinegar for about 15 minutes before using.) Bring the dressing to a boil and pour over eel. Add salt and pepper in light sprinkles. Stir and cover for 10 minutes. Mix several times and allow to cool. Serve with Italian bread and drink a bottle of good Chianti. Serves 6 to 8.

Chilled Fresh Salmon with Herb Mayonnaise

2 pounds fresh salmon	1 medium onion, sliced
Pinch of black pepper	2 celery stalks with leaves, cut
Pinch of salt	into halves
1 cup wine vinegar	Herb Mayonnaise (see below)

Have fishman prepare fish for cooking. Place salmon in a shallow pan and cover with warm water. Add all other ingredients except mayonnaise. Bring to a boil. Lower heat and simmer for 30 to 40 minutes. Check to see if fish is cooked. Remove from water, drain, and allow to cool. Split down the center and remove all bones. Arrange salmon on platter. Cover with herb mayonnaise. Serves 6 to 8.

HERB MAYONNAISE

2 garlic cloves, mashed	1 can (5 ounces) pimientos
2 cups mayonnaise	8 ounces fresh peas, cooked, or 8
10 fresh parsley sprigs, leaves only	ounces canned peas, drained
	1 teaspoon dried orégano
2 whole fresh green scallions	

Mixed mashed garlic into mayonnaise, then discard the bits of garlic. Chop parsley leaves fine and dice entire scallions. Drain pimientos and cut into cubes. Mix all ingredients together and blend well. Spoon over the top of salmon.

Snails with White Wine

24 canned snails with shells
6 tablespoons sweet butter
8 fresh parsley sprigs, leaves only
2 large garlic cloves, mashed
Dash of salt
Dash of freshly ground black pepper
¼ cup dry white wine

Rub the insides of the snail shells lightly with butter. Melt remaining butter (snails require lots of butter). Chop parsley and garlic together and add to butter along with salt, pepper, and wine. Simmer for 5 minutes. Add snails. Mix well and heat slowly for 5 minutes. Do not boil. Preheat oven to hot (400° F.). Spoon a little butter mixture into each shell, then insert snails. Place shells on special snail dish or in pie tin or oven dish. Spoon remaining butter mixture over shells. Bake for 15 minutes. Serves 6 as an antipasto, or 3 as a main course.

Calamari Salad

1 pound fresh calamari (squid)
4 anchovy fillets, mashed
2 large garlic cloves
¼ cup olive oil
10 fresh parsley sprigs, leaves only
Pinch of crushed red pepper
½ teaspoon salt
½ teaspoon freshly ground black pepper
1 sweet onion (Italian, Texas or Bermuda), sliced very thin
1 medium-sized green pepper, sliced thin
6 tablespoons wine vinegar
Juice of 1 fresh lemon

Have a fishman clean calamari well. Wash again before cooking, and dry. Place in boiling salted water and cook for 1 hour. Test for doneness. When cooked, drain, cut into short thin strips, and place in a bowl.

Add mashed anchovies and 1 mashed garlic clove to the oil. Chop the other garlic clove with the parsley. While squid is still warm, add oil with anchovies and garlic. Mix well. Add red pepper, garlic with parsley, salt and black pepper; mix well. Add onion, green pepper, vinegar and lemon juice; mix well. Allow to marinate for several hours before refrigerating. Serves 4 to 6.

Boiled-Beef Salad

½ pound boiled beef, cubed
1 head of Boston or iceberg lettuce, shredded
2 medium-sized ripe tomatoes, sliced thin
1 boiled potato, cut into cubes
4 whole scallions or 1 medium-sized sweet Bermuda onion, diced

2 celery stalks, diced
4 pimientos, drained and diced
4 thin slices of prosciutto or Italian salami, diced
Salad Dressing Luisa (see below)

Instead of beef, cooked ham, veal, tongue, chicken, or any leftover meat can be used. Place all ingredients in a bowl and spoon dressing over. Mix well. Serves 4.

SALAD DRESSING LUISA

6 tablespoons olive oil
1 hard-cooked egg, mashed with a fork
Juice of 1½ lemons
1 teaspoon prepared mustard
1 teaspoon capers

1 garlic clove, mashed
¼ teaspoon freshly ground black pepper
4 anchovy fillets, mashed with a fork

Mix all ingredients well. Pour over salad.

Pâté of Fresh Chicken Livers alla Leone

¼ cup olive oil
½ cup butter
½ pound salt pork, diced
1 pound onions, peeled and diced
¾ pound fresh chicken gizzards, cut into small pieces
8 bay leaves, broken up

1 teaspoon black pepper
1 garlic clove, mashed
1¼ pounds fresh chicken livers, chopped coarsely
½ teaspoon salt, approximately
1 can (3½ to 4 ounces) white Italian truffles

Combine the oil, 2 tablespoons of the butter, and all of the salt pork in a saucepan; heat. Add onions and brown slowly for 5 minutes. Add gizzards and cook for 10 minutes. Add bay leaves, pepper, garlic and livers and simmer for 25 minutes. Remove from the heat and cool for 10 minutes.

Put through food grinder or chop very fine, but do not lose juice. Place juice and solids back in saucepan and simmer for 20 minutes. Place in a bowl or crock. Add balance of butter to the warm pâté and let the butter melt into the pâté. Mix well. Taste for salt and add if necessary. Shave the truffles over the warm pâté.

Serve warm on toast or crackers, or refrigerate and serve cold. Offer a platter of crackers or toasted Italian bread with the pâté and have guests serve themselves. They will love it. For wine, serve one of these: natural sparkling Freisa, Grignolino, Nebbiolo or Dolcetto Spumante. Serves 15 to 20.

Meat and Cucumber Salad

1 cucumber
Salt
4 whole fresh green scallions, diced, or 2 tablespoons chopped sweet onion
2 medium-sized red or green peppers, sliced thin
2 medium-sized tomatoes, sliced thin
2 celery stalks with leaves, minced
2 slices of Swiss cheese, diced

½ teaspoon freshly ground pepper
1 garlic clove, mashed
⅓ cup Italian Salad Dressing (page 49)
2 tablespoons Mother Leone's Shrimp Sauce (page 22)
1 head of Boston lettuce, shredded
1½ cups roast veal or ham, boiled beef, pot roast, or any cooked meat, cut into cubes

Lightly scrape the cucumber and cut into thin slices. Sprinkle slices with salt, arrange on absorbent paper, and drain for 30 minutes. Put scallions, peppers, tomatoes, celery, and cheese in a bowl. Sprinkle with ½ teaspoon salt, the pepper and garlic. Add salad dressing and shrimp sauce. Stir well.

Place lettuce, drained cucumber, and meat in a larger bowl and pour the first mixture over all. Toss and serve. Serves 4 to 6.

Green Peppers and Anchovies

1/4 cup olive oil
6 medium-sized green peppers, quartered
2 garlic cloves, mashed
Pinch of salt
4 anchovy fillets

2 tablespoons sweet butter
1 tablespoon Spanish capers
Pinch of crushed red pepper
Pinch of freshly ground black pepper
1/4 cup wine vinegar

Place olive oil in a saucepan and heat. Add quartered peppers and the garlic. Cook for 5 minutes, stir, and cover. Cook for 20 minutes, or until done. Remove from the heat and season lightly with salt. Mash the anchovies with a fork and mix into the butter. Stir the mixture into the peppers and add capers, red and black pepper, and vinegar; mix and stir. Place in a bowl and cool. Serves 6 to 8.

Anchovies with Pimientos and Mozzarella

4 pimientos, cut into halves
4 slices of mozzarella cheese, diced
8 anchovy fillets
6 fresh parsley sprigs, leaves only
1 garlic clove, mashed
1 teaspon dried orégano
1/2 teaspoon grated onion

Pinch of freshly ground black pepper
1/4 cup olive oil
2 tablespoons wine vinegar
Juice of 1/2 lemon
1 teaspoon salted capers, mashed lightly

Arrange pimientos on plates, cover with pieces of mozzarella, and add 2 anchovy fillets on top of each serving. Chop parsley and garlic together and mix with remaining ingredients. Spoon the sauce over the anchovies and cheese. Serves 4.

Mozzarella in Carrozza

(from southern Italy)

12 slices of white bread, crusts trimmed
2 large eggs, beaten in a bowl
1/2 cup milk
6 slices of fresh mozzarella cheese, 1/4 inch thick
Flour

6 thin slices of chicken or prosciutto
1/4 cup olive oil
2 tablespoons fresh creamery butter
Tiny pinch of freshly ground black pepper

Cut slices of bread into halves and dip into eggs, then into milk. Dust the cheese with a tiny bit of flour. Place a half slice of cheese and a half slice of chicken or prosciutto between 2 half slices of bread. Pin with food picks. Place oil and butter in a skillet and heat well. Place sandwiches in skillet. Cook until light brown, turn, and cook until light brown on the other side and cheese begins to melt. To serve, spoon a little of the hot oil over the sandwich and grind fresh pepper on the top. Serve on the antipasto or as an entrée. Serves 4 to 6.

Cheese-Stuffed Celery

¼ pound Roquefort or blue cheese
2 tablespoons fresh creamery butter
2 tablespoons olive oil
1 teaspoon paprika
Pinch of black pepper
1 tablespoon Worcestershire sauce
Celery stalks (narrow and tender stalks)

Mash cheese and butter together on plate, using a fork. Add olive oil. Add paprika, pepper and Worcestershire sauce. Mix until you have a smooth soft paste. Wash and dry celery stalks. If too wide, cut lengthwise into halves. Stuff cheese mixture lightly into stalks for about an inch from the bottom end. Sprinkle lightly with paprika. Refrigerate. Enough for about 2 dozen celery stalks.

Cranberry-Bean Salad

(fagioli della regina, *the "Queen's beans"*)

2 pounds fresh cranberry beans in shells
4 cups cold water
2 ounces salt pork, diced
1 medium-sized sweet onion
1 large garlic clove, mashed
Pinch of black pepper
½ teaspoon salt
2 medium-sized ripe tomatoes, chopped fine, or 2 tablespoons tomato paste
Dressing (page 33)
8 slices of Genoa-style Italian salami or prosciutto, cut into thin strips

This amount of fresh beans in the shell is equal to 1 pound shelled beans or 1 pound dried beans. If using dried cranberry beans, soak them in lukewarm water overnight.

Put the water in a large pot and add the shelled beans. Bring to a boil, lower the heat, and add salt pork and all other ingredients except dressing and salami. Cook at a slow boil for 45 to 60 minutes. Do not overcook. Drain well. While beans are still warm, pour the dressing over them and add the salami or prosciutto. Mix gently. Serve as an antipasto or as a luncheon dish. It is also delicious served over quartered hard-cooked eggs. Serves 6 to 8.

Note: You may use a good tuna in olive oil instead of salami. The liquid drained from the beans can be used to cook pastina.

DRESSING

6 tablespoons olive oil	Pinch of salt
Juice of 1 lemon	Pinch of black pepper
2 tablespoons wine vinegar	

Mix well and pour over beans while beans are still lukewarm.

Green-Bean Salad

1 medium-sized baking potato	½ teaspoon salt
1½ pounds fresh green beans	½ teaspoon pepper
¼ cup olive oil	8 fresh parsley sprigs, leaves only,
6 tablespoons wine vinegar	chopped
1 large garlic clove, mashed	6 thin slices of prosciutto or
2 whole green scallions, minced	salami, or leftover ham, diced

Boil the potato in its jacket. When cool enough to handle, peel and dice, but keep warm. Trim beans and cook in boiling salted water for about 20 minutes. Test to avoid overcooking. Drain well. Place warm beans in a salad bowl and add potato over top.

Combine olive oil, vinegar, garlic, scallions, salt and pepper. Mix well. Discard bits of garlic. Pour dressing over warm beans and potatoes. Add chopped parsley and diced prosciutto and toss at the table. Serves 6 to 8.

Ceci-Bean Salad

½ pound dried ceci beans (chickpeas) or red cranberry beans	2 tablespoons olive oil
2 quarts water	¼ pound onions, peeled and diced
2 ounces salt pork, diced	½ celery stalk, minced
1 garlic clove, mashed	Dressing (see page 34)

Wash the beans and then soak in the water overnight. In the same water, bring beans to a boil, lower the heat, and add the salt pork, garlic, olive oil, onions, and celery. Cover, and cook for about 1½ hours. (If you use cranberry beans, watch the cooking as cranberry beans cook faster.) Check cooking in the meantime. Do not overcook. Add more boiling water if necessary. When tender, drain the beans, put them back in the warm pot, cover, and keep warm. Cover with dressing and mix gently. Serves 4 to 6.

DRESSING

5 fresh or dried sage leaves
1 jar or can (7 ounces) red pimientos
10 fresh parsley sprigs, leaves only, chopped fine
1 garlic clove, mashed
½ cup olive oil
½ teaspoon salt
½ teaspoon black pepper
3 tablespoons wine vinegar
1 teaspoon prepared mustard
4 whole green scallions, diced, or 3 tablespoons diced sweet onion

If using dried sage leaves, soak them in wine vinegar for about 15 minutes before using. Drain the pimientos and cut them into medium-sized pieces. Place all dressing ingredients in a bowl and mix well. Pour dressing over the warm beans.

Beet Salad

This was a favorite dish for Rudy Vallee, our friend, and perennial American college youth. With it, he usually enjoyed Mother's shrimps and spaghetti and roast chicken.

2 pounds medium-sized red beets
6 anchovy fillets, minced
2 garlic cloves, mashed
¼ cup olive oil
½ cup wine vinegar
½ teaspoon black pepper
Salt

Wash the beets. Boil in their skins in 4 quarts of water. (If you have a roast in the oven, wrap beets in aluminum foil and bake in the oven for about 1½ hours, or until cooked. This will give beets more flavor than the usual boiling.) When cooked, skin and slice. Then place in a bowl and cover.

Combine dressing ingredients, using salt to taste, and pour over warm beets. Cover. Allow to cool, then refrigerate. Naturally, the fresh beets make a better salad than canned beets. If baked, they will have even more flavor. Serve on the antipasto or as a salad. Serves 6 to 8.

Coleslaw

This is a little different from the usual mayonnaise coleslaw. Mother was noted for cooking or making things simple, different and delicious.

1½ to 2 pounds cabbage
Black pepper
½ cup white-wine or cider vinegar
2 large garlic cloves, mashed

1 tablespoon grated carrot
1 tablespoon grated onion
½ cup olive oil
8 anchovy fillets, chopped

Slice or shred the cabbage into a bowl. Grind black pepper over it. Pour the vinegar into a pan and heat. Add garlic, carrot, onion, and olive oil; bring to a boil. Take from the heat immediately as it boils. Add anchovies, stir, and pour over cabbage. Toss, and cover for 15 minutes. Cool and refrigerate. Serves 6 to 8.

Finocchio, Artichoke and Celery Salad

1 large head of finocchio
1 head of celery
12 artichoke hearts in olive oil
12 small pitted black olives, halved
1 teaspoon capers
4 anchovy fillets, cut into small pieces
4 ounces pimientos, cut into ½-inch strips
2 hard-cooked eggs, quartered

6 slices of medium-sized Italian salami, cut into thin strips
4 whole fresh green scallions, sliced lengthwise and diced
1 garlic clove, mashed
¼ cup olive oil
Juice of ½ lemon
2 tablespoons wine vinegar
Pinch of freshly ground black pepper
Salt

Halve the finocchio and slice into strips. Dice a few of the tender leaves. Remove tough outer stalks from celery (save for soup) and dice the tender celery. Arrange the first ten ingredients in a large bowl. Mix garlic into the olive oil and stir well. Add lemon juice, vinegar and pepper. Mix well and pour over salad. Taste for salt when salad is dressed. Serves 4.

Potato Salad

2 pounds potatoes
15 fresh parsley sprigs, stems and all
2 garlic cloves, mashed
6 tablespoons olive oil
1/4 cup wine vinegar
Pinch of black pepper
Pinch of crushed red pepper

1 teaspoon salt
Juice of 1 lemon
2 heaping tablespoons grated onion, or 4 green scallions, minced
1 celery stalk with leaves, minced

Boil the potatoes in their jackets. When cooked, peel immediately. Cut into 3/4-inch cubes. Chop parsley and garlic together. Put with all other ingredients in a bowl and mix well. Pour over potatoes while they are still warm. Taste for salt and add more if necessary. Cool, cover, and refrigerate. Serves 6 to 8.

Insalata Russa

1/2 cup fresh green peas
1 cup fresh green beans, cut into 1-inch pieces
1/2 cup 1/2-inch pieces of carrot
1 cup 1/2-inch pieces of potato
1/2 cup very small white onions

1/2 cup red pimientos
2 cups mayonnaise
Salt and pepper
4 hard-cooked eggs, sliced
8 parsley sprigs, leaves only, chopped fine

Cook each raw vegetable separately until just tender. Drain well. Place all vegetables in a bowl. Drain the pimientos, pat dry, and dice. Add to the cooked vegetables. Add two thirds of the mayonnaise to the vegetables, season with salt and pepper to taste, and mix gently. Arrange the salad nicely on a large platter. Decorate top with slices of eggs and spoon the remaining mayonnaise over top. Sprinkle all with parsley. Serves 4 to 6.

Celery-Root Salad

1 pound celery root (celeriac)	½ teaspoon powdered mustard
¼ cup olive oil	Juice of 1 lemon
2 tablespoons wine vinegar	Salt and pepper
1 garlic clove, mashed	

Cook celery root as for Buttered Celery Root (page 210) and chill the drained strips. Mix dressing ingredients well. Discard bits of garlic. Pour the mixture over the chilled root. Serves 4.

Fresh Figs with Prosciutto

Serve ripe fresh green or black figs with prosciutto. Take a little of the skin off the top of the fig. Split each fig into halves and place a thin slice of ham over each half fig. Grind a little black pepper over fig and prosciutto and serve 2 halves per person. They are delicious.

Melon with Prosciutto

Use ripe cantaloupe, honeydew, casaba or Spanish melon. Melon must be ripe and chilled. Cut melon into halves, remove seeds, and slice into pieces ¾ inch wide. Cut along the bottom of the flesh near the rind, but do not separate or detach rind from melon for better appearance when serving. Place 2 wide, thin slices of prosciutto at an angle over each melon slice. Do not cover entire melon with prosciutto. Grind a little black pepper over prosciutto when serving. Serve 2 melon slices per person.

Sardines and Chopped Eggs

4 hard-cooked eggs, mashed with a fork	Juice of 1 lemon
	Salt and pepper
6 fresh parsley sprigs, leaves only, chopped fine	4 pieces of Italian bread, toasted
	4 good-sized imported sardines in olive oil
2 whole fresh green scallions, minced	Worcestershire sauce
2 heaping tablespoons olive oil	Lemon wedges

Combine mashed eggs, parsley, scallions, olive oil, lemon juice, and salt and pepper to taste; mix together. Spoon egg mixture on toast pieces and arrange a sardine on each serving. Mix a few drops of Worcestershire sauce with oil from sardines or with regular olive oil and spoon over the sardines. Serve with wedges of lemon. Serves 4.

Stuffed Hard-Cooked Eggs

8 hard-cooked eggs
3 tablespoons Mother Leone's Shrimp Sauce (page 22)
3 tablespoons Marinara Sauce (page 94), warmed
6 leaves of chives or 1 teaspoon dried chives
2 tablespoons sweet butter, melted

1 teaspoon prepared mustard
2 whole fresh green scallions, minced
2 tablespoons toasted bread crumbs
Salt and pepper

Halve the eggs and remove yolks. Mash yolks with a fork. In a bowl mix the shrimp sauce and marinara sauce. If using fresh chives, chop fine; if using dried chives, add to the melted butter. Stir in butter and chives, mustard, scallions, mashed egg yolks and bread crumbs. Mix well. Taste for salt and pepper. If too liquid, add more bread crumbs. Stuff egg whites with the mixture. Serves 8 to 16.

Eggs with Green Pepper, Tomato and Prosciutto

1 green or red pepper
2 tablespoons olive oil
2 tablespoons sweet butter
1 small onion, diced
1 garlic clove, mashed

2 thin slices of prosciutto, diced
1 large ripe tomato, sliced thin
4 fresh eggs
Pinch each of salt and pepper

Dice the pepper into small pieces, place in a strainer, and drain for 10 minutes. Place oil and butter in a skillet and heat. Add onion and garlic and cook until medium brown. Discard bits of garlic. Add green pepper, prosciutto and tomato. Stir, cover, and cook for

15 minutes. Beat the eggs well and pour them into the skillet. Cook to taste and season. Serve caffè espresso, black or with a few drops of cream, and Italian bread. Serves 2.

Artichokes Vinaigrette

8 medium-sized artichokes	5 tablespoons olive oil
2 egg yolks	Juice of 1 fresh lemon
1 teaspoon prepared mustard	3 tablespoons wine vinegar
Salt and pepper	

First break off at the base several of the really tough outside leaves. Open up leaves from the inside. Cut off about 1 inch of the tough outside leaves, cutting on a slant toward the tip. Rub with lemon to prevent turning black. Boil in salted water for 30 to 40 minutes, or until tender. Lift artichokes from the water and place upside down to drain.

Have dressing ingredients at room temperature. Beat egg yolks lightly. Add mustard and salt and pepper to taste. Stir. Spoon oil slowly into mixture, add a little lemon juice, and stir. Add more oil and stir. Add remaining lemon juice and the vinegar and stir. Add balance of oil and mix well. Pour over artichokes. Serve 1 artichoke to each person. To eat, peel off leaves and dunk into the dressing. Serves 8.

Marinated Baked Eggplant

2 garlic cloves, mashed	Salt and pepper
1/4 cup olive oil	1 teaspoon minced rosemary
1 eggplant (about 1 1/2 pounds), cut into cubes	1/4 cup wine vinegar
	1/4 cup olive oil
2 large ripe tomatoes, thinly sliced	2 heaping tablespoons grated onion
2 ounces salt pork, diced	Pinch of crushed red pepper

Mash garlic into olive oil with a fork. Mix oil and garlic with eggplant. Place in a baking dish with sliced tomatoes on top. Sprinkle with salt pork, a little salt and pepper and the rosemary. Bake in preheated slow oven (300° F.) for 30 minutes. Lower heat and cook for about 20 minutes longer. Remove from oven and place in a bowl. Mix dressing ingredients together and pour over warm eggplant. Add more salt and pepper if needed. Marinate for 2 hours. Stir again before serving. Serves 6 to 8.

Stuffed Green, Red or Yellow Peppers

8 medium- to large-sized green, red or yellow peppers
2 garlic cloves, mashed well
10 fresh parsley sprigs, leaves only
4 slices of Italian bread (fresh or dry), diced
1/4 cup olive oil
Pinch of freshly ground black pepper
Pinch of crushed red pepper
6 anchovy fillets, chopped
Salt

Cut off tops of peppers and remove cores and seeds. Save the tops, cores and seeds. Chop the garlic and parsley leaves with the cores and seeds of the peppers. In a bowl mix the bread, garlic, parsley, pepper cores and seeds, olive oil, black and red pepper and anchovies. Add salt to taste. Stuff the peppers and replace tops of peppers. Pour a few drops of olive oil onto the bottom of a roasting pan. Arrange peppers standing up. Bake in preheated slow oven (300° F.) for 35 to 40 minutes. Do not burn. Serve cold. If peppers are very large, serve half a pepper to each person. Serves 8 to 16.

Tomatoes Stuffed with Risotto

8 medium-sized firm tomatoes
1/4 cup uncooked rice
2 tablespoons olive oil
2 tablespoons butter
1 ounce salt pork, diced
3 tablespoons chopped onion
1 garlic clove, mashed (optional)
3 chicken livers, chopped very fine
Pinch each of salt and pepper
1 egg, slightly beaten
16 parsley sprigs, leaves only, chopped fine
1/4 cup grated Parmesan cheese
Dressing (see page 41)

Cut off the tops of the tomatoes and scoop out some of insides. Turn upside down to drain. Boil the rice in 3/4 cup salted water for 15 minutes; drain well. Combine in a skillet the olive oil, butter and salt pork; heat the mixture. Add onion and simmer for 5 minutes. Add garlic, chicken livers, and salt and pepper; cook for 10 minutes. Remove from heat. Stir in cooked rice, egg, parsley and cheese; mix well. Add more salt if necessary. Stuff tomatoes right up to top. Place tomatoes in an oiled (olive oil) baking pan. Bake in preheated moderate oven (350° F.) for about 15 minutes. Spoon 1 teaspoon or more of the dressing over each tomato while they are still warm, and serve at once. Serves 8.

DRESSING

2 tablespoons olive oil
1 tablespoon wine vinegar
Juice of 1 lemon

Pinch of powdered mustard
Pinch each of salt and pepper

Mix all ingredients well to make a dressing. Spoon over warm baked tomatoes.

Tomatoes Stuffed with Chicken Salad

6 medium-sized firm tomatoes, unpeeled
1 cup diced boiled chicken (any leftover pieces will do)
½ cup diced celery stalks with leaves
1 cup mayonnaise

3 pimientos, drained and diced
2 whole scallions, minced, or 1 teaspoon grated onion
8 fresh parsley sprigs, leaves only, chopped fine
Pinch each of salt and pepper

Cut a cap off each tomato and reserve. Scoop a deep hollow in each tomato and turn upside down to drain for about 15 minutes. Place all other ingredients in a bowl and mix well. Stuff tomatoes with the mixture and press caps on. Refrigerate. Serves 6.

Pickled Mushrooms

2 pounds small (or button) mushrooms
1 quart cider vinegar
2 quarts water
½ teaspoon salt
½ teaspoon black pepper

½ teaspoon crushed red pepper
4 bay leaves
2 garlic cloves, mashed
6 whole cloves
2 cinnamon sticks
Dressing (see below)

Remove stems from mushrooms and save for another purpose. Place vinegar and water in a saucepan and bring to a boil. Add salt, black and red pepper, bay leaves, garlic, cloves, and cinnamon; stir. Add mushrooms and boil for 15 minutes. Turn off heat and cool in the liquid for 15 minutes. Drain well and place in bowl. Cover with dressing. Allow to cool, and refrigerate. Serves 4 to 6.

DRESSING

6 tablespoons olive oil
1 large garlic clove
2 bay leaves, broken up
2 tablespoons wine vinegar

Pinch of black pepper
Pinch of salt, if needed
1 teaspoon prepared mustard

Put all ingredients in a bowl and mix well. Pour over mushrooms.

Pickled Eggplant with Jalapeño Peppers

3 jalapeño peppers, diced, all seeds removed
3 garlic cloves, mashed well
½ teaspoon salt
½ teaspoon freshly ground black pepper
2 medium-sized ripe tomatoes, diced

12 slices of Genoa-style salami, cut into thin strips
1 teaspoon dried orégano
½ cup olive oil
3 tablespoons wine vinegar
4 cups diced eggplant

Place the peppers, garlic, salt, pepper, tomatoes, salami, orégano, olive oil and vinegar in a bowl. Mix well and pour over eggplant. Toss well and refrigerate for 2 days. Then place in a skillet and simmer slowly for about 40 minutes. Remove from the heat and allow to cool. Mix well when cold and refrigerate. Great with cold meats. Can also be eaten as an antipasto if you like *hot* peppers. Makes about 4 cups.

Bagna Cauda

½ cup butter
½ cup olive oil
4 garlic cloves, mashed
10 anchovy fillets

½ teaspoon freshly ground black pepper
Pinch of crushed red pepper
Italian white truffles (canned)

Combine butter and oil in an earthenware crock with heat underneath. (Crocks especially designed for *bagna cauda* can be purchased in Italian kitchen supply houses.) Or you may use a double boiler. Heat the oil and butter. Add garlic, anchovies, and black and red pepper. Stir and bring to a boil. Cook for a few minutes until anchovies are dissolved. Shave truffles over top.

Place the crock in the center of the table and dip, family style. Dunk raw carrots, celery, finocchio, fresh tomatoes, fresh green peppers, Italian peppers in vinegar, and *cardo* (a bitter type of celery). Naturally, good fresh Italian bread goes well with this. Keep *bagna cauda* warm over a warmer or by reheating. To complete a delectable dish, add a bottle of Barbera, Freisa or Barolo. Serves 6 to 8.

3

Salads and Salad Dressings

Spring Dandelion Salad

At the first sign of spring, a delicious salad grows in our lawns, gardens, fields and meadows. It is the dandelion, a great natural spring tonic. Pick lots of them while they are young, sweet and tender. They become too tough after the flowers bloom. If you live in a city apartment, buy them from your vegetable man as soon as they reach the market. To prepare dandelions, cut off the leaves close to the root, soak in plenty of fresh water, wash well, dry in a large towel, and refrigerate. Serve with Italian Salad Dressing (page 49), or try this dressing.

2 slices of Italian bread, cut into cubes
1 garlic clove
1 tablespoon fresh creamery butter, melted
4 hard-cooked eggs
6 tablespoons virgin olive oil
2 tablespoons wine vinegar

1 teaspoon salt
1 teaspoon freshly ground black pepper
½ cup minced cold cooked chicken, boiled ham or cooked beef
2 fresh tomatoes, sliced very thin

Place bread cubes in a bowl. Mash the garlic and mix well into the butter. Spoon the butter over bread cubes and toss well. Mash the eggs with a fork. Mix with the bread and add all other ingredients. If you have no cooked meat available, use a little prosciutto or salami. Whip with a wire whisk or kitchen fork. Place lots of dandelion greens in a very large bowl and pour dressing over top. Toss well. Serve a large portion to each person, with a Bel Paese, Stracchino or fresh mozzarella cheese and a bottle of Bardolino. Add Bugie (page 231) and caffè espresso and you have a simple healthful luncheon meal. Serves 4.

Note: Enjoy this three or four times while dandelions are tender, and to get the full benefit from them in taste and mineral content. As the dandelions go out of season, cicoria comes in, then the tender field salad, rugola. Also watercress and the green leaf lettuces such as Bibb lettuce, curly endive, and others. Eat plenty of these wonderful salads every day.

Belgian-Endive and Radish Salad

1 good-sized head of Belgian endive per person
3 good-sized red radishes per person
6 tablespoons olive oil
2 tablespoons white-wine vinegar
Juice of 1 fresh lemon
1 garlic clove, mashed
1/3 teaspoon freshly ground black pepper
1/3 teaspoon salt
2 tablespoons heavy cream
3 hard-cooked egg yolks, mashed with a fork

Trim the endives, wash, and dry well. Scrape the radishes lightly at the tops and trim the roots. Wash and dry radishes and cut into 1/4-inch slices. Combine dressing ingredients in a bowl. Mix well. Discard bits of garlic. Add sliced radishes and refrigerate. When ready to serve endive, separate leaves and arrange on a serving plate. Spoon dressing over top. Serves 4 to 6.

Cicoria and Cicoria-Root Salad

1 pound fresh cicoria
1 pound cicoria salad roots
1/4 cup olive oil
1 garlic clove, split
1 teaspoon freshly chopped parsley
Juice of 1 fresh lemon
Salt and pepper
1/4 to 1/2 cup Leone's Master Salad Dressing (page 50)

Cicoria is usually found at Italian vegetable markets. The very bitter roots are usually sold separately from the greens. Cut off close to the root crown, scrape the roots, and cut off the ends. Wash and dry. Place the roots in a pan, cover with hot water, and boil for about 30 minutes, or until tender. Drain and place in a bowl. Mix olive oil, garlic, chopped parsley, and lemon juice. Pour the mixture over the still warm roots. Toss and set aside to cool. Then refrigerate. It will keep.

Wash cicoria leaves and shred coarsely. Refrigerate. At serving time, discard the garlic and place cicoria roots in a good-sized bowl. Add the shredded leaves. Season with salt and pepper to taste. Pour the salad dressing over all and toss well. Serve with a rare roast beef or steak, Italian bread, and a bottle of Saint-Julien, a red Bordeaux. Serves 4 to 6.

Raw Spinach Salad

1 pound uncooked fresh spinach
2 red pimientos, drained and diced
1 small ripe tomato, chopped
¼ cup olive oil
2 tablespoons wine vinegar
Tiny pinch of salt
Pinch of freshly ground black pepper

1 garlic clove, mashed
2 hard-cooked eggs, mashed with a fork
3 anchovy fillets, minced or mashed
Juice of ½ fresh lemon

Wash the spinach carefully several times to get rid of all sand. Or buy prewashed and trimmed fresh spinach at the supermarket, give it a quick wash, and dry well. Place spinach in a bowl, add pimientos and tomato, and refrigerate.

Combine oil and vinegar in a bowl. Add salt, pepper, garlic, mashed eggs, minced anchovies and lemon juice. Mix well. When ready to serve, discard bits of garlic. Pour over spinach and toss well. Serves 4 or 5.

Watercress Salad

2 full bunches of watercress
1 sweet red onion (Italian, Bermuda, California or Texas), sliced very thin
6 tablespoons olive oil
2 tablespoons wine vinegar

Juice of ½ lemon
Pinch of black pepper
2 anchovy fillets, minced
6 salted capers, chopped fine
1 small garlic clove, mashed
½ teaspoon prepared mustard

Trim stem ends of watercress. Wash and drain the watercress, place in a towel or napkin, and shake water out of it. Shred, and refrigerate. Arrange sliced onion on 4 individual serving plates. Place watercress over onion. Combine dressing ingredients and mix well. Discard bits of garlic. Spoon dressing over the watercress. Serves 4.

Tomatoes and Sweet Onions with Roquefort Dressing

4 medium-sized ripe tomatoes, chilled and sliced
1 medium-sized sweet onion, sliced very thin
2 ounces nice ripe Roquefort, mashed with a fork

6 tablespoons Italian Salad Dressing (page 49)
2 fresh green scallions, minced
1 teaspoon dried orégano
Salt and pepper

For those who like cheese, this is a simple, good salad combination. Arrange tomatoes on 4 serving plates with onion over top. Place dressing ingredients in a small bowl and mix well. Spoon over tomatoes and onions. Serves 4.

Tomatoes, Scallions and Cucumbers with Gorgonzola Cheese

2 good-sized tomatoes, sliced thin
4 whole fresh green scallions, diced
2 cucumbers, scraped lightly and sliced thin
2 celery stalks with leaves, minced
¼ cup virgin olive oil
2 tablespoons wine vinegar
Juice of ½ lemon

½ teaspoon salt
½ teaspoon freshly ground black pepper
1 teaspoon dried orégano
8 fresh parsley sprigs, coarsely chopped
2 hard-cooked eggs, mashed with a fork
1 garlic clove, mashed
4 slices of Gorgonzola cheese

Place tomatoes, scallions, cucumbers, and celery in a bowl. Mix oil, vinegar, lemon juice, salt, pepper and orégano together. Add parsley, eggs and garlic. Pour over salad and toss. Serve 1 slice of cheese on each salad plate. Serve with a loaf of fresh Italian bread and a bottle of Valpolicella. Serves 4.

Egg, Cucumber and Tomato Salad

½ head of Boston lettuce, shredded
4 hard-cooked eggs, sliced
1 medium cucumber, sliced
1 celery stalk with leaves, diced
6 red radishes, sliced
2 medium-sized ripe tomatoes, sliced thin
½ teaspoon freshly ground black pepper
Pinch of salt
1 garlic clove, mashed
3 tablespoons virgin olive oil
1 tablespoon wine vinegar
2 whole fresh green scallions, diced
Juice of ½ lemon

Place the shredded lettuce, sliced eggs, sliced cucumber, celery, radishes and tomatoes in a bowl. Mix the dressing ingredients together. Discard bits of garlic. Spoon dressing over the vegetables and eggs. Serve as an antipasto or as a salad. Serves 4.

Waldorf Salad

6 whole pimientos
1 cup diced apples
½ cup shelled walnuts, chopped
1 cup diced celery
¾ to 1 cup mayonnaise
Juice of ½ lemon
¼ teaspoon white pepper
Lettuce leaves
Salt
8 walnut halves

Drain the pimientos and cut into ¼-inch squares. Place first four ingredients in a bowl. Add mayonnaise, lemon juice, and pepper; mix well. Add salt if needed. Refrigerate until ready to serve. Arrange over leaves of crisp lettuce on individual serving plates. Garnish each serving with 2 walnut halves. Serve as an antipasto or as a salad. Serves 4.

Persimmon and Avocado Salad

1 ripe persimmon, peeled and halved
1 ripe avocado, peeled and halved
Lettuce leaves
¼ cup Leone's Master Salad Dressing (page 50)

Place half a persimmon and half an avocado on individual serving plates over several leaves of lettuce. Spoon dressing over top. Serve with a soft Camembert cheese. This is an unusual and delicious combination.

Another way to serve this is to cut both persimmon and avocado lengthwise into thin slices and arrange them alternately on individual plates. They may be dressed with Italian Salad Dressing (below) instead of the other. Serves 2.

Pimiento, Tuna and Apple Salad

4 ounces red pimientos
1 large green or red pepper, cut into very thin slices
4 ounces Italian tuna (*ventresca*) in olive oil, or a good American tuna
4 whole fresh green scallions, diced
1 large apple, peeled, cored and diced
6 fresh parsley sprigs, leaves only, chopped fine
8 ounces mozzarella, Bel Paese or Swiss cheese, diced
Pinch of salt
Pinch of freshly ground black pepper
6 tablespoons mayonnaise
6 tablespoons Leone's Master Salad Dressing (page 50)

Drain the pimientos and cut into ½-inch strips. Place in a bowl and add all other ingredients except mayonnaise and salad dressing. Mix mayonnaise and salad dressing together and pour the mixture over the salad; toss. Taste and add more salt if necessary. Refrigerate. Serve as an antipasto or as a salad. Serves 4.

Italian Salad Dressing

6 tablespoons virgin olive oil
1 garlic clove, mashed
2 tablespoons wine vinegar
Juice of ½ lemon
1 teaspoon salt
1 teaspoon freshly ground black pepper

Place oil in a bowl, add garlic, and stir well. Discard bits of garlic. Add all other ingredients and beat well with a wire whisk or kitchen fork. Refrigerate. A good salad dressing must be well beaten and blended. This is a simple oil and vinegar dressing. Add any seasoning to your taste, such as basil, orégano, anchovies, crushed red pepper, chopped fresh green scallions, powdered mustard or others. Makes about 1 cup.

Leone's Master Salad Dressing

1 cup plus 2 tablespoons virgin olive oil
1 garlic clove, mashed
⅓ teaspoon freshly ground black pepper
⅓ teaspoon salt
6 tablespoons wine vinegar

1 whole green scallion, chopped fine, or 1 teaspoon minced sweet Italian or Bermuda onion
1 teaspoon minced celery leaves
1 small hard tomato, chopped fine

Combine oil with garlic. Stir well to extract garlic flavor, then discard bits of garlic. Add all other ingredients, beat or stir with a wire whisk or egg beater, and refrigerate. Take out of the refrigerator 1 hour before using.

The secret of making a good salad dressing is to use good ingredients and give the mixture lots of beating. Prepare an extra amount of the dressing and store it in the refrigerator for future use. Serve over Bibb, iceberg, or Boston lettuce; chicory or curly endive; escarole, romaine, field salad (rugola), cicoria, dandelion greens, or mixtures of these. Makes about 2 cups.

Mayonnaise

6 egg yolks
2 tablespoons powdered mustard
4 cups virgin olive oil
1 teaspoon salt

Juice of 2 fresh lemons
¼ cup good white-wine vinegar
½ teaspoon freshly ground white pepper

Have all ingredients and utensils at room temperature. Place egg yolks in a bowl and beat well with a wire whisk. Add mustard, a little olive oil, and the salt. Beat well. Mix lemon juice and vinegar together. Add 1 teaspoon of the mixture very slowly, beating constantly. Then slowly add more oil, drop by drop, alternating with lemon-vinegar, always beating as mixture thickens. Always beat in the same direction. Add pepper and more salt if necessary. This is the old way of making mayonnaise and it is still the best. Makes about 5 cups.

Vinaigrette Dressing

2 egg yolks
1 garlic clove, mashed
1 teaspoon powdered mustard
Pinch of freshly ground black
  pepper

½ cup olive oil
Juice of 1 fresh lemon
1 teaspoon finely chopped capers
3 tablespoons wine vinegar
Salt

Beat egg yolks in a bowl. Add the garlic, mustard and pepper. Mix oil in slowly. Add lemon juice and capers; beat. Add vinegar, beat well, and add salt to taste. Refrigerate. Serve over cold asparagus, broccoli, cauliflower, Brussels sprouts, artichokes and artichoke hearts. Makes about 1 cup.

4

Mother's Delicious Soups

MOTHER was never in favor of having a great variety of soups on her menu, but she did want her very best ones to please her customers and friends. The most popular soup in Italy is minestrone and Mother's version is mouth-watering and irresistible. It was always a great favorite at Leone's.

Among the recipes following, you will find a number of hearty and nutritious soups that you can serve proudly as complete meals.

Mother's Minestrone

(with fagioli della regina, *Queen's beans, and all fresh vegetables)*

1 pound dried cranberry beans
5 quarts water
1 pound fresh green beans, broken into halves
6 ounces salt pork, diced
1 pound potatoes, peeled and diced
3 tablespoons olive oil
1 pound onions, peeled and diced
2 cups (one 1-pound can) peeled plum tomatoes or 2 pounds ripe tomatoes, chopped
3 medium-sized garlic cloves, mashed
½ teaspoon freshly ground black pepper
1 teaspoon salt
1 medium-sized carrot, scraped and diced
1 celery stalk with leaves, minced
1 pork hock or hambone
1 ounce spaghettini per person
¼ cup butter

Soak the dried cranberry beans in water overnight. Drain and discard water. If using fresh beans, shell 2 pounds to have 1 pound shelled. Do not soak the fresh beans. Add beans to the water and bring to a boil. Lower the heat and add all other ingredients except butter and spaghettini. Cook slowly for 2 hours.

When beans are cooked, measure 1 generous cup of soup for each person into another pot. Bring to a boil and add 1 ounce spaghettini, broken into 1½-inch pieces, for each person. Cook for 8 minutes. Add the butter, stir and serve. Serve grated Parmesan cheese on the side, and for wine, a Valpolicella.

Pour the remainder of the soup into several containers, and cool. When cold, freeze for serving at a later time. When ready to serve the frozen soup, just reheat it slowly, stirring occasionally. Serves 15 or 16.

The Peasant's Minestrone

(with fresh spareribs, Savoy cabbage and fagioli della regina)

1 pound dried cranberry beans
3½ pounds fresh spareribs
5 quarts cold water
3 tablespoons olive oil
1 pound onions, peeled and diced
2 large garlic cloves, mashed
2 pounds fresh Savoy cabbage, shredded
6 ounces salt pork, chopped
1 cup canned peeled plum tomatoes or 1 pound ripe tomatoes, chopped
½ teaspoon minced fresh basil
½ teaspoon black pepper
Pinch of crushed red pepper
1 pound potatoes, peeled and diced
1 pound fresh green beans, broken into halves
1 medium-sized carrot, scraped and diced
1 celery stalk with leaves, diced
¼ cup butter
1 ounce spaghettini per person

Soak the dried beans as in Mother's Minestrone (page 52), or use 1 pound shelled fresh beans. Have spareribs cut into 2-inch pieces (butcher will do this). Pour the water into a large pot. Add beans and spareribs and cook for 45 minutes. Skim all grease off top and discard. Add the amount of hot water that was discarded with the grease. Check spareribs occasionally to be sure you do not overcook them. Add olive oil and all other ingredients except butter and spaghettini. Cook slowly for 2½ hours, but be sure to remove the spareribs as soon as they are cooked, even when a little underdone.

Place spareribs in a separate pan and keep warm. When soup is cooked, return spareribs to soup pot, add butter, and bring soup to a boil. (At this point, if you do not intend to serve all of the soup at once, take out what you are putting aside.) Add 1 ounce spaghettini, broken into 1½-inch pieces, per person. Boil for 8 minutes. Serve a large portion of beans, spareribs and cabbage in individual bowls or large deep dishes. Freeze what is left over, just as with regular minestrone. When ready to serve the frozen soup, heat in the same way. A good wine as accompaniment is aged Chianti. Serves 15 or 16.

Mezzo e Mezzo Carne e Fagioli Zuppa del Mezzardo

(half and half meat and bean soup of the share cropper)

¼ pound dried lima beans
¼ pound dried white navy beans
2 tablespoons olive oil
2 tablespoons sweet butter
2 ounces salt pork, diced
½ pound onions, peeled and diced
1 good-sized garlic clove, mashed
½ pound Italian sweet sausage (not the thin sausage)
½-pound chunk of lean pork

½ pound shoulder of lamb
¼ teaspoon freshly ground black pepper
¼ teaspoon salt
2 good-sized ripe tomatoes, chopped
½ head of iceberg lettuce
½ pound potatoes, peeled and diced
8 ounces spaghettini
Grated Parmesan cheese

Combine lima and navy beans in a strainer, wash well, and place beans in a soup pot with 2 quarts cold water. Soak overnight. In the morning, add 1 cup cold water to beans and bring to a boil. Add 1 tablespoon olive oil and simmer slowly.

In another saucepan combine 1 tablespoon olive oil, the butter and salt pork; heat. Add onions and cook for 3 minutes. Add garlic and cook to medium brown. Add sausage and pork. Trim fat from lamb shoulder and cut the meat into 2 pieces. Add to pork. Brown slowly for 15 minutes. Add pepper and salt, stir, and add the tomatoes. Cook for 5 minutes, stir, and add all this mixture to the beans. Add a little of the hot bean soup to the saucepan just emptied and stir to get all the drippings and flavor, then return all to soup. Cover the pot and continue to cook for about 45 minutes.

Check cooking of meats; remove any meat that is cooked and set aside. Do not overcook any of the meats. Wash the lettuce and

coarsely shred it. Add with the potatoes, cover, and cook for about
1 hour. Taste for salt. Slice the pork and cut the sausage into 2-inch
pieces. Return all to soup pot. Add spaghettini, broken into 1½-
inch pieces. Stir well and cook for 8 minutes. Serve the soup with
grated Parmesan cheese on top. A loaf of well-crusted Italian bread,
a green salad with Italian Salad Dressing (page 49), and a bottle of
Barbera or aged Chianti will complete the meal. Serves 8.

Note: In cooking a soup like this one or other bean soups, I always cook a larger quantity to get the full flavor of the ingredients.
I freeze what I do not use. Always set aside for freezing before
adding spaghettini.

Mezza Zuppa di Fagioli Bianchi con Prosciutto e Lingua de Vitello alla Napoli

(half soup of white beans with prosciutto and veal tongue alla Napoli)

½ pound dried white beans
2 fresh leeks
2 tablespoons virgin olive oil
4 ounces salt pork, diced
1 celery stalk with leaves, minced
1 fresh veal tongue (about 1⅓ pounds)
4 small tomatoes or ½ cup canned peeled plum tomatoes, chopped fine
½ teaspoon freshly ground black pepper

10 fresh parsley sprigs, leaves only
2 large garlic cloves, mashed
6 whole fresh green scallions, diced
1 pound potatoes, peeled and diced
5 thin slices of prosciutto, diced
5 tablespoons uncooked rice
2 tablespoons butter

Wash the beans and soak in 4 cups cold water overnight. Wash
the leeks thoroughly and dice only the tender part. Place 4 cups
cold water in a large soup pot and add the beans with the water
they soaked in. Add the oil, salt pork, leeks, celery and tongue.
Bring to a boil, lower the heat, and add tomatoes and black pepper.
Chop the parsley and garlic together and add to the soup. Add half
of diced scallions (save half to serve with finished soup). Cover and
simmer for 1 hour. Uncover and check beans and tongue for cooking. Add potatoes and prosciutto, cover again, and simmer for

about 40 minutes. Check again 25 minutes before serving. Add the rice, check carefully for salt, stir, and cover again. Cook for 20 minutes longer.

Remove the tongue from the soup. When cool enough to handle, trim skin and slice. Serve sliced tongue with the soup. Add the butter to the soup and stir in. If soup is too thick, add a little boiling water and reheat. Garnish with diced green scallions. Serve with a loaf of Italian bread and a bottle of Valpolicella. Serves 4 to 6.

Minestra di Trieste

(soup of Trieste)

2½ pounds pigs' knuckles
1 pound dried cranberry beans
2 large garlic cloves, mashed
12 fresh parsley sprigs, leaves only
5 quarts cold water
½ pound onions, peeled and diced
6 ounces salt pork, diced
1 prosciutto hambone or hock
½ pound potatoes, peeled and diced

4 medium-sized ripe tomatoes, chopped
1 carrot, scraped and diced
1 celery stalk, minced
3 tablespoons olive oil
½ teaspoon freshly ground black pepper
½ teaspoon salt, approximately
3½ cups (one 1-pound, 4-ounce can) sauerkraut
1 pound fresh green beans
¼ cup butter, melted

Wash the pigs' knuckles and cut into halves; or have the butcher prepare them. Wash the cranberry beans and soak them overnight as in Mother's Minestrone (page 52); or use 1 pound shelled fresh beans. Chop the garlic and parsley together.

Place the water in a large soup pot. Add drained or fresh cranberry beans. Bring to a boil and add all other ingredients except sauerkraut, green beans and butter. Lower the heat and cook slowly for 1½ hours. Soak the sauerkraut in water for 30 minutes, then drain, discarding the water. Wash the green beans, cut off the stem and blossom ends, and cut beans into halves. Add drained sauerkraut and green beans to the soup. Cook for 40 minutes. Lift out bones and discard. Check carefully to see if more salt is needed. When cooked, add the butter and stir. If there is any soup left over, it freezes well. Makes about 4 quarts.

Lentil Soup

1 pound dried lentils
4 quarts water
3 garlic cloves, mashed
1 celery stalk, diced
1/4 cup olive oil
4 ounces salt pork, diced
1 1/2 pounds onions, peeled and diced
1/2 teaspoon black pepper
1 teaspoon salt
2 good-sized ripe tomatoes or 1 cup canned peeled plum tomatoes, chopped

1 pound potatoes, peeled and diced
1/4 pound carrots, scraped and diced
2 large leeks, diced
1 can (9 ounces) pitted black olives
1/4 cup butter
8 slices of boiled Italian salami or mortadella, diced

Wash the lentils and soak in 2 quarts water overnight. Drain and discard the water. Bring the 4 quarts water to a boil and add all the ingredients except the olives, butter and salami. Cook slowly for 1 1/2 hours. Add olives, salami or mortadella, and butter. Cook for 30 minutes longer. Taste for seasoning and add more if necessary. Serves 6.

Green Split-Pea Soup

2 1/2 cups green split peas
3 quarts water
3 tablespoons olive oil
1/2 pound carrots, scraped and diced
1 celery stalk, diced
1 1/2 cups diced onions
1 medium-sized baking potato, peeled and diced
1 ham hock

6 ounces salt pork, diced
1 bay leaf, crumbled
1 large garlic clove, mashed
1 teaspoon salt
1/2 teaspoon black pepper
1 pound fresh peas, shelled
1/2 pound vermicelli
1/4 cup sweet butter
1/2 cup freshly grated Parmesan cheese

Soak the split peas in water overnight. Drain and discard the water. Place the 3 quarts water in a large soup pot and heat. Add drained split peas and the oil and bring to a boil. Add next ten ingredients. Cook slowly for 1 hour.

Remove soup from the heat and discard the ham bones. Pass the soup through a strainer or purée in a blender. Place soup back in the pot, bring to a boil, and add the fresh peas. Cook slowly for 1 hour. Check for doneness. Do not burn. Add the vermicelli and cook for 6 minutes. Take the soup off the heat and stir in the butter. Let stand for 4 minutes. Sprinkle some of the cheese over each serving. Serves 6 or more.

Ceci-Bean Soup

1 pound dried ceci beans (chick-peas)
3 large garlic cloves, mashed
8 fresh parsley sprigs, leaves only
¼ cup olive oil
½ cup sifted all-purpose flour
¾ pound onions, peeled and diced
4 whole green scallions, diced
4 ounces salt pork, diced
2 celery stalks, diced
4 medium-sized ripe tomatoes or 2 cups canned tomatoes, chopped
2 carrots, diced
3 fresh sage leaves or 1 teaspoon dried leaf sage
2 tablespoons butter, melted
¼ teaspoon salt
¼ teaspoon freshly ground black pepper
½ cup uncooked rice

Wash the ceci beans and soak in water overnight. Drain the soaked beans and measure the water. Add enough to make 4 quarts water. Chop the garlic and parsley together. Place the drained beans in a large soup pot. Pour the oil over the beans and blend. Sprinkle with the flour. Mix very well with a spoon. Add the water, chopped garlic and parsley, and next eight ingredients. Bring to a boil, then add the salt and pepper. Lower the heat and cook slowly for 1½ to 2 hours. Add the rice, stir, and cover. Cook for 20 minutes. Taste; add more seasoning if necessary, and check to see that all ingredients are cooked.

When soup is cooked, lift out one third of the ceci beans and put them through a sieve or purée in a blender. Pour the purée back into the soup pot and mix. Serve with cheese sprinkled over the top. Serves 8.

Zuppa di Aglio alla Napolitana

(garlic soup)

¼ cup olive oil	5 cups beef or chicken broth, boiling hot
¼ cup butter	4 fresh eggs
4 slices of Italian bread, cut into cubes	½ teaspoon freshly ground black pepper
8 garlic cloves, mashed well	Salt
8 fresh parsley sprigs, leaves only, chopped fine	¼ cup freshly grated Parmesan cheese
6 tablespoons dry red wine	

Place olive oil and butter in a soup pot and heat. Add bread cubes and garlic. Allow to cook to a golden color, but do not burn. Add parsley and wine. Cover and cook for 1 minute, then add the broth and bring to a boil. Break the egg shells, one at a time, and drop each egg separately into boiling broth. Boil for 1 minute, then remove the pot from the heat. Add the pepper, and salt if needed; remember, broth and cheese contain salt. Ladle 1 egg with some of the bread cubes into a hot individual soup bowl. Fill with broth and sprinkle a spoonful of cheese over top. Serve with a bottle of Barolo. Serves 4.

Leek and Potato Soup

1 pound fresh leeks	1 teaspoon salt
2 quarts water	½ teaspoon freshly ground black pepper
2 pounds potatoes, peeled and quartered	¼ cup sweet butter
2 heaping tablespoons grated onion	½ cup heavy cream
2 cups milk	½ cup freshly grated Parmesan cheese

Wash the leeks thoroughly; dice and put aside about 2 ounces of the tender white heart. Cut the rest of the leeks into ½-inch pieces. Place the water in a soup pot and add the potatoes, leeks and grated onion. Bring to a boil, then add the milk, salt and pepper.

Cook slowly for 30 minutes. Lift out the cooked potatoes and leeks and force them through a ricer or sieve, or purée in a blender, and return to the soup pot. Add the tender diced leeks, the butter, and cream; bring to a boil. Be sure to stir and do not allow to burn. Cook slowly for 15 minutes. Stir in the cheese and taste for seasoning. Add toasted Italian bread when serving.

To serve cold, add 1 tablespoon heavy cream and 1 tablespoon cold milk for each cup of soup. Chill. Add a pinch of freshly chopped chives before serving. Serve in chilled cups. Serves 6 to 8.

Mushroom Soup

1 pound fresh mushrooms, washed and dried	1/4 cup diced onion
1/3 ounce dried Italian mushrooms	Pinch of black pepper
	Pinch of cayenne pepper
1/2 cup lukewarm water	5 cups boiling beef broth
3 tablespoons olive oil	1/2 cup dry sherry
1/4 cup butter	Salt
2 garlic cloves, mashed	1/2 cup heavy cream

Remove mushroom stems and chop fine. Then slice the caps thin and chop coarsely. Soak the dried mushrooms in the lukewarm water. Drain, saving the water, and chop the mushrooms.

Place olive oil and butter in a medium-sized saucepan or soup pot. Heat and add garlic. Stir well to extract flavor of garlic. Discard bits of garlic. Add onion and sauté until medium brown. Add dried mushrooms with water, fresh mushrooms and chopped stems, and sauté slowly for 15 minutes. Add black and cayenne pepper, beef broth and sherry. Add salt to taste if needed. Bring to a rapid boil for 5 minutes. Remove from the heat and stir in cream. Serve immediately. The recommended wine is sherry. Serves 4 or 5.

Onion Soup with Spinach

Prepare Onion Soup (see page 61). When adding the boiling broth to the soup, also add 1 package (10 ounces) prewashed fresh spinach which has been rewashed and chopped, and 1 teaspoon pastina per person. Cook for about 6 minutes, or until spinach is cooked. Sprinkle a little Parmesan cheese over the top.

Onion Soup

2 tablespoons olive oil
3 tablespoons butter
4 cups thinly sliced onions
1 large garlic clove, mashed
1 teaspoon salt
1 teaspoon freshly ground black pepper

1½ tablespoons all-purpose flour
1 cup dry red wine
8 cups beef or chicken broth
6 to 8 medium-sized slices of Italian bread, toasted
1½ cups grated Parmesan cheese

Combine olive oil and butter in a heavy saucepan and heat. Add onions, cover, and sauté slowly for 12 minutes. Uncover and cook slowly to a dark brown. Add garlic, salt and pepper. Sprinkle in flour and stir. Add wine and simmer for 3 minutes. Add boiling broth and cook slowly for 10 minutes.

Pour soup into a crock or heatproof glass dish and cover with the slices of toast. Cover the entire surface with the cheese. Place under broiler (low heat) and brown. Serve with more cheese if desired. Serve a bottle of aged Barolo. Some gourmets like an extra touch of a dry red wine in their onion soup. Serves 6 to 8.

Fresh Vegetable Soup without Meat

2 large fresh leeks
1 pound fresh green beans
2 pounds fresh peas in shells
3 quarts cold water
1½ carrots, scraped and diced
½ celery stalk, diced
1 bunch of whole fresh green scallions, diced
½ pound potatoes, peeled and diced

½ pound white turnips, peeled and diced
¼ pound onions, peeled and diced
2 tablespoons olive oil
Pinch each of salt and pepper
6 tablespoons fresh creamery butter
⅓ cup grated Parmesan cheese

Wash the leeks thoroughly and dice them. Wash and trim the green beans and cut them into halves. Shell the peas; there will be about 1 pound when shelled; or use 1 pound frozen peas or a 1-pound can of peas.

Place the water in a large soup pot. Bring to a boil and add all ingredients except butter and cheese. Cover and cook slowly for 2 hours. Taste for salt and add more if necessary. Remove soup from the heat and add the butter. Sprinkle cheese over the top, stir, and serve. Serves 6 to 8.

Zuppa di Pesce Fresco del Pescatore

(fisherman's soup of all fresh fishes)

8 ounces red snapper
8 ounces bass
8 ounces halibut
8 ounces cod
36 fresh littleneck clams in the shell
1 pound jumbo shrimps (15 to 20 to the pound)
1 cup sifted all-purpose flour
3 eggs, beaten
½ cup sifted bread crumbs
½ cup olive oil
½ cup butter

3 firm ripe tomatoes, sliced very thin
3 garlic cloves, mashed
12 fresh parsley sprigs, leaves only
½ teaspoon crushed red pepper
½ teaspoon black pepper
2 bay leaves, crumbled
2 cups dry white wine
2 cups boiling water
2 loaves of Italian bread
1 garlic clove, cut

Cut the four kinds of fish into 2-inch pieces. Do not open the clams. Wash them under cold running water and scrub with a brush. Check to see if they are sound by hitting them together. Discard any open ones. Shell the shrimps, and wash and devein them while still raw. Split down the middle lengthwise.

Sprinkle the fish with flour, shake off any excess, and then dip into the beaten eggs. Roll in bread crumbs. Place 6 tablespoons of the oil in a large skillet and heat. Sauté the fish pieces on each side for 5 minutes. Remove the skillet from the heat, but leave the fish in the skillet.

Place the butter and the remaining olive oil in the bottom of a large soup pot. Heat. Add the raw shrimps, clams still in their shells, and the sliced tomatoes. Cover and cook for 10 minutes. Chop the mashed garlic and parsley together and add to the soup with the red and black pepper and the bay leaves. Cover and cook for 10 minutes longer. Add sautéed fish to the pot and pour in the oil and juices from the skillet. Pour the white wine into the pot, cover, and cook slowly for 5 minutes. Add the boiling water and cook, uncovered, for 10 minutes. Turn off the heat and keep pot covered.

Slice the bread and rub the slices with the cut garlic clove. Toast in the oven. Do not burn. Place 2 slices of toast in each individual soup bowl. Arrange pieces of fish over the toast and then the clams and shrimps, divided evenly. Pour all of juices over the clams and the fish, and enjoy a real fisherman's dish. For a wine, serve a good Soave. Serves 8 to 10.

Fresh Clam Soup

2 dozen medium-sized cherry-stone clams
1 pound calamaretti or calamari (squid)
1/4 cup olive oil
2 tablespoons butter
1/3 pound onions, peeled and diced
2 baking potatoes, peeled and diced
1 carrot, scraped and diced

1 cup bread crumbs
3 garlic cloves, mashed
8 fresh parsley sprigs, leaves only
1/4 teaspoon crushed red pepper
1/2 teaspoon freshly ground black pepper
6 tablespoons dry white wine
2 medium-sized ripe tomatoes, sliced thin
3 cups boiling water

Wash clams and scrub with a stiff brush under cold running water to remove sand. Open and save natural juice. To make it easier to open them, after they are washed and dried place them in a bowl in the freezer for 1 hour. The cold will make them start to open. Or have your fishman open them. Ask him to save the natural juice, with no water added. Have fishman clean and wash the squid. Dry them and cut into dice.

Combine olive oil and butter in a soup kettle and heat. Add the onions and cook until medium brown. Add potatoes and carrot, stir, and cook slowly for 5 minutes. Add calamari. Meanwhile toast the bread crumbs in the oven. Do not burn. Sprinkle toasted bread crumbs over top and mix well. Cook for 15 minutes. Chop garlic and parsley together. Add to the soup with red and black pepper, and cook for 2 minutes. Add wine, cover, and cook for 2 minutes longer. Add all of the clam juice, the clams, tomatoes and boiling water.

Stir, cover, and cook for 10 minutes. Taste to see if salt is needed. A cold bottle of Orvieto will go nicely with this. Serves 4 or 5.

Fresh Lobster Bisque

2 lobsters (about 1½ pounds each)
2½ cups simmering water
2½ cups simmering milk
2 bay leaves, crumbled
2 large ripe tomatoes, sliced thin
6 peppercorns, cracked slightly
2 celery stalks
1 onion, sliced
2 garlic cloves, mashed
½ cup butter
¼ cup sifted all-purpose flour
1 cup heavy cream, hot
Pinch of grated nutmeg
Pinch of paprika
½ cup dry sherry

Place lobsters in a large saucepan and cover with the water and milk. Add bay leaves, tomatoes, peppercorns, celery, onion and garlic. Cook for 20 minutes. Remove lobsters from the liquid and set aside to cool for 10 minutes. Strain the liquid. Split lobsters into halves and remove head sacs and intestinal veins. Remove all meat from shells, including roe if any, and chop fine. Return chopped lobster to the strained liquid.

Put a fine sieve over a saucepan, and pound all shells and the chopped lobster and liquid through the sieve. Discard shells. In another pan melt the butter, stir in the flour, and gradually stir in 2 cups of the sieved broth. When the mixture is smooth, add it to rest of the liquid and simmer for 3 minutes. Remove from the heat and add the hot cream, grated nutmeg, and paprika. Heat but do not boil. Lastly stir in the sherry. Serve in heated bowls or cups. Serves 4 to 5.

Fresh Clam Bisque

2 dozen fresh cherrystone clams, in the shell
3 cups cold water
1 medium-sized tomato, chopped
2 celery stalks, diced
1 medium-sized onion, sliced
⅓ teaspoon black pepper
¼ cup butter, melted
¼ cup sifted all-purpose flour
2 cups clam broth, hot
¾ cup heavy cream, hot
Chopped fresh chives or parsley

Scrub the clams thoroughly under cold running water. Place in a saucepan and cover with the cold water. Add the tomato, celery, onion and pepper. Cover and cook for 15 minutes. Remove clams from pot, saving broth. Allow to cool for 5 minutes before taking clams out of shells. Chop clams fine. Strain broth through a triple thickness of cheesecloth or a wet kitchen towel, leaving a very little broth at bottom of pan as there may be sand settled there. Clean the pan and put clams and broth back.

Melt the butter, add the flour, and stir. Slowly add 2 cups hot clam broth, stirring constantly. When smooth, add to clams and broth. Simmer for 3 minutes. Turn off heat and add the hot cream. Taste for seasoning. Serve in hot cups, adding a sprinkle of chives or parsley, preferably chives. Serves 6.

Simple Chicken Soup

Chicken necks, wings, backs, second joints, livers and gizzards
3 quarts cold water
1 carrot
2 celery stalks
2 medium onions, cut into halves
Salt and pepper
3 tablespoons uncooked rice

This tasty soup uses the less-wanted parts of the chicken that you may be preparing for another dish.

Place the chicken parts in a large soup pot and cover with the water. Bring to a boil and add carrot, celery, onions, and salt and pepper to taste. When wings and second joints are cooked, remove from pot. Cook soup slowly for 1 hour longer. Then add the rice, stir, cover, and cook for another 20 minutes. Uncover, stir, and put back the pieces removed earlier. Cook just long enough to reheat them, about 5 minutes. Serve the soup in deep plates. Serves 6.

Chicken and Chicken Broth

$2\frac{1}{2}$ pounds chicken wings, necks, backs, feet and giblets
1 stewing chicken or fowl (6 to 7 pounds)
5 quarts water
2 garlic cloves, mashed
$\frac{1}{4}$ teaspoon black pepper
1 teaspoon salt
6 fresh parsley sprigs, cut into 1-inch pieces
1 bay leaf
2 medium onions, each cut into 8 wedges
3 celery stalks with leaves, each cut into 4 pieces
2 medium-sized ripe tomatoes, sliced

Soak chicken feet in boiling water for 15 minutes. Then peel off skin with a knife. Mash all the wings, necks, backs, feet and giblets with a mallet or the flat side of a heavy cleaver. Wash the fowl well. Place water and fowl in a large soup pot and bring to a boil. Lower the heat and add all other ingredients. Simmer for 1½ hours. Skim fat off top. Check cooking of stewing chicken after 1 hour. When the bird is cooked, remove it from the pot, salt it lightly, and set aside. Cook soup with other ingredients for 1 hour longer.

Remove soup from the heat and strain it through a sieve. Discard the mashed chicken parts. Cut up the fowl at the joints and slice the breasts. Return chicken and strained soup to the pot and add more salt if necessary. Reheat. Serve broth with a sprinkle of Parmesan cheese on top. Serve the chicken on a warm platter, garnished with boiled potatoes and parsley. Add a green salad (dandelion, rugola, field salad or watercress), dressed with Leone's Master Salad Dressing (page 50). This meal calls for a Château Haut-Brion. Serves 6 to 8.

Save any broth and pieces of chicken that are left. They may be used in other soup preparations. Here are several delicious ways to use broth and chicken pieces.

Chicken Broth with Escarole

Wash 1 head of escarole thoroughly and drain well. Shred the escarole. Bring 5 cups broth to a boil, add escarole, and cook for 15 to 20 minutes. Serve with a teaspoon of cheese on top. Serves 4.

Chicken Broth with Rice and Diced Chicken

Bring 5 cups broth to a boil. Add ¼ cup uncooked rice, cover, and cook for 25 minutes. Dice the meat from wings, legs and backs of the fowl. Add to the rice and broth. Serve with a teaspoon of cheese on top. Serves 4.

Chicken Broth with Noodles and Sliced Chicken

Bring 5 cups broth to a boil and add 4 ounces thin noodles. Cook noodles for about 12 minutes. Taste a strand of noodles during the cooking to be sure they are not overcooked. Serve noodles and broth together in soup cups. Add slices of chicken to the broth and sprinkle a little Parmesan cheese over it. Serves 4.

Chicken Broth with Sherry

Serve 1 cup chicken broth with 2 tablespoons dry sherry stirred into it. Add a sprinkle of Parmesan cheese. Serves 1.

Stracciatella in Brodo di Gallina

3 cups chicken broth	Pinch of freshly ground pepper
4 fresh pullet eggs or 2 medium to large eggs	4 slices of white meat of chicken or turkey
2 teaspoons pastina	Salt

Bring the broth to a boil and remove from the heat. Beat the eggs in a medium-sized bowl. Slowly spoon and stir half of the hot broth into the beaten eggs. Put all back into the soup pot with remaining broth. Bring to a boil again and add the pastina, pepper, and sliced chicken. Cook for about 5 minutes. Taste to see if pastina is cooked and add salt if necessary. Serve in hot deep soup bowls. Sprinkle cheese over the top. For a wine, cream sherry. To finish off this simple, light, but nourishing dinner, have Bibb lettuce or Belgium endives in a salad with a soft Camembert, then a red Delicious apple. Serves 2.

Beef Broth

4 pounds veal and beef bones	6 tablespoons canned tomatoes or 2 medium-sized ripe tomatoes, chopped
1 beef marrowbone	
2½ pounds beef short ribs	
5 quarts water	1 large garlic clove, mashed
4 whole medium-sized onions	8 parsley sprigs, coarsely chopped
2 celery stalks, each cut into 4 pieces	Pinch of freshly ground black pepper
2 carrots, cut into halves	Salt
2 medium potatoes	

Wash the bones well in cold water. Place the meat and bones in a large kettle. Add the water, bring to a boil, and cook for 30 minutes. Skim grease off the top and add all the rest of the ingredients with salt to taste. Cover and simmer for 45 minutes. When the meat and vegetables are fully, but not over, cooked, remove them and set aside. Simmer the soup for another 40 minutes.

When ready to serve return meat and vegetables to the soup just long enough to reheat. Serve them on a hot platter with a pungent sauce. A good sauce can be made by mixing 1½ cups mayonnaise with 2 tablespoons prepared horseradish. Serve a cup of steaming hot broth first. Put in each serving of broth 1 ounce (2 tablespoons) good dry red wine. If there is broth left over, save it for another soup (see below). Serves 6 to 8.

Beef Broth with Little Meat Balls and Pastina

6 fresh parsley sprigs
6 leaves of fresh chives or ½ teaspoon dried chives
½ slice of bread
½ pound lean beef, finely chopped
1 large shallot or 2 whole fresh scallions, minced
1 tablespoon grated onion
1 tablespoon olive oil
2 slices of prosciutto, chopped fine
7 teaspoons grated Parmesan cheese
1 egg, lightly beaten
Salt and pepper
6 cups beef broth (page 67)
4 teaspoons pastina

Chop parsley and chives together and place in a bowl. Soak the bread in a little milk, then squeeze dry and shred into the bowl. Add the beef, shallot, onion, olive oil, prosciutto, 3 teaspoons of the cheese, the egg, and salt and pepper to taste. Mix well and make into small meat balls.

Bring beef broth to a boil. Add meat balls, lower the heat, cover, and cook for about 20 minutes. Add the pastina and cook for about 5 minutes more. Sprinkle remaining cheese on top. Serve with hot toasted Italian bread, a bottle of Dolcetto or Barbera Spumante, a soft Bel Paese cheese, and nice ripe pear for a perfect light dinner. Serves 4.

5

Mother's Pasta, Rice and Polenta, and Her Delicious Sauces

HERE are the basic rules on how to cook spaghetti and macaroni. Use plenty of water. Using too little water makes the spaghetti sticky and pasty. Cook about 2 ounces of pasta per person. You should use at least 4 quarts of water. Use only fresh cold water to start with. Bring to a furious, steaming boil. Add 1 heaping tablespoon salt for 4 persons. This is important: Do not cook spaghetti without salt. It will never taste right. Now place your spaghetti gently into the boiling water. Allow the boiling water to soften it. Stir immediately and often. Do not allow the pasta to stick to the bottom of the pan.

Spaghettini, a favorite size, cooks in about 10 minutes. A heavier spaghetti cooks in about 12 minutes. If you are cooking a heavier pasta such as ziti, cook for 20 to 25 minutes. The Italians usually like pasta firm, *al dente* (to the teeth), but Americans like it a little softer. Taste a strand occasionally to test its doneness.

As soon as the pasta is cooked, drain it well. Do not allow it to stay in the water. Drain it in a colander or a strainer. Do not rinse it in or under cold water. After draining, put the spaghetti back into the hot pot it was cooked in. Add a little butter, cheese and sauce and gently stir with a fork. Cover the pot until you are ready to serve. The sauce should be put on each individual serving and the cheese should be served separately to the guests.

Spaghetti with Italian-Sausage and Eggplant Sauce

1 pound Italian sweet sausage
1 fresh eggplant (about 1½ pounds)
2 large garlic cloves, mashed
10 fresh parsley sprigs, leaves only
3 tablespoons olive oil
¼ cup fresh creamery butter
2 ounces salt pork, diced
¼ pound onions, peeled and diced

1 teaspoon salt
½ teaspoon black pepper
3 green peppers, sliced very thin
2 cups (one 1-pound can) peeled plum tomatoes, chopped or sieved
3 large ripe tomatoes, chopped fine
Spaghetti
Parmesan cheese

Remove the casing from the sausage and cut the meat into small pieces. Wash and dry the eggplant but do not peel it. Cut it into 6 crosswise slices and then into ½-inch cubes. Chop the garlic and parsley together.

Combine olive oil, butter and salt pork in a saucepan; heat. Add onions and cook until medium brown. Add sausage and brown for 10 minutes. Add garlic and parsley, salt and pepper, and cook for 10 minutes longer. Add green peppers and eggplant cubes, stir, and cook for 5 minutes. Add canned and fresh tomatoes and cook for 30 minutes, slowly. Taste to see if sauce is cooked and add more salt if necessary.

Cook 3 ounces spaghetti per person in boiling salted water for about 12 minutes, until done to your taste. Drain well and place in a large bowl. Pour sausage and eggplant sauce over the pasta. Sprinkle Parmesan cheese over it. Mix and serve on warm individual plates. Enjoy this dish with a bottle of aged Barolo. Makes about 6 cups sauce.

Spaghettini with Clam Sauce

24 medium-sized cherrystone clams
¼ cup virgin olive oil
¼ cup fresh creamery butter
1 ounce salt pork, diced
3 medium-sized garlic cloves, mashed

12 fresh parsley sprigs, leaves only
Pinch of flour
Pinch of crushed red pepper
Pinch of freshly ground black pepper
1 pound spaghettini

Open the clams, saving any juices, and coarsely chop the clams. Combine olive oil, butter, and salt pork in a skillet; heat. (For a meatless meal, omit the salt pork.) Chop garlic and parsley together and add to skillet. Cook slowly for 2 minutes. Do not burn. Add chopped clams and cook for 5 minutes. Add flour and red and black pepper and stir well. Do not add salt as the clams are salty. Cook for 3 minutes. Add about 1/4 cup of the clam juice, but be careful not to make the sauce too liquid. Bring to a boil and mix and the clam sauce is ready.

In the meantime have boiling salted water ready for the spaghettini. Cook for 10 minutes. (If a heavier spaghetti is used, cook a little longer.) Always taste a strand before removing from the heat to be sure it is cooked to your taste. Drain immediately and place back in the hot pot in which it was cooked. Pour a little sauce over it and mix. Serve in a warm bowl and add the rest of the sauce. Serves 4 or 5.

Note: You may add a dash of Tabasco and a squeeze of lemon to the balance of the clam juice for an invigorating and refreshing cocktail. Or mix clam juice with a glass of Champagne and a dash of Tabasco.

Salsa di Olio di Olive, Aglio e Acciughe per Spaghettini

(olive-oil, garlic and anchovy sauce for spaghettini)

1/2 ounce dried French or Italian mushrooms
1/4 cup lukewarm water
1 pound spaghettini
1/4 cup virgin olive oil
2 tablespoons fresh creamery butter
3 large garlic cloves, mashed
Pinch of crushed red pepper

1/2 teaspoon freshly ground black pepper
8 anchovy fillets, mashed with a fork
1/4 cup freshly ground Parmesan cheese
1 loaf of Italian bread
8 thin slices of mortadella or Italian salami

Soak the dried mushrooms in the 1/4 cup lukewarm water for 30 minutes. Drain, saving the water, and chop the mushrooms fine. Combine olive oil and butter in a skillet and heat. Add garlic and red and black pepper; heat but do not burn. Add chopped mushrooms with 2 tablespoons of the mushroom water. Stir and cook for 5 minutes. Meantime, cook spaghettini in unsalted boiling water.

(Unsalted water is unusual in cooking pasta, but in this case it is best because the anchovies are salty.)

When spaghettini is ready, drain well and place back in the hot pot in which it was cooked. Take sauce from the heat and add anchovies to it, stirring well. Pour sauce over spaghettini, mix, and add the cheese. Place on warm individual plates and serve immediately with slices of Italian bread and the mortadella or salami arranged on the bread; for wine, Bardolino. Serves 4.

Salsa di Lumache Tarantese con Lumache per Spaghettini

(snail sauce Tarantese with snails for spaghettini)

36 snails (imported canned)
6 large fresh oysters
10 fresh parsley sprigs, leaves only
2 large garlic cloves, mashed
1 whole hot cherry pepper
1/3 ounce dried Italian mushrooms
2 tablespoons warm water
2 tablespoons olive oil
1 ounce salt pork, diced
1/2 cup sweet butter

4 whole green scallions, sliced lengthwise and diced
1/4 cup chopped red onion
1/2 teaspoon freshly ground black pepper
1/4 cup red wine
4 medium-sized ripe tomatoes, chopped fine
Pinch of salt
1 to 1 1/2 pounds spaghettini
1/4 cup freshly grated Parmesan cheese

Chop 6 of the snails to add more flavor to the sauce and cut the rest of them into halves. Open the oysters, saving any juice, and coarsely chop the meat. Set aside oysters and juice separately. Chop parsley and garlic together. Cut the hot pepper into halves and discard the seeds. Wash and dry the pepper and cut into fine slices. Soak the mushrooms in the warm water for 20 minutes. Save the mushroom water and chop the mushrooms fine.

Combine olive oil, salt pork and 6 tablespoons of the butter in a saucepan; heat. Add scallions and red onion and cook slowly for 3 minutes. Add snails and oysters and cook for 3 minutes longer. Add parsley and garlic, black pepper and sliced cherry pepper and cook for 2 minutes. Stir. Add the wine, shake the skillet, and cook for 2 minutes more. Add mushrooms, tomatoes, mushroom water, salt and oyster juice. Cook slowly for 3 minutes. Do not burn. Check for salt and add more if necessary. Cook for 10 minutes more, uncovered.

In the meantime, cook spaghettini. When cooked, drain, place back in the hot pot, and add the remaining 2 tablespoons butter. Add 6 tablespoons of the snail sauce and the grated cheese. Mix, and cover until ready to serve. Place spaghettini on individual serving plates and spoon all of sauce over top. Snail sauce can also be served over toast as a main course. Drink a Bardolino or a Soave with this dish. Serves 4 to 6.

Macaroni and Clams with Clam Sauce

18 good-sized fresh cherrystone clams
24 fresh littleneck clams
3 garlic cloves, mashed
10 fresh parsley sprigs, leaves only
1/4 cup olive oil
1/4 cup fresh creamery butter
Pinch of crushed red pepper
Pinch of black pepper
2 good-sized ripe tomatoes, chopped
1 tablespoon tomato paste
Pinch of flour
3/4 pound ziti, millerighe, or other large macaroni
Grated Parmesan cheese

Open the cherrystone clams, saving natural juices, and chop the clams medium-fine. Do not open the littleneck clams, but wash under cold running water and scrub with a brush. Be sure all are tightly closed; discard any that are opened or broken. Chop the garlic and parsley together.

Combine olive oil and butter in a skillet and heat. Add chopped clams and cook for 3 minutes. Add garlic and parsley, red and black pepper, and stir. Do not add salt as clams are salty. Cook for 2 minutes. Add tomatoes, tomato paste, 2 tablespoons of the reserved clam juice, and the flour. Add unopened littleneck clams, cover, and cook for about 10 minutes, or until clams are open.

In the meantime cook the pasta in boiling salted water for 20 to 25 minutes. Taste for doneness before removing from the heat. Drain well and place in a warm bowl. Sprinkle cheese and a little of the sauce over the pasta and mix. Serve macaroni in deep soup bowls or plates and spoon all of the clams and sauce over pasta. Serve a chilled bottle of California rosé. Serves 4 to 6.

Ziti with Broccoli

1¼ to 1½ pounds fresh broccoli
8 fresh parsley sprigs, leaves only
2 large garlic cloves, mashed
¾ pound ziti
¼ cup olive oil

2 tablespoons butter
¼ cup freshly grated Parmesan
   cheese
½ teaspoon freshly ground black
   pepper

Cut stems off broccoli and wash thoroughly. Chop parsley and garlic together. Steam broccoli in a little water in a covered saucepan for about 25 minutes. In another pot cook the ziti in boiling salted water for about 20 minutes. Combine olive oil, butter, parsley and garlic. Stir to get flavor of garlic. Warm this sauce for 2 minutes, but do not cook or burn.

Drain broccoli and ziti as soon as cooked. Place both in the hot pot the ziti was cooked in and pour the sauce mixture over both. Sprinkle on the cheese and black pepper, stir, and serve immediately. Have a loaf of good Italian bread and a bottle of Barolo. Instead of dessert, try a mixed rugola and dandelion salad with Italian Salad Dressing (page 49) and a soft Brie or Bel Paese cheese. Serves 4 to 6.

An Impromptu Pasta Sauce with Farfalle

1 ounce salt pork minced
6 tablespoons olive oil
¼ cup butter
1 pound lean beefsteak, ground
   twice
½ teaspoon salt
½ teaspoon pepper
2 large garlic cloves, mashed
⅓ bunch of fresh parsley, leaves
   only, chopped

4 cups (two 1-pound cans) peeled
   plum tomatoes, sieved
1 heaping tablespoon tomato
   paste
1 pound farfalle (butterflies)
¼ cup freshly grated Parmesan
   cheese

Combine salt pork, olive oil, and butter in a skillet; heat. Add beef and brown slowly for 10 minutes. Add salt, pepper, garlic and parsley; cook for 10 minutes. Add tomatoes and tomato paste and cook slowly for 30 minutes. Add more salt if necessary.

Meantime cook farfalle about 20 minutes. As soon as ready, drain and return to the pot with a little sauce and the grated cheese stirred in well. Cover. Serve the rest of the sauce on top. To complete the meal, try a green salad, a loaf of Italian bread, a good bottle of red Chianti, fresh ripe pears with Bel Paese cheese, and caffè espresso. This sauce is also good with ziti. Serves 4 to 6.

Fettucini al'Alfredo of Rome

One of the outstanding restaurants in Rome is Alfredo's. My good friend Alfredo was always a perfect host and showman and a master at cooking his specialty. He knew how to make his guests happy and had a great memory for faces and names. I didn't take too many vacations, especially to Rome, but whenever I did he always treated me royally.

I can still see his beaming face as he recognized and welcomed me. He would shout, with all the gestures of a true Roman, *"Ecco il mio caro amico, Eugenio Leone di New York. E lui che mi ha insegnato il mio buon mestiere."* (Here is my dear friend Gene Leone of New York. It is he who taught me my wonderful trade.)

Even though it wasn't true at all, it sounded awfully good, especially when I was entertaining friends. It was during one of these welcomes that I convinced him to give me the recipe for his world-famous Fettucini al'Alfredo.

It's a rather simple dish, easy to prepare and very delicious. Like Mother's famous shrimp sauce, it is a dish that the world has tried to copy but with little success.. I was very proud to add his wonderful fettucini to Leone's menu.

2 cups sifted all-purpose flour	Cornmeal
3 eggs	¾ cup fresh creamery butter
¼ teaspoon salt	6 tablespoons freshly grated Parmesan cheese
2 tablespoons cold water	

Place the flour on a pastry board, make a well in the center, and add eggs, salt, and 1 tablespoon of the water. Mix well with fingers and knead. Add rest of water as needed. Knead until the dough forms a ball and comes away from your hands clean. Cover and let stand for 1 hour.

Cut dough into 4 pieces. Roll out paper thin, as thin as possible. Place on a towel to dry for 20 minutes. Now roll each sheet into a scroll about 2½ inches wide. Place on a board and cut into ¼-inch strips. Pick up with both hands and lightly shake loose, spreading the strips on wax paper. Sprinkle a little cornmeal over the fettucini. (You can buy the pasta ready-made in a package, but it won't taste quite the same.)

Cook the fettucini in salted boiling water for 10 minutes. Check to see if it is cooked the way you like it. When ready, drain well and place back in the hot pot. Add about half of the butter; mix well. Add half of the cheese and mix again. Place in a warm bowl. Add the rest of the cheese and butter and mix well. Place the bowl in a hot oven for 2 minutes. Remove, and serve from bowl onto hot plates at table. Serves 4.

Spinach Noodles

1 package (10 ounces) fresh spinach	Cornmeal
3 cups sifted all-purpose flour	¼ cup sweet butter
4 eggs	6 tablespoons grated Parmesan

Cut stems off spinach and wash the leaves. Cook, covered, in very little salted water. Drain well, saving the cooking water, and chop spinach fine. Set aside to cool.

Place the flour in a bowl, add eggs, and mix well with hands. Slowly add about 2 tablespoons of spinach water, then the chopped spinach. Knead well. Dough must be very firm. If necessary, add a little more flour. Divide dough into 3 sections. Roll dough out on a floured board with a floured rolling pin to a very, very thin sheet. Place on a towel and let stand for 20 minutes. Fold 1 sheet at a time to about a 2-inch strip. Cut into ¼-inch-wide noodles. Gently lift noodles to a platter. Sprinkle with a little cornmeal and set aside until ready to cook.

Cook noodles in rapidly boiling water for 10 to 12 minutes. When tender, drain immediately and put back in the hot saucepan. Add the butter and cheese and a little sauce of your choice; stir. Cover until ready to serve. Serves 6.

Note: Italian-Sausage and Tomato Sauce (page 98) was specially created for noodles, and is particularly good with these.

Ravioli

Enrico Caruso, after his performances at the Metropolitan Opera, often came in for what he called a snack, a great big plate of Mother's ravioli.

SAUCE FOR RAVIOLI

1½ pounds lean beef (flank or bottom round)
1 pound fresh lean pork shoulder
3 garlic cloves, mashed
1 teaspoon fresh rosemary
½ cup olive oil
¼ cup butter
4 ounces salt pork, diced
¾ pound onions, peeled and diced
2 bay leaves, crumbled

Tiny pinch of ground allspice
1 teaspoon freshly ground black pepper
½ cup good dry red wine
1 cup canned peeled plum tomatoes, chopped or sieved
2 medium-sized ripe tomatoes, chopped
2 cups boiling water
1 teaspoon salt

Cut the beef and pork shoulder into small cubes. Chop garlic and rosemary together. Combine olive oil, butter and salt pork in a saucepan; heat. Add onions and sauté slowly to medium brown. Add beef and pork cubes and simmer for 20 minutes. Add bay leaves, allspice, black pepper, and garlic and rosemary mixture. Cook for 10 minutes. Add wine, stir, cover, and cook for 3 minutes. Add canned and fresh tomatoes, boiling water and salt; simmer for 20 minutes. Remove from heat. Remove all meat from the sauce and put through a food chopper. Place half of the chopped meat back in the sauce, stir, and bring to a boil, slowly. Remove from heat. Put remaining chopped meat aside for the stuffing.

STUFFING FOR RAVIOLI

1 package (10 ounces) fresh spinach
Half of meat from sauce, chopped (see above)
1 cup grated Parmesan cheese

3 eggs
Pinch of black pepper
Pinch of freshly grated nutmeg
Salt

Wash the spinach, cook it until tender, then drain thoroughly and chop fine. Mix with meat, cheese, eggs, pepper and nutmeg. Add salt to taste. Mix well and your stuffing is ready.

HOMEMADE DOUGH FOR RAVIOLI

3½ cups sifted all-purpose flour	4 to 5 tablespoons water
4 eggs	1 tablespoon salt

Place flour on a long pastry or baker's board. Make a well in the center and drop eggs in. Add water, a little at a time, and the salt. Blend together and knead until smooth and elastic. Cover and let stand for 30 minutes. Divide into 4 parts. Roll out the dough, wrapping it around rolling pin until it is very thin, as thin as you can make it. Spread out dough on a flat surface.

ASSEMBLING RAVIOLI

Make a row of little mounds of stuffing on the rolled-out ravioli dough, using about 1 teaspoon for each. The mounds should be 2 inches from the edge of the dough and 1½ inches apart. When row is complete, cover by folding the dough over top; then press firmly between the mounds of stuffing with the side of your hand. Cut along the full length of strip and in between mounds with pastry wheel cutter, bearing down on wheel. Separate and allow to dry for at least 40 minutes. Continue until all dough and stuffing are used.

When ready to cook, place ravioli in boiling salted water and cook for about 12 minutes. Drain in a strainer, handling carefully, and place in a warm bowl. Spoon a little sauce over and sprinkle with grated Parmesan cheese. Mix gently. If you are making them for the next day or if you have some left over, refrigerate immediately, or freeze for future use. The sauce by itself and the uncooked ravioli freeze well. Serves 6 to 8.

Baked Homemade Lasagne

Even though I retired from the restaurant in 1959, my association with West Point has continued. I hope it never ends. On September 20, 1960, I received a letter from Major General W. C. Westmoreland, who was then Superintendent of the U.S. Military Academy.

He asked if I could spare the time to make a tour of the Cadet Mess facilities to help cope with the problem "of offering an attractive, well-balanced menu appealing to many regional tastes within a limited budget."

After a thorough inspection and investigation I made several suggestions and recommendations which resulted in several new seasoning agents being purchased and butter and pork being used to accentuate the flavor of appropriate foods. But what pleased me the most was that several new items were added to the Cadet menu including lasagne, which has proven to be very popular with the Cadets.

TOMATO SAUCE

½ pound lean beef
½ pound lean pork
10 fresh parsley sprigs, leaves only
2 large garlic cloves, mashed
¼ cup olive oil
¼ cup butter
2 ounces salt pork, diced
¾ pound onions, peeled and diced

1 teaspoon salt
½ teaspoon freshly ground black pepper
1½ pounds canned peeled plum tomatoes, chopped or sieved
1 small green pepper (2 to 3 ounces)
Chopped Meat Balls (see below)
3 tablespoons tomato paste

Grind beef and pork together. Chop parsley and garlic together. Combine olive oil, butter and salt pork in a skillet; heat. Add onions and sauté to medium brown. Add ground meat and brown. Stir well. Add parsley and garlic, salt and pepper, and cook for 20 minutes. Add tomatoes and green pepper and cook for 10 minutes. Taste for salt. Add meat balls and cook slowly for 1½ hours. When cooked, add tomato paste, stir well, and again taste for salt.

MEAT BALLS

1 pound lean beef
1 pound lean pork
½ small garlic clove
8 fresh parsley sprigs, leaves only
½ cup bread crumbs

½ cup grated Parmesan cheese
1 large egg
½ cup small raisins
1 teaspoon salt
½ teaspoon black pepper

Chop the beef and pork together. Chop the garlic and parsley together. Place all ingredients in a bowl and mix well. Taste for salt. Make meat balls about 1 inch across. You should get about 32.

SAUCE FOR TOP OF LASAGNE

2 tablespoons butter, melted	¾ cup Tomato Sauce (page 79)
2 tablespoons heavy cream	2 tablespoons all-purpose flour

Combine butter, cream and tomato sauce in a saucepan; heat. Stir and add flour.

LASAGNE PASTA

You may make your own pasta by using Homemade Dough for Ravioli (page 78). Roll out the dough into a thin sheet and cut it into strips 2½ inches wide and 10½ inches long. Or you may buy lasagne pasta ready-made in 1-pound packages. Homemade are better, of course.

Place 1½ pounds lasagne in boiling salted water with 1 tablespoon olive oil. Cook for 12 minutes. Remove from water and drain. Place on a towel until ready to use.

ASSEMBLING BAKED LASAGNE

Tomato Sauce (page 79)	1½ cups grated Parmesan cheese
Cooked lasagne	Sauce for Top of Lasagne (see
2 pounds ricotta cheese	above)
Meat Balls (page 79)	

Pour a thin layer of tomato sauce into the bottom of a rectangular baking pan and cover with a layer (3 strips) of lasagne. Spread half of the ricotta over it and add some meat balls and ½ cup of the Parmesan cheese. Cover with another layer of lasagne. Place remaining ricotta, the rest of the meat balls, and a layer of tomato sauce on top. Cover with a third layer of lasagne and spoon the sauce for top of lasagne over it. Cover pan with foil and bake in preheated moderate oven (350° F.) for 20 minutes. Remove foil and continue baking for about 20 minutes longer. Serves 8.

Cannelloni alla Romana

(a delicacy of the Romans)

CRÊPE BATTER

1 cup cold water	½ teaspoon salt
1 cup cold milk	1 cup sifted all-purpose flour
4 eggs	¼ cup butter, melted

Place water, milk, eggs and salt in a bowl and beat well. Add flour, then butter. Cover and refrigerate overnight, or not less than 3 hours. Batter should be like a thin cream. If too thick after your first crêpe, beat in a little water.

Use a 6- to 6½-inch skillet. Brush a little olive oil over entire skillet. Heat until pan is very hot. Remove from heat. Place 2 table-spoons of the batter in center of pan, then tilt pan in all directions until bottom of pan is covered, even the sides. Return pan to heat for about 70 seconds. Shake pan sharply to loosen the crêpe. Lift edge of crêpe to see if it is light brown, then turn to cook on the other side for about 30 seconds. Slide crêpe onto a plate. Oil skillet again and cook another crêpe, and so on until all batter is used. Prepare these ahead. If prepared the day before, refrigerate until ready to use. Makes 12 to 14 crêpes.

MEAT SAUCE

¼ cup butter	¼ pound fresh chicken livers
¼ cup olive oil	2 bay leaves
4 ounces salt pork, diced	2 garlic cloves, mashed
¾ pound onions, peeled and diced	8 fresh parsley sprigs, leaves only
1½ pounds beef, ground	1½ pounds canned peeled plum tomatoes
1 pound Italian sweet sausage	1 tablespoon tomato paste

Combine butter, olive oil and salt pork in a saucepan; heat. Add the onions and brown slowly. Add beef, sausage, chicken livers, and bay leaves. Cook slowly for 10 minutes. Taste for salt. Chop garlic and parsley together and add to the sauce. Stir and cook for 5 minutes. Add tomatoes and simmer slowly for 30 minutes. Stir well, remove from the heat, add tomato paste, and allow to cool.

Remove all meat from the sauce and put through a food grinder twice, or chop very fine. Return half of ground meat to the sauce and simmer slowly for 20 minutes longer. Put remaining ground meat aside for the stuffing.

Stuffing for Cannelloni

1 pound fresh spinach	Pinch of freshly grated nutmeg
Half of meat from sauce, ground	¼ teaspoon freshly ground
2 eggs, beaten	pepper
¼ cup freshly grated Parmesan cheese	Salt

Cook the spinach in very little salted boiling water for 10 minutes. Drain thoroughly and chop fine; drain again so that it is quite dry. Add the ground meat, beaten eggs, the cheese, nutmeg and pepper. Taste and add salt if necessary. Mix well.

Sauce Béchamel

2 tablespoons butter	½ teaspoon salt
2½ tablespoons all-purpose flour	Pinch of freshly grated nutmeg
1 cup boiling milk	¼ cup heavy cream

Stir butter and flour in a saucepan over low heat for 2 minutes. Remove from heat and add boiling milk and seasonings. Boil, stirring, for 1 minute. Lower the heat and slowly add cream, stirring constantly until thick. Remove from the heat.

Assembling Cannelloni

Spread out the crêpes. Place some stuffing evenly across the center of each crêpe, making a mound about ¾ inch thick. Fold crêpe twice over the filling. When all crêpes are filled, arrange them in a buttered baking pan. Spoon enough meat sauce (page 81) over the crêpes to cover them. Sprinkle with ¼ cup grated Parmesan cheese. Stir ½ cup of the meat sauce into the warm sauce Béchamel and mix well. Spoon this over everything. Place the baking pan in a preheated moderate oven (350° F.) for about 12 minutes. If any sauce is left over, use with other pasta. For each serving allow 2 of the filled crêpes. Serves 6 or 7.

Manicotti

This favorite dish was often enjoyed by my very good friend—and a fine artist—Willard Mullin.

3 cups sifted all-purpose flour	1 tablespoon olive oil
4 eggs	Stuffing for Manicotti (see below)
4½ tablespoons cold water	3 cups Meat Sauce (page 91)
Pinch of salt	¼ cup grated Parmesan cheese

Place flour on a pastry board and make a well in the center. Break the eggs into the well and add water, a little at a time, and the salt. Knead for about 10 minutes. Let stand, covered, for about 1 hour. Cut dough into 4 pieces and roll as thin as you can. Cut into rectangles 4 inches wide and 6 inches long. Place between pieces of wax paper. You should have about 12 pieces. Cook half at a time in 4 quarts salted boiling water with the olive oil added. Cook for 5 minutes. Drain and place between 2 towels.

Divide stuffing into 12 parts. Place a mound of stuffing on each dough rectangle about ⅓ inch from the edge; mound should be about ½ inch thick and ½ inch wide. Fold dough over twice. Spread a thin layer of the meat sauce on the bottom of a baking pan. Arrange manicotti about ¼ inch apart in the pan and spoon the rest of the sauce over the top. Sprinkle a teaspoon of Parmesan cheese over each of the manicotti. Bake in a preheated slow oven (300° F.) for 15 to 20 minutes. Serves 6 or 7.

STUFFING FOR MANICOTTI

¾ cup ricotta or cottage cheese	2 tablespoons grated Parmesan cheese
¾ pound mozzarella cheese, diced	½ teaspoon salt
3 eggs, lightly beaten	Pinch of black pepper
2 tablespoons butter	

Drain the ricotta or cottage cheese. Combine ricotta, mozzarella, eggs, butter, Parmesan cheese, salt and pepper in a bowl. Mix well.

Gnocchi

2 pounds best-quality baking po-
    tatoes
1 cup sifted all-purpose flour
1 whole egg
1 extra egg yolk

2 tablespoons butter, softened
1 teaspoon salt
Grated Parmesan cheese
Tomato Sauce alla Piemontese
    (see below)

Boil the potatoes in jackets until cooked. Peel and put through a ricer. While potatoes are still warm, blend them with the flour. Add lightly beaten egg and yolk, the butter and the salt. Place on a floured board and knead lightly. Keep dough soft. Roll into sticks 1 inch thick and about 10 inches long. Cut into ¾-inch pieces. Dent each piece in the middle with a fork.

When ready to serve, place gnocchi in boiling salted water. Cook until they rise to the top of the water. Drain and place in a warm bowl. Sprinkle the cheese and the sauce over them. Serve immediately. A Grignolino will go nicely with this pasta, or Nebbiolo Spumante. Serves 6 to 8.

TOMATO SAUCE ALLA PIEMONTESE

¼ cup butter
¼ cup olive oil
4 ounces salt pork, diced
¼ cup diced onions
½ pound Italian sweet sausage
½ pound lean beef, diced
2 garlic cloves, mashed
10 fresh parsley sprigs, leaves only
5 fresh basil leaves or ½ teaspoon
    dried basil
1 bay leaf, crumbled

½ teaspoon black pepper
18 slices of dried Italian mush-
    rooms
1 cup warm water
2 cups (one 1-pound can) peeled
    plum tomatoes
2 large ripe tomatoes, chopped
    fine
½ cup dry white wine
1 teaspoon tomato paste

Combine butter, olive oil and salt pork in a saucepan; heat. Add onions and sauté slowly to golden brown. Remove casing from sausage and cut the meat into ½-inch pieces. Add sausage pieces and diced beef to the saucepan and brown for 10 minutes. Chop garlic, parsley and basil together and add to the sauce along with bay leaf and pepper. Soak the mushrooms in the warm water for 20 minutes. Drain, saving the water, and chop the mushrooms. Meanwhile stir and cook the sauce slowly for 20 minutes. Put the canned tomatoes through a ricer or food mill and add to the sauce. Add fresh tomatoes, wine, mushrooms and mushroom water. Stir and cook slowly for 1 hour. Turn off the heat and cool for 10 minutes. Strain and put all solid pieces through a food grinder. Place all back in sauce. Add the tomato paste, stir, bring to a boil, and sauce is ready to serve.

Risotto alla Milanese with Truffles

This risotto is complicated, but it is a luxurious and delicious meal all by itself.

1 cup finely chopped cooked chicken
1 cup uncooked rice
1/8 teaspoon ground saffron
3 cups boiling chicken broth, or more if needed
2 tablespoons olive oil
6 tablespoons fresh creamery butter
3/4 pound onions, peeled and diced
1/2 teaspoon freshly ground black pepper
1 bay leaf, crumbled
1 can (4 ounces) white Italian truffles
4 fresh chicken livers, chopped fine
1/2 teaspoon salt
1/4 cup freshly grated Parmesan cheese

If you make your own chicken broth, save the best part of the chicken to slice for chicken Tetrazzini or other important uses, but use the wings, legs, backs, etc., to chop for this dish. Soak the rice in warm water for 15 minutes and drain. Dissolve the saffron in a little of the hot broth. Combine olive oil and butter in a saucepan and heat. Add onions and sauté for 4 minutes, or until medium brown. Add pepper, bay leaf and drained rice. Stir and cook for 2 minutes. Add 2 cups of the hot broth and the juice drained from truffles. Cover and simmer for 15 minutes. Add chopped chicken and the rest of the chicken broth with saffron and chicken livers. Taste for seasoning and salt and add the salt if needed.

This risotto should not be too liquid and must not be too dry. If necessary, add more broth, a little at a time. Do not overcook;

slightly underdone is better. Spoon onto a warm platter and shave the truffles over top of steaming rice. (Of course you can use more truffles; it's up to you. More truffles make the dish even more luxurious and delicious.) Sprinkle cheese over all and mix lightly. Serve immediately. This calls for a well-chilled bottle of Champagne. Serves 4 to 6.

Risotto alla Milanese alla Leone

1/4 cup butter
2 ounces salt pork, diced
2 tablespoons olive oil
3/4 pound onions, peeled and diced
4 fresh or frozen chicken livers, chopped fine

1/2 teaspoon salt
1/3 teaspoon freshly ground black pepper
1 cup uncooked rice
3 cups boiling chicken broth, or more if needed
1/8 teaspoon ground saffron

Place butter, salt pork and olive oil in a skillet; heat. Add onions and cook until medium brown. Add chopped livers, salt and pepper, and stir. Brown for 5 minutes. Add rice, stir well, and cook for 2 minutes. Add the boiling broth. Stir well, cover, and simmer for 18 minutes. Test for doneness and salt. Add saffron and stir. If the rice is too dry, add a little more broth. Do not overcook. Serve on warm plates with cheese sprinkled over top. A green salad with a slice of soft Bel Paese cheese and a bottle of Barbera Spumante tops off this delicious dinner. Serves 4 to 6.

Risotto alla Piemontese

1 cup uncooked rice
1/2 pound fresh mushrooms
1/4 cup olive oil
1/4 cup butter
1 ounce salt pork, diced
3/4 pound onions, peeled and diced
12 fresh chicken livers, coarsely chopped

6 fresh chicken gizzards, finely chopped
2 bay leaves, crumbled
1 large tomato, chopped fine
4 cups boiling chicken broth
Salt and pepper
Grated Parmesan cheese

Soak the rice in lukewarm water for 15 minutes and drain. Remove mushroom stems and chop very fine. Slice the caps. Or use ⅓ ounce dried mushrooms, soak them in ½ cup lukewarm water for 15 minutes, and drain, saving the water. Chop the soaked mushrooms.

Combine olive oil, butter and salt pork in a saucepan; heat. Add onions and cook slowly until light brown. Add chopped livers and gizzards and the bay leaves and brown slowly for 10 minutes. Add the tomato and mushroom caps and stems or dried mushrooms and water. Cover and cook for 10 minutes. Add rice, stir well, and brown for 2 minutes. Add 3 cups of the chicken broth and use balance of broth as needed. Cover and simmer for 17 minutes. Add salt and pepper as needed. Salt may not be needed as broth and salt pork may be salty enough. When cooked, remove from the heat; do not overcook. Sprinkle cheese over top. Serve immediately. A bottle of Barbera Spumante or Barolo will complete this dinner. Serves 4 to 6.

Risotto with Shrimps

36 raw jumbo shrimps	1 celery stalk with leaves, minced
2 garlic cloves, mashed	2 heaping tablespoons grated carrot
12 fresh parsley sprigs, leaves only	¼ teaspoon salt
3 fresh sage leaves or 1 teaspoon dried leaf sage	¼ teaspoon freshly ground black pepper
¼ cup olive oil	⅔ cup dry white wine
¼ cup fresh creamery butter	1 cup uncooked rice
2 ounces salt pork, diced	4 cups boiling chicken broth
1 pound onions, peeled and diced	Grated Parmesan cheese

Shell and devein the shrimps, wash them, and dry thoroughly. Chop half of them (18) into small pieces and slice the remainder lengthwise down the middle. Chop garlic and parsley together. If using dried sage, soak the leaves in lukewarm water for 15 minutes before using.

Combine olive oil, butter and salt pork in a saucepan; heat. Add onions and cook to medium brown. Add celery and carrot, stir, and cook for 5 minutes. Add all the shrimps and cook for 10 minutes.

Add garlic with parsley, sage, salt and pepper; stir and cook for 2 minutes. Add wine, cover, and cook for 3 minutes. Add the rice and cook for 2 minutes longer. Add 3 cups of the boiling broth, stir, and add more broth as needed. Cover and simmer for about 20 minutes; then check for cooking and seasoning. Do not overcook. Place on a warm platter and sprinkle cheese lightly on top. A semidry Orvieto (*abboccato*) goes well with this. Serves 6 or 7.

Note: For a meatless dish, omit the salt pork and add an additional 2 tablespoons butter.

Risotto con Tonno

1 cup uncooked rice	1 large garlic clove, mashed
2 tablespoons tomato paste	1/8 teaspoon freshly ground black
1/2 cup dry white wine	pepper
2 tablespoons olive oil	2 1/2 cups boiling broth or water
1/4 cup butter	1 pound Italian *ventresca* tuna in
2 ounces salt pork, diced	olive oil
1/2 pound onions, peeled and diced	Salt
Pinch of crushed red pepper (optional)	1/4 cup freshly grated Parmesan cheese

Soak the rice in lukewarm water for 15 minutes. Drain. Stir the tomato paste into the wine. Place olive oil, butter and salt pork in a skillet; heat. Add onions and cook until medium brown. Add garlic, red and black pepper, and wine with tomato paste. Stir and cook for 2 minutes. Add broth or water, stir, and cook for 3 minutes. Add drained rice, stir, cover, and simmer for 15 to 20 minutes. Then add the tuna and cook for 2 minutes. Test the rice at this point and taste for salt. Tuna may be salty enough so that no additional salt is needed. Risotto should not be too dry, so don't overcook. Arrange on a warm platter and sprinkle the cheese over top. I personally like Valpolicella, a delicious light red wine, with this dish. Serves 4 to 6.

Note: For a meatless dish, omit the salt pork and add an additional 2 tablespoons butter.

Wild Rice with Chicken Livers and Mushrooms

1 cup uncooked wild rice
½ pound fresh mushrooms
15 chicken livers
¼ cup olive oil
¼ cup sweet butter
2 ounces salt pork, diced
¾ cup diced onions
3 chicken gizzards, chopped fine
Pinch of freshly ground black pepper

About 30 fresh parsley sprigs, leaves only, chopped
3½ cups hot chicken broth, or more if needed
Salt
¼ cup freshly grated Parmesan cheese

Wash the wild rice in several changes of water, then soak in cold water for 15 minutes and drain. Cut the mushrooms into thin slices; or use ½ ounce dried mushrooms and soak them in ½ cup lukewarm water for 15 minutes; drain, saving the water, and chop the mushrooms. Chop 3 of the chicken livers into very small pieces.

Place olive oil, butter and salt pork in a saucepan; heat. Add onions and cook to light brown. Add all the livers, the gizzards, and black pepper and cook for 5 minutes. Add drained rice and stir. Add sliced mushrooms, or dried mushrooms and mushroom water if used, and the parsley; stir. Add broth slowly, stir, cover, and simmer for about 20 minutes. Test for doneness and add salt if needed. (Salt pork and chicken broth may have enough salt.) Serve rice on individual serving plates, allowing 3 whole livers per person. Sprinkle the cheese on top. For wine, a Barolo. Serves 4.

Polenta

1 cup yellow cornmeal
1 cup cold water
1 teaspoon salt
4 cups boiling water

2 tablespoons butter
½ to ¾ cup melted butter
½ to ¾ cup grated Parmesan cheese

Combine cornmeal, cold water and salt. Stir into the boiling water. Stir constantly over low heat for about 15 minutes. Add 2 tablespoons butter and stir. Sprinkle each individual serving with some of the melted butter and some of the grated cheese. Serve hot. Serves 4 to 6.

SAUTÉED POLENTA

Put any leftover polenta in a shallow pan and refrigerate. Cut into ½-inch slices and slowly sauté the slices in a mixture of half olive oil and half butter. Serve with grated Parmesan cheese, or with Marinara Sauce (page 94).

Polenta with Beef and Sausage Stew

1½ pounds lean beef
¾ pound Italian sweet sausage
2 garlic cloves, mashed
10 parsley sprigs, leaves only
½ pound fresh mushrooms
3 tablespoons olive oil
¼ cup butter
2 ounces salt pork, diced
½ pound onions, peeled and diced
¼ teaspoon freshly ground black pepper

1 bay leaf, crumbled
½ cup dry white wine
2 tablespoons minced celery
2 tablespoons minced carrot
1 medium-sized fresh tomato or ½ cup canned peeled plum tomatoes, chopped fine
½ cup hot water
Pinch of freshly grated nutmeg
Salt
Polenta (page 89), freshly cooked

Cut the beef into ½-inch cubes. Remove casing from the sausage and cut the meat into 1-inch pieces. Chop garlic and parsley together until almost puréed. Cut the mushrooms into thin slices; or use ½ ounce dried mushrooms and soak them in ½ cup lukewarm water for 15 minutes. Drain, saving the water, and chop the mushrooms.

Combine olive oil, butter and salt pork in a saucepan; heat. Add onions and sauté slowly until medium brown. Add beef and sausage and brown for 10 minutes. Add garlic and parsley, black pepper and bay leaf. Stir and cook for 10 minutes. Add wine, stir, cover, and simmer for 10 minutes. Add celery, carrot, tomatoes and mushrooms. Stir and cook for 10 minutes longer. Add hot water and water from dried mushrooms if any. Stir, cover, and simmer for 40 minutes. Grate a little nutmeg over the top and simmer, uncovered, for 10 minutes longer. Test beef for doneness; taste for salt and add if necessary, but salt pork may have added enough.

Divide the hot polenta among 4 to 6 warm plates. Serve the stew and gravy over polenta. Enjoy a bottle of Valpolicella with it. Serves 4 to 6.

Mother Leone's Meat Sauce

(for spaghetti)

½ pound salt pork, diced
¼ cup olive oil
¼ cup butter
¾ pound onions, peeled and diced
1 pound lean beef, cut into ½-inch cubes
½ pound lean pork shoulder, cut into ½-inch pieces
4 chicken livers, chopped fine
4 chicken gizzards, cut into small pieces
2 bay leaves, crumbled

5 garlic cloves, mashed
1 tablespoon fresh rosemary
½ teaspoon ground allspice
1 teaspoon freshly ground black pepper
5 pounds ripe fresh tomatoes or 6 cans (1 pound each) peeled plum tomatoes, chopped fine
¼ pound carrots, scraped and minced
¼ pound celery, minced
Salt
7 ounces tomato paste

Combine salt pork, olive oil and butter in a large saucepan; heat. Add onions and sauté to medium brown. Add beef, pork, chicken livers and gizzards and bay leaves; stir. Cook slowly, uncovered, for 30 minutes. Chop garlic and rosemary together and add to the sauce with allspice and pepper. Stir well and continue to cook over low heat for 20 minutes, and inhale the aroma. Cover and cook for 5 minutes. Add tomatoes, carrots, celery, and ½ tablespoon salt. Simmer slowly for 1½ hours, stirring occasionally. Do not hurry the cooking for a good sauce.

Remove sauce from the heat and allow to cool for 10 minutes. Then strain the sauce. Put whatever remains in the strainer through a food mill and return it to the sauce. Add the tomato paste, stir well, and bring to a boil. Check for salt, adding more if necessary. Any sauce that is not for immediate use can be frozen for a future occasion. Makes 3½ quarts.

Mother Leone's Tomato Sauce

3½ to 4 pounds veal knuckle
1 beef marrowbone
6 ounces salt pork, diced
¼ cup olive oil
¼ cup butter
¾ pound onions, peeled and diced
4 garlic cloves, mashed
14 fresh parsley sprigs, leaves only
5 fresh basil leaves or 1 teaspoon dried basil

5 pounds ripe fresh tomatoes, chopped fine, or 4 cans (1 pound, 1 ounce each) peeled plum tomatoes, sieved
2 medium-sized green peppers, chopped
1 teaspoon salt
½ teaspoon black pepper
3½ ounces tomato paste

Have the butcher crack the veal and beef bones. Combine the salt pork, olive oil and butter in a saucepan; heat. Add onions and sauté to medium brown. Add veal and beef bones and brown slowly for 20 minutes. Chop the garlic, parsley, and basil together and add it to the mixture. Stir and cook for 20 minutes. Add tomatoes and green peppers, cover, and cook slowly for about 2 hours. Stir occasionally. Do not allow to burn. Remove and discard all bones. Add salt, pepper, and tomato paste; stir well. Any sauce that is not for immediate use can be frozen. Makes 3 quarts.

Anchovy and Garlic Butter

12 anchovy fillets
2 good-sized garlic cloves, mashed
¼ cup sweet butter
2 tablespoons olive oil

Pinch of crushed red pepper
Pinch of freshly ground black pepper

Mash anchovies with a fork. Work in the mashed garlic and the cold butter, making a paste. Place in a bowl. Add olive oil and red and black pepper, and mix all ingredients together well. Do not add salt as anchovies make the spread salty enough. Do not cook or heat the butter sauce, but use just as it is over freshly cooked hot spaghetti. Add Parmesan cheese, mix, and serve with a bottle of red Chianti and fresh Italian bread. Simple, but delicious. Serves 4.

Note: Refrigerate any butter that is left over and spread over Italian bread as a tasty snack.

Ricotta-Tuna-Tomato Sauce

(with no garlic or onions)

4 good-sized ripe tomatoes	5 ounces tuna
½ cup fresh butter	½ cup ricotta cheese
Pinch each of salt and freshly ground black pepper	¼ cup grated Parmesan cheese

Drop the tomatoes into boiling water for 2 minutes, lift out, and remove skins. Chop the tomatoes. Place the butter in a saucepan and bring to a boil. Add the tomatoes and sauté for 20 minutes. Add salt and pepper. Remove from the heat and stir in tuna and ricotta. Pour over spaghetti or any pasta. Sprinkle Parmesan cheese on top. Place pasta under broiler for 2 minutes. Serves 4.

Tuna and Green-Pea Sauce

3 tablespoons olive oil	2 medium-sized ripe tomatoes, chopped fine
6 tablespoons fresh creamery butter	2 heaping tablespoons tomato paste
½ pound onions, peeled and diced	2 cups (one 1-pound can) small green peas, well drained
2 garlic cloves	6 ounces Italian *ventresca* tuna in olive oil
8 parsley sprigs, leaves only	8 anchovy fillets, mashed with a fork
Pinch each of black and crushed red pepper	
1 cup canned peeled plum tomatoes, chopped or sieved	

Combine olive oil and butter in a saucepan and heat. Add onions and brown. Chop garlic and parsley together and add to the onions along with the black and red pepper; stir. Cook slowly for 3 minutes. Add canned and fresh tomatoes, tomato paste, and peas. Stir and cook slowly for 20 minutes. Add tuna and anchovies, stir, and cook for 2 minutes. Serve. This sauce is delicious over a thin pasta like spaghettini, or just as good with a heavier pasta like ziti. Serves 4.

Marinara Sauce

6 tablespoons olive oil
¼ cup butter
3 large garlic cloves, mashed
16 fresh parsley sprigs, leaves only
½ teaspoon freshly ground black pepper

½ teaspoon salt
6 cups (three 1-pound cans) peeled plum tomatoes
1 tablespoon dried orégano
8 anchovy fillets, chopped
2 heaping tablespoons tomato paste

Combine olive oil and butter in a saucepan and heat. Chop garlic and parsley together and add to the pan. Cook slowly for 5 minutes, then add salt and pepper. Drain the tomatoes and chop the solids. Add the chopped tomatoes and orégano to the sauce and cook slowly for 30 minutes. Add anchovies and tomato paste, stir well, and remove from the heat. At the end of cooking, taste for salt and add some if necessary, but remember, the anchovies will make the sauce salty. Serve over macaroni, spaghetti, green beans, hard-cooked or scrambled eggs. Makes about 5 cups.

Champagne and Truffles Spaghetti Sauce

(lavish and most delectable)

3 tablespoons olive oil
6 tablespoons fresh creamery butter
4 ounces salt pork, diced
½ pound onions, peeled and diced
¾ pound lean beef, cut into ½-inch pieces
2 slices of prosciutto, minced
2 fresh chicken livers
2 fresh chicken gizzards
2 garlic cloves, mashed
8 fresh parsley sprigs, leaves only
½ teaspoon freshly ground black pepper

1 bay leaf, crumbled
½ teaspoon salt
1 heaping tablespoon finely grated carrot
1 heaping tablespoon finely chopped celery
1 can (4 ounces) white Italian truffles
2 cups (one 1-pound can) peeled plum tomatoes, sieved
2 medium-sized ripe tomatoes, chopped fine
3 tablespoons heavy cream
½ cup good Champagne
1 teaspoon tomato paste

Combine olive oil, 4 tablespoons of the butter and the salt pork in a saucepan; heat. Add onions and sauté until medium brown, slowly. Add beef and prosciutto. Chop chicken livers and gizzards together and add to the sauce. Brown for 15 minutes, slowly. Chop garlic and parsley together and add to the sauce with bay leaf, pepper and salt. Cook slowly for 30 minutes. Add carrot and celery and the juice drained from the canned truffles. Cook for 5 minutes. Add canned and fresh tomatoes and cook slowly for 30 minutes. Remove the mixture from the heat and allow to cool for 10 minutes. Put through a food mill and put all back in the saucepan. Cover and keep warm.

About 20 minutes before serving, place the heavy cream and the remaining butter in a bowl. Shred, slice, or shave the truffles into the same bowl, making very thin slivers; mix. Add the Champagne. Stir this mixture gently and smoothly into the reserved sauce. Add tomato paste and bring to a boil. Cook very slowly for 5 minutes. Remove from the heat, taste, and add more salt if necessary. Serve with a tender pasta like spaghettini, adding grated cheese with the sauce. Makes about 6 cups.

Squid Sauce for Pasta

1½ pounds fresh squid
3 tablespoons olive oil
3 tablespoons sweet butter
2 ounces salt pork, diced
¼ pound onions, peeled and diced
2 good-sized garlic cloves, mashed
12 fresh parsley sprigs, leaves only
½ teaspoon freshly ground black pepper

Pinch of crushed red pepper
¼ cup red dry wine
3 tablespoons freshly grated Parmesan cheese
6 small ripe tomatoes or 1 cup canned peeled plum tomatoes, chopped fine
⅓ teaspoon salt
½ teaspoon dried orégano
6 anchovy fillets, mashed with a fork

Have fishman cut off heads of squid, wash squid, and prepare for cooking. Dice the squid. Combine olive oil, butter and salt pork in a saucepan or skillet; heat. Add onions and cook until medium brown. Add squid, stir, and cook slowly for 15 minutes. Chop garlic and parsley together and add to the squid with red and black pepper.

Stir and cook for 2 minutes. Add wine, cover, and simmer for 5 minutes. Then add the cheese, chopped tomatoes, salt and orégano. Stir, cover, and cook slowly for 50 minutes. Taste for cooking and salt. When the sauce is ready to be taken off the heat, put in the anchovies. This sauce is good with a heavier pasta such as ziti, rigatoni, or mostaccioli. Makes about 4 cups.

Meatless Tomato Sauce

¼ cup olive oil
6 tablespoons fresh creamery butter
½ pound onions, peeled and diced
3 garlic cloves
10 parsley sprigs, leaves only
1 teaspoon salt
½ teaspoon black pepper

2 medium-sized green peppers, chopped
1½ cups canned peeled plum tomatoes, chopped or sieved
2 large ripe tomatoes, chopped fine
2 heaping tablespoons tomato paste

Combine olive oil and butter in a skillet and heat. Add onions and brown slowly for 10 minutes. Chop garlic and parsley together and add to onions along with salt and pepper. Cover and cook for 10 minutes. Add green peppers and cook for 5 minutes. Add canned and fresh tomatoes and cook slowly for 40 minutes. Add tomato paste, stir well, and remove from the heat. Add more salt if necessary. Serve over spaghettini or a pasta of your choice. Makes about 4 cups.

Bolognese Sauce

¼ cup olive oil
¼ cup fresh creamery butter
2 ounces salt pork, diced
¼ pound onions, peeled and diced
½ pound Italian sweet sausage
½ pound lean beef, ground
4 chicken livers, chopped fine
2 garlic cloves, mashed
½ teaspoon fresh rosemary

1 bay leaf
¼ teaspoon ground black pepper
6 tablespoons dry white wine
1 cup canned peeled plum tomatoes, sieved
2 medium-sized ripe tomatoes, chopped fine
Tiny pinch of freshly grated nutmeg
1 cup boiling water

Combine olive oil, butter and salt pork in a saucepan; heat. Add onions and brown slowly. Remove sausage casing and cut the meat into ½-inch pieces. Add to the onions with the beef and chicken livers. Brown slowly for 15 minutes. Chop garlic with the rosemary and add to the sauce with the bay leaf and pepper. Stir well and cook for 10 minutes. Add wine, stir, cover, and cook for 10 minutes. Remove sausage, chicken livers, and all chunks and chop fine; place back in the sauce. Add sieved and chopped tomatoes and the nutmeg. Remove and discard bay leaf. Add boiling water and cook, uncovered, for 40 minutes, slowly. This sauce is especially delicious over fettucini or spaghetti. Makes about 4 cups.

Ravioli and Pasta Sauce

If you do not make your own ravioli, there are ready-made ravioli on the market. You can make your own sauce by this recipe and use it for noodles, spaghetti, and macaroni, too.

1 pound lean beef (top or bottom round or flank)
¾ pound sweet Italian sausage
2 garlic cloves, mashed
1 teaspoon fresh rosemary
¼ cup butter
¼ cup olive oil
4 ounces salt pork, diced
½ pound onions, peeled and diced

Tiny, tiny pinch of ground allspice
½ teaspoon salt
⅓ teaspoon freshly ground black pepper
4 medium-sized ripe tomatoes or 2 cups canned peeled plum tomatoes, chopped
1 cup boiling water

Cut the beef into small cubes. Remove sausage casing and cut the sausage into small pieces. Chop the garlic and rosemary together. Combine butter, olive oil and salt pork in a skillet; heat. Add onions and sauté slowly until medium brown. Add beef and sausage, allspice, salt and pepper. Brown for 15 minutes. Add garlic and rosemary, stir, and cook for 2 minutes. Add tomatoes and boiling water, stir, cover, and cook slowly for 45 minutes. Uncover and cook for 5 minutes more. Test for doneness. When meat is tender, remove sauce from heat and serve plentifully over freshly cooked ravioli or pasta. Also delicious over slices of Italian bread. Makes about 4 cups.

Italian-Sausage and Tomato Sauce

1¼ pounds Italian sweet sausage
3 garlic cloves, mashed
¼ bunch of parsley, leaves only
⅓ ounce dried mushrooms
1 cup warm water
2 tablespoons olive oil
2 ounces salt pork, diced
2 tablespoons sweet butter
½ pound onions, peeled and diced

3 cups canned peeled plum tomatoes, sieved
2 medium-sized ripe tomatoes, chopped
2 tablespoons tomato paste
6 tablespoons heavy cream, warm (not hot)

Remove casing from sausage and cut meat into ½-inch pieces. Chop the garlic and parsley together. Soak the mushrooms in the warm water for about 10 minutes. Drain, saving the water, and chop the mushrooms.

Combine olive oil, salt pork and butter in a saucepan; heat. Add onions and cook slowly until golden brown. Add sausage and brown slowly. Add garlic and parsley, cover, and cook slowly for 4 minutes. Add mushrooms and mushroom water, sieved and chopped tomatoes, cover, and cook slowly for 40 minutes. Add tomato paste. Cook for 2 minutes. Just before serving add the cream to sauce and stir. Makes about 6 cups.

Beef Sauce for Polenta

1½ pounds beef chuck
1 teaspoon fresh rosemary
2 garlic cloves, mashed
10 slices of dried mushrooms
⅓ cup warm water
2 tablespoons olive oil
2 ounces salt pork, diced
½ pound onions, peeled and diced

¼ cup butter
1 teaspoon salt
½ teaspoon ground black pepper
¼ teaspoon ground allspice
4 medium-sized ripe tomatoes or 2 cups canned peeled plum tomatoes, chopped
1½ cups boiling water

Cut the beef into very small cubes. Chop rosemary and garlic together. Soak the mushrooms in the warm water for 10 minutes. Drain, saving the water, and chop mushrooms fine. Or use ½ pound fresh mushrooms and cut into thin slices.

Combine olive oil, salt pork and butter in a saucepan; heat. Add onions and cook to medium brown. Add beef, salt and pepper. Brown for about 15 minutes. Add rosemary and garlic and allspice, cover, and cook for 2 minutes. Then add tomatoes and mushrooms with mushroom water. Stir, cover, and cook for 3 minutes. Add boiling water and cook slowly for 1 hour, or until meat is tender. Serve on freshly cooked hot Polenta (page 89) with extra melted butter and a little cheese on top. If there is extra sauce, it keeps well for future use. Makes about 5 cups.

6 🌿

Fish and Shellfish

FISH and shellfish, many people maintain, are good brain and health foods. Whether or not we eat seafood to help our thinking and to keep us healthy, we should in any case use our heads and take it where and when it is at its best.

In my book, fresh fish is best. Out of the water and into the frying pan, oven or broiler. Then only will you get the best flavor and substance. When you are traveling, let's say in Venice or Naples or Gloucester, Massachusetts, all noted fishing towns, get your fill of fresh fish. Get your meats and poultry in the inland country and cities. While I was the owner and chef of my restaurant, I always carried a large reserve supply of jumbo shrimps, frogs' legs, and quality fishes. On Saturday nights alone we cooked, washed, deveined, dried, dressed, and served over a ton of shrimps. Some other best sellers were pompano, shad, mussels and lobster.

Freshwater Bass

2 freshwater bass (1½ to 2 pounds each)
1 eggplant (1¼ pounds)
Salt
10 fresh parsley sprigs, leaves only
2 large garlic cloves, mashed
4 fresh sage leaves or 1 teaspoon crumbled dried sage
¼ cup sifted all-purpose flour
¼ cup olive oil
½ cup butter, melted
½ teaspoon freshly ground black pepper
1 teaspoon salt
½ cup dry white wine
¼ cup freshly grated Parmesan cheese

Have fishman scale the fish and remove head, tail and fins. Have the fish boned. Cut the eggplant into ½-inch slices and then into

100

cubes. Parboil eggplant for 20 minutes, drain, and place on brown paper. Sprinkle lightly with salt and allow to stand for 30 minutes. Chop parsley and garlic together. If using dried sage, soak the crumbled leaves in warm water for 15 minutes and drain before using.

Preheat oven to moderate (375° F.). Wash and dry fish well and dredge with flour. Oil a baking pan with some of the olive oil and place the fish, skin side down, in center of pan. Add eggplant around edge of pan, circling fish. Combine the butter, remaining oil, the parsley-garlic mixture, pepper, sage and salt in a bowl; mix. Spoon the mixture over fish and eggplant. Cook for 5 minutes. Add wine, cover with lightly buttered brown paper, and bake for 20 minutes. Uncover and sprinkle cheese over the top. Cook for 15 minutes. Check for doneness, and taste for seasoning.

Serve *spaghettini al burro* on same plate with this dish. Spoon gravy and drippings over fish and eggplant. A bottle of chilled Soave or a white California wine is just great with this. Serves 4.

Bluefish alla Leone

1 fresh bluefish (2½ to 3 pounds)	Pinch of black pepper
1 large garlic clove, mashed	Pinch of salt
7 fresh parsley sprigs, leaves only	3 tablespoons butter
7 slices of dried mushrooms	3 medium-sized potatoes
½ cup good dry white wine	¼ cup olive oil
Pinch of crushed red pepper	½ cup milk

Have fishman cut fins, tail, and head from the bluefish and remove the bones. If fresh fish is not available, use frozen, but there is a big difference. Chop garlic and parsley together. Soak the dried mushrooms in the white wine for 30 minutes. Drain, saving the wine, and chop the mushrooms. (Remember, the better the wine used in cooking, the better will be the flavor of the completed dish.) Preheat broiler. Place garlic-parsley mixture, chopped mushrooms, the wine, red and black pepper, salt, and butter in a bowl. Set aside.

Parboil the potatoes, skin, and slice. Oil a shallow baking dish or oven pan with some of the olive oil. Pour the milk into the pan. Arrange fish, skin side down, in the pan and brush with oil. Place under the broiler 8 inches from the source of heat. Broil for 4 minutes. Remove from broiler. Arrange the sliced potatoes around edge of pan. Spoon the other mixed ingredients over the top. Place back in the broiler and broil for 20 to 25 minutes. Watch carefully and check for doneness. Serve with a green salad with Italian Salad Dressing (page 49), toasted Italian bread and caffè espresso. Serves 4.

Baccalà with Polenta and Tomato Sauce

Polenta (cornmeal) is considered a pasta throughout the northern Italian mountain regions, the Dolomites and the Alps.

2 pounds baccalà (dried salt codfish)
½ cup fresh creamery butter
½ cup virgin olive oil
1 pound onions, peeled and diced
3 garlic cloves, mashed
12 fresh parsley sprigs, leaves only
½ teaspoon freshly ground black
  pepper

½ cup dry white wine
3 medium-sized ripe tomatoes or
  1½ cups canned peeled plum
  tomatoes, chopped
1½ cups cornmeal
1½ cups cold water
4 cups boiling water
1 teaspoon salt
Grated Parmesan cheese

Pound the dried salt codfish with a mallet or the flat side of a heavy cleaver. Soak the fish in cold water for 2 days, changing water twice. Rinse well, drain, and dry. Cut the fish into 1-inch cubes.

Place half of the butter and all of the olive oil in a skillet and heat. Add onions and brown them. Add cubed fish and brown for 15 minutes. Chop the garlic and parsley together and add to the fish along with the pepper; stir. Cook for 10 minutes. Add wine, cover, and cook for 3 minutes. Add tomatoes and cook for 30 minutes; cook slowly, and if the liquid reduces too much add ¼ cup hot water.

Meanwhile soak the cornmeal in the cold water. Stir it into the boiling water and add the salt and 2 tablespoons of the butter. Stir constantly while simmering for 20 minutes. Taste, and add more salt if needed. When polenta is cooked, spread it on a warm platter, spread remaining butter over it, and sprinkle with a little cheese.

Arrange the cooked baccalà on the polenta. Spoon sauce over top and cap with more grated cheese. Serve with a Beaujolais. Serves 6.

Note: This recipe is also suitable for fresh codfish, but cooking time will be less, and of course the preliminary soaking will not be needed.

Baked Fresh Halibut

1 medium-sized garlic clove, mashed
8 parsley sprigs, leaves only
2 medium-sized green or red peppers
¼ cup olive oil
10 tablespoons melted butter
½ cup chopped onion

Pinch each of salt and black pepper
3 pounds fresh halibut, 2 inches thick
2 tablespoons all-purpose flour
¼ cup heavy cream
¾ cup Marinara Sauce (page 94)

Chop garlic and parsley together. Wash peppers and remove cores and seeds. Chop into very small pieces and drain them in a strainer for 10 minutes before using. Preheat oven to moderate (350° F.). Combine oil and 6 tablespoons of the butter in a baking pan and heat. Add onion and cook slowly for 5 minutes on top of the stove. Add garlic and parsley, drained green peppers, salt and pepper, and cook for 5 minutes. Remove from heat. Arrange halibut on top of the chopped vegetables, cover, and bake in the oven for 10 minutes.

Put the remaining butter in a small saucepan and blend in the flour. Add the cream. When sauce thickens, add marinara sauce, stirring well. Spoon the sauce over the halibut, cover, and bake for 20 minutes longer. Serve halibut with *spaghetti al burro* and spoon drippings and sauce over both. Serves 4 to 6.

Baked Pompano

2½ pounds baking potatoes
8 pieces of dried mushrooms
½ cup milk
10 tablespoons butter
1 large garlic clove, mashed
3 teaspoons olive oil
6 tablespoons sifted all-purpose flour
3 to 3½ pounds fresh or frozen pompano

Salt and freshly ground black pepper
8 fresh parsley sprigs, leaves only, chopped
2 tablespoons heavy cream
¼ cup freshly grated Parmesan cheese

Boil the potatoes in jackets for 20 minutes. Drain, cool enough to handle, peel, and cut into cubes. Set aside. Preheat oven to slow (300° F.). Soak the mushrooms in 1/4 cup of the milk for 15 minutes. Drain the mushrooms, reserving the milk, and chop the mushrooms. Melt 2 tablespoons of the butter and add mashed garlic. Oil a baking pan with some of the olive oil and place on top of stove. Lightly flour the pompano, shaking off any excess, and arrange fish in the oiled pan. Brush well with balance of oil and sprinkle with salt and pepper. Remove bits of garlic from the butter and discard garlic. Spoon the butter over fish. Add chopped parsley and mushrooms. Cover and cook slowly on top of the stove for 5 minutes. Uncover and arrange cubed potatoes around edge of pan.

Heat the remaining butter, stir in remaining flour (there should be about 5 tablespoons), and add the remaining milk and the milk drained from mushrooms. Simmer over low heat, stirring constantly. When smooth and thickened, fold in the cream and add salt and pepper to taste. Pour the sauce over the fish and potatoes. Sprinkle the cheese over top, cover with buttered aluminum foil, and bake for 30 minutes. Serve immediately. A suggested wine, Montrachet. Serves 4 to 6.

Broiled Red Snapper

3 pounds fresh or frozen red snapper	6 tablespoons sweet butter, melted
1 tiny slice of garlic	1/3 teaspoon each salt and freshly ground black pepper
5 parsley sprigs, leaves only	

Cut the fish into serving pieces. Chop garlic and parsley together. Place 2 tablespoons of the butter, the salt and pepper, garlic and parsley, in a bowl and set aside. Preheat broiler. Brush fish well on both sides with butter and butter a broiler pan. Place the fish, skin side down, in the broiler pan, and broil slowly for 10 minutes. Turn, brush with more butter, and cook for 10 minutes longer. Pour the butter and seasoning mixture over the fish and cook for about 5 minutes more, or until done. Serves 4 or 5.

Note: You may also cook whitefish or striped bass using this recipe.

Baked Boned Fresh Shad

2 tablespoons olive oil
½ cup fresh sweet butter, melted
¼ cup finely chopped shallots or grated onion
2½ to 3 pounds boned fresh shad
2 tablespoons all-purpose flour
½ teaspoon salt
Pinch of freshly ground black pepper
¼ cup milk, hot
2 egg yolks, beaten
¼ cup heavy cream
¼ cup dry white wine

Preheat oven to moderate (350° F.). Oil a baking pan with some of the olive oil. Combine remaining oil and half of the butter in the pan and heat on top of the stove. Add chopped shallots and slowly sauté for 5 minutes. Arrange the shad on the shallots. Put pan in the oven and bake for 10 minutes.

Combine flour and the remaining butter, the salt and pepper, and stir over low heat. Add the milk and cook for 1 minute, stirring constantly. Beat the egg yolks in a bowl, add the cream, and beat again. Dribble eggs and cream into the hot sauce, beating all the while. Spoon the sauce over the fish and pour the wine over top. Bake for 15 minutes, then transfer from oven to preheated broiler for 10 minutes. Taste for salt and cooking.

Serve with hot boiled potatoes on same plate. Spoon chives and hot butter over potatoes and shad. This goes well with a chilled bottle of Chablis. Serves 4 to 6.

Sole or Flounder with Smoked Salmon

2 fresh sole or flounder fillets (6 to 8 ounces each)
2 thin slices of smoked salmon
3 very large raw shrimps
1 teaspoon dried chives
6 tablespoons dry white wine
3 tablespoons olive oil
3 tablespoons fresh sweet butter
1 large garlic clove, mashed
¼ cup canned mushrooms, sliced thin
Pinch of salt
½ teaspoon freshly ground black pepper
Pinch of crushed red pepper (optional)
3 tablespoons grated Parmesan cheese

Be sure fish fillets are cut lengthwise of the fish and that the salmon has been freshly sliced. Shell and devein the shrimps, wash and dry them, and cut lengthwise into thin slices. Soak the dried chives in the wine. Heat olive oil, butter and garlic in a shallow oven pan on top of the stove. Stir garlic well around pan. Add shrimps, mushrooms and salt. Sauté for 5 minutes. Stir and remove from the heat. Discard the bits of garlic. Remove shrimps and mushrooms to a small plate.

Place 1 fillet on the bottom of the same pan; then place the 2 slices of salmon on top of the fillet. Sprinkle black and red pepper over the salmon, then spoon shrimps and mushrooms over top. Spoon some of the butter and oil drippings over. Place the other fish fillet on top. Cook over low heat for 5 minutes, basting several times. Add wine and chives and cover. Cook for 2 minutes. Uncover, sprinkle cheese over the top, and baste with the liquid in the pan. Put under preheated broiler about 8 inches from the source of heat for 8 minutes. To serve, cut into 2 portions and spoon sauce over each serving. Serve a chilled Chablis. To complete the meal, serve a salad of Belgian endives with lemon and olive-oil dressing, a large red Delicious apple, a slice of Gorgonzola, and caffè espresso. Serves 2.

Broiled English Sole

3 pounds frozen English sole
½ cup fresh creamery butter, melted

Salt and pepper
4 fresh parsley sprigs, leaves only, minced

Preheat broiler. Brush fish on both sides with butter. Grease bottom of broiler pan and place fish on it. Broil on each side for 12 minutes. Take from the heat, and remove bones. Place on a warm platter and season with salt and pepper to taste. Add parsley to melted butter, heat it, and spoon over the boned hot fish. Slip the platter under the broiler for 1 minute. Serve with lemon wedges. For the wine, a bottle of Liebfraumilch. Serves 4.

Fried Fillets of Gray Sole

3 pounds fillets of gray sole
⅓ cup all-purpose flour
¼ cup olive oil
Salt and freshly ground pepper

½ cup sweet butter, melted
18 leaves of fresh chives, chopped fine, or 1 tablespoon dried chives

The gray sole is our best American flounder. Wash the fillets, dry them, and dip into flour. Place olive oil in a large heavy-bottomed skillet and heat. Lay fish on the bottom of pan without crowding. Cook on each side for 5 minutes. Season lightly with salt and pepper. Combine melted butter and chives and spoon over fish. Cover and cook for 10 minutes. Check for doneness.

Arrange fillets on warm plates and spoon oil and butter drippings over fish. Place a good helping of Shoestring Potatoes (page 216), or any potatoes you choose, on the plate with the fish and serve immediately. Add a green salad and a slice of ripe Gorgonzola or Roquefort. A dry white or a rosé wine is appropriate. Serves 4 to 6.

Fillets of Gray Sole with Clam Sauce

2 pounds fillets of gray sole	1/4 cup olive oil
1/4 cup all-purpose flour	Pinch each of salt and pepper
1/4 cup fresh sweet butter	Clam Sauce (see below)

Preheat broiler and oil a broiler pan. Wash and dry fillets and flour lightly. Place fillets in the pan and pour over them a mixture of butter, olive oil, salt and pepper. Place under medium heat and broil for 10 minutes.

Spoon clam sauce over the fish, cover, and cook slowly for 15 minutes. Uncover, and test for doneness. Serve on a hot platter with au gratin potatoes and a fresh dandelion or other green salad with hard-cooked-egg dressing. Add Italian bread, a piece of ripe Brie or soft Camembert, and for wine a Moselle. Serves 4 or 5.

CLAM SAUCE

6 fresh cherrystone clams	2 tablespoons olive oil
2 tablespoons tomato paste	2 tablespoons butter, melted
3 garlic cloves, mashed	4 shallots, chopped fine
10 fresh parsley sprigs, leaves only	1/4 cup dry white wine

Open the clams and chop them, saving all juices from both steps. Stir the tomato paste into the clam juice. Chop garlic and parsley together. Combine olive oil and butter in a skillet and heat. Add shallots and cook for 2 minutes. Add chopped clams and garlic and parsley mixture, and cook for 2 minutes. Add tomato paste and clam juice and the wine, cover, and cook very slowly for 5 minutes. Remove from the heat.

Broiled Sole alla Vikki

½ cup clam juice
½ cup dry white wine
½ cup water
1 lemon slice or wedge
1 celery stalk
2 pounds fresh lemon or gray sole
½ cup fresh creamery butter
1 garlic clove, mashed

1 tablespoon all-purpose flour
¼ cup heavy cream, warmed
Pinch each of salt and black pepper
2 egg yolks
¼ cup olive oil
Juice of 1 lemon
¼ cup cream sherry

Mix the clam juice, wine and water, and add the lemon slice and celery stalk. Place fish on an oiled poaching rack, or tie in a long piece of cheesecloth. Lower rack or cheesecloth into a shallow saucepan large enough to hold the fish. Cover with the clam-juice mixture. Simmer gently for 5 minutes. Lift fish from the saucepan, discard cheesecloth if used, and move fish to an oiled oven dish.

Melt butter with garlic over low heat. Stir in flour, then discard bits of garlic. Remove from the heat, add the warmed cream and salt and pepper, and blend well. Beat the egg yolks with the olive oil and the lemon juice and stir into the sauce. Add sherry. Pour the sauce over the poached fish. Place in the broiler and broil under low heat for 20 minutes. Check carefully for doneness. Serves 4.

Baked Swordfish

2½ pounds fresh or frozen swordfish
All-purpose flour
Salt and pepper
½ cup Marinara Sauce (page 94)

6 tablespoons butter
¼ cup olive oil
4 shallots, sliced fine
1 loaf of Italian bread
1 teaspoon minced chives

Cut the fish into ½-inch slices, dry well, and sprinkle lightly with flour, salt and pepper. Mix the marinara sauce with 4 tablespoons of the butter. Place the oil in a baking pan and add the fish. Cook for 5 minutes on each side on top of stove. Remove from the heat. Add the marinara-sauce mixture and sliced shallots. Cover. Bake in a slow oven (300° F.) for 20 minutes.

Slice the Italian bread but do not detach slices. Mix remaining butter and the chives and spoon this mixture between the slices. Wrap in aluminum foil and place in the oven for 10 minutes. Do not allow to burn. For each serving place 2 slices of hot bread in a deep dish, arrange some of the fish on top, and spoon sauce over all. Try a cold bottle of white Chianti with the swordfish. Serves 4 or 5.

Brook Trout Sauté Meunière

At one time our friends and customers were served trout that they themselves caught in a stream running in the beautiful gardens on our property. John McGraw and Heywood Broun were the first friends of Mother's to catch their own trout and to have her cook the fish for them. Here is the recipe.

4 trout (10 to 12 inches long)	2 tablespoons olive oil
All-purpose flour	Juice of 1 lemon
Salt and pepper	Chopped parsley
½ cup butter, melted	

Prepare trout for cooking and sprinkle lightly with flour and salt and pepper. Place 2 tablespoons of the butter and the olive oil in a heavy-bottomed skillet and heat. Add the trout and sauté until firm and brown. Arrange trout on large warm platter.

Add the rest of the butter to the skillet and cook for 1 minute. Add the lemon juice. Shake the skillet, stir, and add a sprinkle of chopped parsley. Pour the mixture over trout. Serve Baked Tomatoes (page 219) and lemon slices dipped into paprika on the same plate, and enjoy a cold bottle of California Riesling. Serves 4.

Poached Brook Trout

Only when a brook trout is fished out of a stream and is still alive when you are ready to cook will you achieve the real *truite au bleu* flavor—a special taste treat!

4 speckled or rainbow trout (12 inches long)
1 lemon, cut into wedges
1 onion, sliced
2 bay leaves, crumbled
Juice of 1 lemon
Pinch of crushed red pepper
1 garlic clove, mashed
6 fresh parsley sprigs, leaves only
6 heaping tablespoons butter, melted
Pinch of freshly ground black pepper
Salt
Parsley sprigs for garnish

Go to your fishman and get the freshest trout he has; have him prepare them for cooking. To a pot of salted boiling water add 2 lemon wedges, the onion, bay leaves, lemon juice, and red pepper. Drop in the trout and boil for 5 minutes. Remove the pot from the heat, cover, and let stand for 5 minutes. Drain.

Chop the garlic and parsley leaves together and stir the mixture with the butter. Add the pepper, and salt to taste. Mix well and heat. Place the trout on a platter. Spoon the butter sauce over the trout and garnish with parsley sprigs and remaining lemon wedges. Serve with buttered parsleyed small potatoes and a chilled bottle of Montrachet. Serves 4.

Poached Fresh Whitefish

2 pounds fresh whitefish or baby halibut
1 tablespoon olive oil
½ cup clam juice
1 garlic clove, mashed
½ teaspoon black pepper
Salt
Sauce Ravigote (page 111)

Have fishman prepare fish for cooking. Place fish, with a little olive oil, on an oiled poaching rack, or wrap fish in cheesecloth and add a few drops of oil to poaching liquid. Lower the rack or cheesecloth package into an oven pan or pot. Add the clam juice and enough additional water to cover the fish. Add the garlic, black pepper, and salt to taste. Cover and steam for about 15 minutes, then test for doneness. When fish is done to your taste, lift from the poaching liquid and cut into 4 portions.

Place the fish on a warm serving plate and spoon sauce ravigote over fish. Serve with *spaghettini al burro* on the same plate, or with parsleyed boiled potatoes. For wine, Barolo, and then a bottle of Champagne, of course, because this is a fish dish. Serves 4.

SAUCE RAVIGOTE

Juice of 1 lemon
1 tablespoon wine vinegar
1 good-sized garlic clove, mashed
8 fresh parsley sprigs, leaves only,
    chopped
⅓ teaspoon freshly ground black
    pepper

⅓ teaspoon salt
2 hard-cooked eggs, mashed fine
    with a fork
¼ cup virgin olive oil
Pinch of crushed red pepper (op-
    tional)

Place all the ingredients in a bowl. Beat well together with a wire whisk. Discard bits of garlic. Spoon over the hot fish.

Anguilla Stufata con Polenta

(eel stew with polenta)

2 pounds fresh eel
¼ cup olive oil
2 tablespoons butter
⅓ pound onions, peeled and
    diced
2 bay leaves, crumbled
2 garlic cloves, mashed
8 fresh parsley sprigs, leaves only
12 small green olives, pitted
6 thin slices of prosciutto, diced
    (about 4 ounces)

1 hot cherry pepper
⅓ teaspoon freshly ground black
    pepper
6 tablespoons dry white wine
2 small ripe tomatoes or ¾ cup
    canned peeled plum tomatoes,
    chopped
½ cup boiling water
Polenta (page 89)

Have fishman skin the eels and prepare for cooking. Cut into 2-inch pieces, wash well, and dry. Combine oil and butter in a skillet and heat. Add onions and cook to medium brown. Add pieces of eel, stir, cover, and cook slowly for 5 minutes. Add bay leaves. Chop garlic with parsley and add to skillet along with olives and prosciutto. Cut the cherry pepper into halves, remove and discard cores and seeds, and dice. Add to the stew with the black pepper, and stir. Cover and cook for 5 minutes. Add wine, cover, and simmer for 5 minutes. longer. Add tomatoes and the boiling water, stir, and simmer slowly, uncovered, for about 30 minutes. Taste carefully to see if the dish needs salt. About 20 minutes before the stew is done, prepare the polenta. Serve the eel in very hot bowls over portions of polenta. Spoon sauce over eel and polenta, and drink Soave with it. Serves 4 or 5.

Capitone Arrosto

Broiled eel (*capitone*) is a Christmas holiday delicacy and, according to ancient Italian custom, a "must" on Christmas Eve, no matter what the price. For this dish the eel must be fresh.

2½ pounds fresh eel
¼ cup olive oil
2 tablespoons butter, melted
4 bay leaves, broken into halves
½ cup wine vinegar
Pinch of salt

⅓ teaspoon crushed red pepper
1 teaspoon freshly ground black pepper
6 tablespoons sifted bread crumbs
1 lemon, cut into wedges

Have fishman save an eel for you and skin and prepare it for cooking. Wash and dry well. Cut into serving pieces. Place the olive oil, butter, bay leaves, vinegar, salt, and red and black pepper in a bowl. Stir. Add the eel and half of the bread crumbs. Marinate for 2 hours. Stir mixture several times.

Preheat broiler. Arrange eel in a broiler pan and pour all marinade mixture over the fish. Place the pan about 8 inches below the source of heat. Cook slowly for 15 to 20 minutes. Turn, baste, and sprinkle remaining bread crumbs over top. Cook slowly for about 20 minutes longer, or until eel is a golden brown. Place on hot plates and spoon juices over top. Add a lemon wedge. Serve with toasted garlic bread and a bottle of chilled Chiaretto del Garda, a delicious rosé from the Lago di Garda region. Serves 4 or 5.

Frogs' Legs Provençale

20 medium-sized fresh frogs' legs
Juice of ½ lemon
¼ cup all-purpose flour
8 leaves of fresh chives, chopped fine, or ½ teaspoon dried chives
¾ cup sweet butter, melted
2 medium-sized ripe tomatoes
4 fresh sage leaves or 1 teaspoon dried leaf sage

¼ cup olive oil
3 garlic cloves, mashed
8 fresh parsley sprigs, leaves only
½ teaspoon salt
¼ teaspoon freshly ground pepper
1 loaf of Italian bread

Trim frogs' legs and soak in cold water with a pinch of salt and the lemon juice for at least 1 hour. Rinse and dry very well. Dip into flour and shake off any excess so that each leg is evenly covered. Place chives in half of the melted butter and set aside. Chop the tomatoes and place them in a strainer to drain. If using dried sage, soak the leaves in a little warm water for 10 minutes before using. Drain.

Place olive oil in a skillet large enough to cook all the legs without crowding. Heat the oil and add frogs' legs. Sauté slowly for 15 minutes. Chop garlic and parsley together and add to the skillet. Sprinkle legs with salt and pepper. Cook for 3 minutes and discard half of the oil. Add remaining butter, the drained tomatoes and the sage. Stir and shake the skillet. Cover and simmer for 10 minutes. Remove pan from the heat and transfer legs to a warm platter. Spoon sauce over.

While frogs' legs are simmering, slice the bread, but do not detach the slices. Spoon butter and chives between slices. Wrap in aluminum foil and bake in a hot oven for 10 minutes. Serve the buttered toasted slices with the legs and sauce and have a chilled bottle of dry white or rosé wine. Serves 4.

Note: You may make this recipe without the tomatoes. The frogs' legs will then be more crisp and more savory of garlic and parsley.

Whale Steak Stew

(a big strong caveman's dish)

2½ pounds whale steak	2 bay leaves, crumbled
2 large garlic cloves, mashed	¼ cup dry red wine
8 fresh parsley sprigs, leaves only	2 carrots, scraped and diced
1 teaspoon fresh rosemary	1 celery stalk with leaves, minced
1½ pounds potatoes, peeled	Pinch each of salt and freshly
1 medium-sized green pepper	ground pepper
3 tablespoons olive oil	2 tablespoons tomato paste
¼ cup butter	1 cup warm water
2 ounces salt pork, diced	1 large loaf of Italian bread
1 pound onions, peeled and diced	

Cut the whole steak into 1-inch cubes and soak in water for 2 hours before starting to prepare the dish. Drain and dry well. Chop garlic, parsley and rosemary together. Cut the potatoes into medium-sized pieces and the green pepper into thin slices.

Combine olive oil, butter and salt pork in a saucepan; heat. Add onions and sauté until medium brown. Add whale meat and brown slowly for 10 minutes; stir. Add garlic, parsley, rosemary and bay leaves. Stir and cook for 8 minutes. Add wine, cover, and cook for 5 minutes. Add carrots, celery, potatoes, green pepper, salt and black pepper; stir. Mix the tomato paste with the warm water and stir well into the stew. Cook slowly for about 1½ hours. Test for doneness.

Slice the bread, but do not detach slices. Rub outside of slices with garlic and brush a little butter over and between slices. Wrap loaf in aluminum foil and place in a hot oven for 5 minutes. For each serving place 2 slices of bread in an individual bowl and spoon out a man-sized portion of stew on top. Serve a red Chianti. Serves 4 lusty eaters or 6 average eaters.

Clams with Fresh Spinach

32 medium-sized cherrystone clams in shells
1 package (10 ounces) prewashed fresh spinach
2 large garlic cloves, mashed
8 parsley sprigs, leaves only
¼ cup olive oil
¼ cup sweet butter
¼ pound onions, peeled and diced
1 green pepper, chopped fine
1 good-sized ripe tomato, sliced thin
4 fresh sage leaves or 4 dried sage leaves
⅛ teaspoon freshly ground black pepper

Open the clams, saving any juice, and chop the clams. Measure ½ of the juice and put any remaining juice aside for other uses. Wash the spinach and drain well. Remove any coarse stems and chop any very large leaves. Chop garlic and parsley together. Place olive oil and butter in a saucepan and heat. Add onions, brown them, and then add green pepper, spinach, tomato and the ½ cup clam juice. Stir, cover, and cook for 15 minutes. Uncover, stir, add the chopped clams, and cook for 2 minutes. Add garlic and parsley mixture, the sage and pepper. Salt should be added if necessary, but it may not be needed as the clams are salty. Stir well, and cook for 4 minutes. Serve clams and juice in deep soup plates. Serve with toasted Italian bread and for wine, a chilled Chablis. Serves 4.

Note: To use remaining clam juice as a cocktail, see note, page 71.

Littleneck Clams Marinara

60 littleneck clams in shells
¼ cup olive oil
¼ cup butter
2 garlic cloves, mashed
8 fresh parsley sprigs, leaves only
Pinch of crushed red pepper

Pinch of black pepper
¾ cup dry white wine
2 cups warm Marinara Sauce
  (page 94)
2 loaves of Italian bread

Wash the clams and scrub under cold running water with a stiff brush. Discard any opened clams. Combine olive oil and butter in a saucepan and heat. Add the clams, still in their shells. Chop garlic and parsley together and add to the clams along with the red and black pepper. Cover and cook for 2 minutes. Add the wine and cook for 3 minutes. Add marinara sauce and cook for 10 minutes.

Slice the bread and rub the slices on one side with raw garlic. Toast slices in the oven. For each serving place 2 slices of toast on the bottom of a deep dish and spoon 10 clams over. Pour plenty of the juice over the clams and toast. Serve with a white wine like that used in the sauce. Dunk the extra toast into the sauce. Serves 6.

Sautéed Soft-Shell Crabs

6 small to medium-sized soft-shell
  crabs
1 garlic clove, mashed
3 tablespoons sweet butter,
  warmed slightly
3 tablespoons all-purpose flour

3½ tablespoons olive oil
Pinch of salt
Pinch of black pepper
12 parsley sprigs, leaves only,
  minced
Lemon wedges

The shells of the crabs are edible. Cut the back of crabs and lift out spongy gills and sand bags. Cut out face. Lift out small apron at lower end. Wash crabs and dry well. Stir mashed garlic into the butter and let stand until just before using, then discard the bits of garlic.

Dip crabs into flour, shaking off any excess. Place olive oil in a skillet and heat. Add crabs and sauté on each side for 5 minutes. Pour garlic-flavored butter over the crabs and add salt and pepper. Shake pan, cover, and cook slowly for 10 minutes. Sprinkle parsley over the top; shake skillet. Arrange crabs on warm serving plates, spoon butter drippings over all, and serve immediately with lemon wedges. Serves 2 if crabs are small; 6 medium-sized crabs may be large enough to serve 3.

Broiled Soft-Shell Crabs

Preheat broiler. Prepare crabs as for sautéing (see page 115). Dip into olive oil. Place crabs on broiler rack about 6 inches below source of heat. Broil on each side for 8 minutes. Warm 3 tablespoons sweet butter, add 1 mashed garlic clove, and stir well. Discard bits of garlic. Add 12 parsley sprigs, chopped fine, to the butter. Place crabs on a warm serving dish and spoon butter mixture over top. Serve with lemon wedges.

Hard-Shell Maryland Crabs

9 hard-shell crabs
¼ cup virgin olive oil
6 tablespoons sweet butter
2 ounces salt pork, diced
¼ pound onions, peeled and diced
6 tablespoons Marsala wine
Pinch of salt
Pinch of freshly ground black pepper

Pinch of crushed red pepper
3 medium-sized ripe tomatoes, chopped
1 teaspoon dried orégano
¼ cup hot broth or water
8 ounces mostaccioli
6 tablespoons freshly grated Parmesan cheese

Wash crabs several times in cold running water. Drop them into salted boiling water, cover, and cook for 3 minutes. Remove from the cooking vessel and cool enough to handle. Break off pointed apron tail, pull upper and lower shells apart, and wash away loose matter under cold running water. Remove intestines and spongy gills. Place crabs on a heavy board and cut or chop into halves and then into quarters.

Combine olive oil, butter and salt pork in a large soup pot or skillet; heat. Add onions and sauté until medium brown. Add crab pieces and brown slowly for 10 minutes. Add Marsala, cover, and cook for 5 minutes. Add salt and black and red pepper, and stir; add tomatoes, orégano and broth or water. Shake skillet, stir, and simmer for 25 minutes.

Drop the mostaccioli into boiling salted water and cook for about

Like Mother . . .

I can still see Mother working in front of her stoves, turning out her wonderful cooking. Seasoning is an art, and cooking, if it's done right, is not easy. Always a perfectionist, Mother basted her roasts a dozen times, because she knew it was necessary. I was often asked how Mother became such a wonderful cook. Did she study at the fine cooking schools in Rome, Florence or Milan? Was she a student at the famous Cordon Bleu in Paris? The answer to all these questions was no. She learned from her mother —just as I learned from mine. When it came to cooking I always felt that I had talent. But Mother was an absolute genius.

. . . like son.

New York Post

Mother was never happier than when she was cooking for friends.

Perfectly cooked pasta with delicious sauces was her specialty.

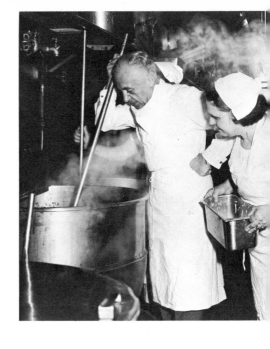

New York World-Telegram

I followed Mother's recipes, her principles and her policies and inherited her desire and capacity for work.

New York Herald Tribune

Harry Truman breaking bread in Leone's with me, Hugh Fulton and Mon Wallgren, former governor and United States Senator from the State of Washington.

U.S. Army Photo

General Dwight D. Eisenhower with the author, Honorary Member of the West Point Class of 1915, at a fiftieth reunion party held at Leone's Farm in Central Valley.

Two wonderful ladies, Mary Margaret McBride and Mrs. Eleanor Roosevelt, added their considerable charm to the atmosphere of Leone's.

Milhollan

Former West Point football coach Earl Blaik and General Douglas MacArthur pore over the menu at a dinner honoring Blaik in 1959 when he retired after eighteen years of splendid leadership. General MacArthur was a rabid football fan.

Richard Hochman

Tommy Weber

Here are some of the women busily engaged in shelling the shrimp we used in the restaurant. It was no easy job, since our customers consumed about one ton of shrimp a night.

When Mother left us, I took full charge of the kitchen and began hiring a group of women as my assistants. They helped in the preparation of soups, sauces, roasts and other dishes that must be cooked in advance.

Foto Attualità Casasole

I sampled some wine from the barrel of Signor Petrurbani's stock in my never-ending search for fine wines to add to my collection. I made many trips to Italy looking for good wine and good recipes.

Italnews

Marchesa Travaglini, Conte Pago Golforelli and the author at the famous Scoglio di Roma. I enjoyed this restaurant so much I called it the "Mother Leone's of Rome."

This is just one corner of one of the thirteen rooms that were open to feed as many as 6,000 patrons on a busy night. The art collection on display throughout Leone's was valued at a quarter of a million dollars.

The forty-fifth reunion of the West Point graduating class of 1915 was held under a gaily decorated tent on the lawn at my farm in Central Valley. President Eisenhower called the 1960 reunion the best one his class ever had.

25 minutes. Drain. Serve pasta and crabs in warm deep soup bowls. Spoon the juices over all. Sprinkle with the cheese. Serve a loaf of Italian bread and a rugola or cicoria salad with Italian Salad Dressing (page 94). Serves 4.

Maryland Crabmeat and Nova Scotia Salmon with Truffles

1/4 cup olive oil
6 tablespoons sweet butter
1 large garlic clove, mashed
1 pound fresh Maryland lump crabmeat
4 whole fresh green scallions or 2 shallots, diced
1/4 pound smoked Nova Scotia salmon, cubed
1/2 cup very good cream sherry
1/2 cup Spanish pimientos

4 ounces imported canned mushrooms *au naturel* (Italian or French) or a good brand of American mushrooms
12 small green olives, pitted
1/2 teaspoon pepper
Pinch of crushed red pepper
2 ounces white Italian truffles
8 fresh parsley sprigs, leaves only, chopped

Combine olive oil, butter and garlic in a large skillet; heat. Discard bits of garlic. Add crabmeat and scallions, cover, and cook slowly for 3 minutes; stir. Add salmon and cook for 2 minutes. Add sherry, cover, and simmer for 2 minutes longer. Drain the pimientos, cut them into halves, and slice into 3/4-inch strips. Cut the mushrooms into thin slices. Add pimientos, olives, mushrooms, and black and red pepper. Cover and simmer for 4 minutes more, and the dish is cooked. Shave the truffles into the dish and add the parsley; stir. Serve immediately. This delicious dish rates a good Champagne. Serves 4 to 6.

Baked King Crab

3 pounds King crab claws
10 fresh parsley sprigs, leaves only
2 garlic cloves, mashed
1/3 teaspoon freshly ground black pepper

Pinch of crushed red pepper
1/3 teaspoon salt
1/4 cup olive oil
6 tablespoons sweet butter
1/2 cup dry white wine

Have fishman crack crab and cut into serving pieces. As this fish comes to our markets frozen, thaw out well the day before preparing this dish. Wash, drain, and dry well. Preheat oven to hot (400° F.).

Chop parsley and garlic together. Mix black and red pepper and the salt and sprinkle over top of garlic-parsley mixture. Arrange crab claws in a baking pan. Brush lightly with olive oil. Combine remaining oil, the butter and seasoning mixture; brush or spoon it over top of claws. Cover with aluminum foil. Place in oven, cook for 5 minutes, and lower the heat to slow (300° F.). Cook for 20 minutes. Baste well with the juices in the pan, then add wine, shake the pan, and bake, uncovered, for another 10 minutes. Serve on warm plates with *ravioli al burro* on the same plate. Spoon juices over all. A bottle of California white wine will add a bit of the atmosphere of the Pacific, the origin of this delicious dish. Serves 3 or 4.

Chicken Lobsters with Vermicelli

4 live chicken lobsters (1 pound each)
6 tablespoons all-purpose flour
6 fresh basil leaves or 1 teaspoon dried basil, chopped
3 garlic cloves, mashed
1/2 cup sweet butter
2 eggs, beaten well
1/4 cup olive oil
1/4 cup diced onion
Pinch of salt
1/2 teaspoon freshly ground black pepper
1/2 cup good cream sherry
8 ounces vermicelli or any thin spaghetti
1/4 cup freshly grated Parmesan cheese

Drop the lobsters into a large pot with 5 quarts salted boiling water. Cook for 10 minutes. Allow lobsters to cool in the water for 10 minutes. Remove from pot, tear off claws and crack, and remove meat. Split lobsters into halves. Remove head sacs and intestinal veins and discard. Remove all meat and fat. Cut lobster meat into large pieces and flour lightly, shaking off any excess.

Mix basil and garlic with 6 tablespoons of the butter; stir, and let stand for 20 minutes. Dip floured lobster chunks into beaten eggs. Place the oil in a skillet, heat it, and cook the onion until medium brown. Add lobster meat and cook for 3 minutes. Add salt and pepper and the butter with garlic and basil. Stir and cook for 2 minutes. Add sherry, cover, and cook for 5 minutes. Simmer slowly for 5 minutes more, uncovered.

During the last 5 minutes of cooking, prepare the vermicelli. When the pasta is ready, drain immediately and put back in hot pot. Add remaining butter, a little sauce, and the cheese to the vermicelli;

mix and cover. Serve the pasta on individual plates and spoon lobster and sauce over top. Sprinkle with more cheese. For wine, a fine Chablis or a Soave. Serves 4.

Lobster Fra Diavolo

4 lobsters (1½ to 2 pounds each)
8 fresh parsley sprigs, leaves only
1 garlic clove, mashed
½ cup fresh sweet butter
¼ cup olive oil
¾ pound onions, peeled and diced
Pinch of salt
¼ teaspoon crushed red pepper
⅓ teaspoon freshly ground black pepper
4 cups warm Marinara Sauce (page 94)
1 pound spaghettini

Split the lobsters lengthwise down the middle. Remove head sacs and intestinal veins and discard. Chop parsley and garlic together. Combine butter and olive oil in a large skillet and heat. Add onions and sauté slowly to medium brown. Add lobsters, meat side down, and sauté for 10 minutes. Turn lobsters, add parsley and garlic, and stir well. Cook for 10 minutes. Add salt, red and black pepper, and marinara sauce. Stir, cover, and cook for 10 minutes longer. Uncover and cook slowly for another 20 minutes.

Have boiling salted water ready; add the spaghettini and cook for about 10 minutes, or until done to your taste. Serve spaghettini on same plate with the lobster and spoon the sauce over all. Serve a chilled Chiaretto del Garda or Soave. Serves 4 to 6.

Baked Fresh Oysters

72 large juicy oysters in shells
20 fresh parsley sprigs, leaves only
2 garlic cloves, mashed
12 fresh or dried basil leaves
4 shallots, minced
1⅓ cups toasted bread crumbs
½ cup grated Parmesan or Swiss cheese
½ cup olive oil
½ cup softened butter
Pinch of black pepper
Pinch of crushed red pepper
Salt

Open the oysters, leaving each on its half shell. Chop parsley, garlic and basil together. Place all ingredients except oysters in a bowl and mix well. Use salt to taste. Place oysters on their shells in an open pan and cover each oyster with some of the dressing. Cover tightly with aluminum foil. Place pan in preheated moderate oven (375° F.) and bake for 20 minutes. Serve very hot. Serves 8 as a main dish. For a smaller serving for antipasto, see page 25.

A Quick Oyster Dish

24 large heavy oysters in shells
3 tablespoons virgin olive oil
¼ cup fresh sweet butter
½ Bermuda or red sweet onion, sliced thin
1 garlic clove, mashed
1 hot cherry pepper
2 ounces canned mushrooms, sliced thin

1 large ripe tomato, sliced thin
Pinch of salt
⅓ teaspoon freshly ground black pepper
8 fresh parsley sprigs, leaves only, chopped fine

Open the oysters, saving any juice. Combine olive oil and butter in a skillet; heat. Add onion and garlic and stir and cook slowly for about 5 minutes. Cut the cherry pepper into halves, discard all seeds, wash carefully, and cut into thin slices. Add to the skillet along with mushrooms and tomato. Cover, and cook slowly for about 10 minutes. Add oysters and juice, salt and pepper, and cook for 3 minutes. Turn oysters, add the parsley, cover, and cook for 3 minutes longer. Spoon onto slices of fresh Italian bread, and serve a green salad. For dessert, serve a red or yellow Delicious apple with a slice of nice ripe Gorgonzola; for wine, Valpolicella. Serves 2 to 4.

Shrimps Marinara

28 fresh jumbo shrimps
6 tablespoons sifted all-purpose flour
6 tablespoons fresh sweet butter
¼ cup olive oil
2 ounces salt pork, diced
¾ pound onions, peeled and diced
3 garlic cloves, mashed
10 fresh parsley sprigs, leaves only
1 tablespoon dried orégano

⅓ teaspoon salt
⅓ teaspoon freshly ground black pepper
Pinch of crushed red pepper
½ cup dry white wine
4 medium-sized ripe tomatoes or 1 cup canned peeled plum tomatoes, chopped
2 bay leaves
2 tablespoons tomato paste
¼ cup warm water

Shell the shrimps, devein, wash under cold running water, and dry thoroughly. Dredge shrimps with the flour, shaking off any excess. Place butter, olive oil and salt pork in a skillet; heat. Add onions and cook to medium brown. Add the floured raw shrimps and stir and cook for 5 minutes. Chop garlic and parsley together and add along with orégano, salt, and black and red pepper. Stir and cook for 3 minutes. Add wine, tomatoes, bay leaves, tomato paste, and water. Stir, cover, and cook for 20 minutes. Then cook, uncovered, for another 5 minutes. Taste and add more salt if necessary.

To serve, place a mound of cooked rice or a piece of garlic toast on each plate. Arrange 6 or 7 shrimps on the rice or toast and spoon all of the sauce over top. Sprinkle some grated cheese over all. For wine, serve a good dry or semidry Orvieto. To make this a meatless dish, omit the salt pork. Serves 4 to 5.

Butterfly Shrimps in the Oven

30 fresh jumbo shrimps	2 large garlic cloves, mashed
¼ cup olive oil	10 fresh parsley sprigs, leaves only
¾ cup toasted bread crumbs	
Pinch of salt	6 tablespoons fresh creamery butter, melted
Pinch of crushed red pepper	
Pinch of freshly ground black pepper	¼ cup freshly grated Parmesan cheese

Preheat oven to slow (300° F.). Slit the shrimps down the back, but leave the shells on. Devein, wash, and dry thoroughly. Arrange the shrimps in an oiled ovenproof pan. Pour olive oil evenly over them. Sprinkle bread crumbs over top and add salt and red and black pepper. Chop garlic and parsley together and sprinkle over the shrimps. Stir all together gently so that shrimps are evenly coated with the oil, crumbs and seasonings. Cover the pan. Put the pan in the oven and bake for 20 minutes. Spoon the butter over shrimps and bake, uncovered, for about 5 minutes longer. Check for doneness.

Serve with *spaghettini al burro*. Serve the pasta on the same plate with shrimps, spooning juices over the spaghettini, too. Top with the grated cheese. For wine, a dry Orvieto. Serves 4 or 5.

Broiled Shrimps Milanese

28 raw jumbo shrimps, fresh or frozen
¼ teaspoon freshly ground black pepper
¼ teaspoon crushed red pepper
¼ teaspoon salt
¼ cup sifted all-purpose flour

2 large eggs, beaten
½ cup sifted bread crumbs
½ cup fresh sweet butter, melted
¼ cup olive oil
Juice of 1 lemon
1 tablespoon Worcestershire sauce

Shell the raw shrimps, devein them, wash in cold water, and dry. Combine the peppers and salt. Flour the shrimps and shake off any excess. Dip them into the beaten eggs, then dredge with bread crumbs. Shake off any excess crumbs. Combine 2 tablespoons of the butter with the olive oil. Oil a broiling pan with some of the mixture. Arrange shrimps in the oiled pan and spoon remaining oil and butter mixture over them. Sprinkle with salt and peppers. Place pan 8 inches below a preheated broiler. Decrease the heat and cook shrimps for 5 minutes. Turn and cook for 15 minutes longer. Check cooking. Place the remaining butter in a small pan and bring to a boil, but do not burn. Add lemon juice and Worcestershire sauce and also, if you like, a few drops of Tabasco. Heat thoroughly and spoon over shrimps. Serve 7 shrimps per person on the same plate with potatoes au gratin. A chilled rosé wine will go nicely with this. Serves 4.

Broiled Northern Deep-Sea Scampi

32 frozen raw hard-shell deep-sea scampi
3 eggs
¼ cup sifted all-purpose flour
5 tablespoons sifted bread crumbs
6 tablespoons sweet butter
¼ cup olive oil
3 tablespoons freshly grated Parmesan cheese
⅓ teaspoon freshly ground black pepper

Pinch of crushed red pepper (optional)
10 fresh parsley sprigs, leaves only
2 garlic cloves, mashed
½ teaspoon salt
1 teaspoon dried orégano
Juice of 1½ lemons
2 tablespoons Worcestershire sauce

Remove scampi from the freezer the night before preparing this dish and let them thaw in the refrigerator. Beat egg yolks and whites separately. Cut scampi shells with a very sharp knife or scissors on the stomach side. Crack shells by placing fingers on back and pressing forward, but do not remove shells. Flour scampi lightly and shake off any excess. Dip them into the beaten egg yolks, then dredge lightly with bread crumbs, then dip into beaten egg whites. Oil a broiler pan lightly.

In a bowl mix together $\frac{1}{4}$ cup of the butter, the olive oil, remaining bread crumbs and eggs, the cheese, and black and red pepper. Chop parsley and garlic together and add to mixture in bowl along with the salt. Spoon this stuffing into and over stomachs of scampi. Sprinkle orégano over the top. Arrange scampi in the oiled broiler pan and put in preheated broiler 8 inches below the source of heat. Broil slowly for about 20 minutes. When done, serve 8 scampi per person on hot plates. Spoon all of drippings into a warm bowl and add remaining butter, the lemon juice and Worcestershire sauce; stir. Heat under the broiler before spooning over scampi. Fettucini al'Alfredo (page 75) will go very nicely on the same plate, and for a wine, a dry Orvieto. Serves 4.

Deep-Sea Scampi Sautéed

32 frozen raw hard-shell deep-sea scampi
$\frac{1}{4}$ cup sifted all-purpose flour
3 egg yolks, lightly beaten
2 tablespoons olive oil
6 tablespoons fresh sweet butter
$\frac{1}{2}$ teaspoon salt
$\frac{1}{3}$ teaspoon freshly ground pepper
2 lemons, halved

Prepare scampi as for Broiled Northern Deep-Sea Scampi (see page 122). Flour scampi lightly, shaking off any excess. Dip into egg yolks. Place olive oil and butter in a large skillet; heat. Add scampi, stomach side down, and cook slowly for 10 minutes. Turn, sprinkle lightly with salt and pepper, cover, and cook slowly for 10 to 12 minutes longer, or until golden brown. Place 8 scampi per person on warm serving plates. Squeeze a little lemon juice over top and spoon drippings over all. Put $\frac{1}{2}$ lemon on each plate. Au gratin potatoes will go nicely with this. Complete the meal with a loaf of

Italian bread, a soft Bel Paese cheese, a delicious ripe pear, and a bottle of dry white Frascati. Serves 4.

Fisherman's Deep-Sea Scampi Stew alla San Gennaro

(San Gennaro or Saint Januarius is the patron saint of fishermen.)

12 fresh oysters in shells
All-purpose flour
1 egg, lightly beaten
Sifted bread crumbs
12 fresh cherrystone clams in shells
12 raw jumbo shrimps
12 deep-sea hard-shell scampi (frozen)
2 large garlic cloves, mashed
12 fresh parsley sprigs, leaves only
½ ounce dried Italian or French mushrooms

1 cup lukewarm water
¼ cup olive oil
¼ cup sweet butter
4 thin slices of prosciutto, diced
½ teaspoon freshly ground black pepper
1 teaspoon dried orégano
¾ cup dry white wine
4 cups boiling water
1 cup finely chopped fresh tomatoes or canned peeled tomatoes
Pinch of crushed red pepper
⅔ cup uncooked rice

Open the oysters, saving any juice. Lightly flour the oysters, dip them into the beaten egg, and then into the sifted bread crumbs. Set aside. Open the clams, saving any juice, and coarsely chop the clams. Combine oyster and clam juices, measure ½ cup of the liquid, and set aside. Wash the jumbo shrimps, devein them, split lengthwise down the middle, and gently dry them. The frozen scampi are already washed and deveined before freezing. With a sharp knife cut the shells on the stomach side, but do not remove them, for scampi will be cooked in the shells.

Chop garlic and parsley together. Soak the dried mushrooms in the lukewarm water for 20 minutes. Drain them, saving the liquid, and chop the mushrooms.

Combine olive oil and butter in a large soup pot and heat. Add breaded oysters and chopped clams. Cook for 3 minutes. Stir lightly. Add prosciutto, shrimps and scampi. Stir and cook for 3 minutes. Add garlic and parsley, pepper and orégano, and stir lightly. Add wine and chopped drained mushrooms, cover, and cook for 2 minutes. Add reserved clam and oyster juice, boiling water, mushroom liquid, tomatoes and red pepper. Simmer for 30 minutes. About 20 minutes before serving, add the rice, stir, cover, and cook until done. Taste for salt, but remember oysters and clams and their juices are naturally salty, so very little or no salt will be needed. Serve with well-crusted Italian bread and a chilled dry white wine; for dessert, sliced red apples with Gorgonzola cheese. If any stew is left over, cool and refrigerate; it is delicious the next day. Serves 4 or 5.

Baked Fresh Bay Scallops

1½ to 2 pounds fresh bay scallops
3 tablespoons all-purpose flour
6 tablespoons fresh creamery butter, melted

6 tablespoons sifted bread crumbs
Pinch each of salt and pepper

Butter a shallow pan or baking dish. Wash the scallops, dry well, and sprinkle lightly with flour. Place scallops in the pan and brush with the melted butter. Sprinkle bread crumbs over scallops and mix well. Brush with more butter and add more bread crumbs. Season lightly with salt and pepper. Place under preheated broiler, broil for 5 minutes, and decrease heat. Stir bottom of pan. Broil slowly for 10 minutes longer. Try this with fettucini. Place cooked fettucini on warm plates and spoon scallops and sauce over all. Serve a dry white Frascati with this. Serves 4.

Snails alla Casalinga

From my experience in the restaurant business, I have observed that snails are getting to be more popular each year. They are very easily prepared, but they can be served with a lot of pomp and ceremony. The secret of making them delicious is to use lots of butter, garlic, parsley, salt and pepper.

32 canned snails with shells
18 fresh parsley sprigs, leaves only
3 large garlic cloves, mashed
¾ cup sweet butter

1 teaspoon freshly ground black pepper
Salt
Italian bread

Put snail shells aside and keep them warm in the top part of a double boiler over hot water, or in a very low oven. Chop parsley and garlic together. Melt the butter in a large skillet. Add garlic with parsley, pepper, and a light pinch of salt. Cook slowly for 1 minute, then stir and add the snails. Simmer slowly for 4 minutes; do not burn. Dip warm shells into the butter mixture and place 1 snail into each shell. Return snails in their shells to the sauce. Stir, cover, and cook slowly for 5 minutes. Serve over toasted slices of Italian bread to absorb drippings. Spoon all the sauce over snails; let it ooze into the toast. Enjoy toast and all with a good bottle of Château Latour. Serves 4.

Breaded Snails in Burgundy

32 canned snails with shells	½ teaspoon salt
Pinch of grated nutmeg	⅓ cup sifted bread crumbs
1 cup sweet butter, melted	3 large garlic cloves, mashed
¼ cup dry red Burgundy	14 fresh parsley sprigs, leaves
1 teaspoon black pepper	only

Place snails in a mixing bowl. Wash and dry the shells and keep them warm as in Snails alla Casalinga (page 125). Grate a little nutmeg over the snails and add ¼ cup of the butter, the Burgundy, pepper and salt. Mix well and allow to stand for 15 minutes. Mix again and sprinkle lightly with bread crumbs. Mix and sprinkle with bread crumbs a second time.

Place remaining butter in a large saucepan and heat. Chop garlic and parsley together and add to butter. Cook slowly for 2 minutes. Do not boil. Add the snails but not the wine mixture. Stir well, and cook for 2 minutes. Remove saucepan from the heat and spoon a little of the garlic butter sauce into each warm shell. Put 1 snail into each shell, and then fill shells with more sauce. Replace them in the pan, bring to a slow boil, and pour the wine mixture over them. Cover and simmer for 5 minutes. Simmer, uncovered, for another 4 minutes. Arrange snails on special plates or in soup plates, 8 for each serving. Spoon all of sauce over shells. Serve with slices of well-crusted Italian bread. Serves 4.

Fresh Calamari Stew

1½ pounds fresh calamari (squid)
¼ cup all-purpose flour
¼ cup olive oil
⅓ cup sweet butter
¼ pound onions, peeled and diced
2 garlic cloves, mashed
12 fresh parsley sprigs, leaves only

2 large ripe tomatoes or ½ cup canned peeled plum tomatoes, chopped
⅓ teaspoon freshly ground black pepper
Pinch of crushed red pepper
Pinch of salt
½ teaspoon minced fresh basil
½ teaspoon dried orégano

Have fishman clean the calamari well, but wash well again before cooking. Cut into 1-inch pieces. Sprinkle with flour.

Combine olive oil and butter in a saucepan and heat. Add onions and cook to medium brown. Chop garlic and parsley together and add to saucepan; stir. Add calamari, stir, cover, and cook for 20 minutes. Add tomatoes, black and red pepper, salt, basil and orégano. Stir, cover, and cook for about 45 minutes. Check for cooking and add more salt if necessary. Serve over a pasta of your choice. Add a chilled bottle of dry white wine. Serves 4 or 5.

7

Poultry and Game

CHICKEN is one of our most economical and versatile foods. It's a staple the world around. It's roasted, fried, made into soups, salads, pies. Its uses seem limitless. There's one point to keep in mind when preparing chicken: it has a bland flavor and needs "taste excitement." This can be added with spices, sauces and stuffings. In the pages following you will find classic chicken dishes as well as a selection of unusual, taste-teasing recipes for other poultry and for game.

Roast Stuffed Chicken

When Will Rogers was playing in the Ziegfeld Follies, he dined three or four nights a week in our place. He especially enjoyed Mother's stuffed whole roast chicken and spaghetti with a bottle of Chianti.

6 ounces salt pork
2 cups dried bread
¼ cup milk
¼ cup olive oil
¼ cup butter
½ cup diced onion
3 chicken gizzards, cut into small pieces
3 chicken livers, chopped
½ cup chopped fresh parsley

Salt and black pepper
1 egg
2 tablespoons grated Parmesan or Swiss cheese
4 whole fresh spring chickens (2¼ pounds each)
1 tablespoon minced fresh rosemary
¼ cup boiling water

Cut the salt pork into very thin slices. Reserve 8 slices for larding the chickens and dice the rest. Moisten the bread with the milk, press out the liquid, and shred the bread. Combine 2 tablespoons of the oil, the diced salt pork, and 2 tablespoons of the butter in a saucepan; heat. Add onion and brown for 5 minutes. Add gizzards and livers and cook for 5 minutes longer. Remove from the heat and let cool for 10 minutes. Take ingredients from the saucepan, chop all again until very smooth, then return to the pan. Add shredded bread, chopped parsley, salt and pepper to taste, the egg and the cheese. Mix well. If too moist, add some bread crumbs.

Stuff chickens with the mixture. Preheat oven to hot (400° F.). Rub a little olive oil over baking pan. Also, rub chickens with a little olive oil. Place the birds, breast side down, in the pan and bake for 10 minutes. Turn chickens breast up, lay 2 thin slices of salt pork over each, and pour remaining drops of olive oil over all. Sprinkle with rosemary, salt and pepper, and return to oven. Reduce heat to slow (300° F.) and cook for 20 minutes, basting at intervals. Turn chicken breast down, baste, and cook for 10 minutes. Turn again and cook for about 10 minutes more. Test for doneness.

When the birds are done, remove them from the pan and keep warm. Drain off grease from pan, leaving drippings. Add the boiling water and remaining butter. Simmer, stirring bottom of pan constantly, until gravy thickens. Strain the gravy and spoon it over the chickens. Serves 6 to 8.

Note: The chickens are also delicious roasted without stuffing. Prepare for roasting, then rub cavities with a mixture of butter, olive oil, salt and pepper. Cooking time for chickens without stuffing should be less.

Chicken au Gratin with Broccoli

1 chicken (3½ to 4 pounds), poached
1¼ pounds tender fresh broccoli
¼ cup butter
3 tablespoons all-purpose flour
¼ cup boiling chicken broth
½ cup heavy cream, warmed
½ cup dry white wine
Salt and pepper
¾ cup freshly grated Parmesan cheese

Slice the breasts and thighs of the poached chicken and lightly pound the meat of the legs between 2 sheets of wax paper. Reserve any remaining chicken for other uses. Trim and wash the broccoli and steam it, heads up, in 1½ inches of water for about 15 minutes. Drain.

Preheat oven to moderate (350° F.). Place butter in a small saucepan and heat. Add flour and stir. Add chicken broth slowly. Stir until mixture thickens. Add the warmed cream and the wine and stir. Remove from the heat. Have 4 individual casseroles ready and warmed. Place a quarter of the drained broccoli in the center of each. Arrange chicken alongside broccoli. Grind a little pepper and a pinch of salt over the top. Now spoon sauce evenly over top. Sprinkle cheese on top and bake for about 20 minutes. For wine, serve a 10-year-old Chianti. Serves 4.

Broiled Chicken

2 fresh broiling chickens (2½ pounds each) Olive oil	Salt and pepper Melted butter

Split each chicken down the back into halves. (Save any giblets for another use.) Wash pieces of chicken well and dry. Preheat broiler. Brush chicken with olive oil on both sides, then sprinkle lightly with salt and pepper. Place the halves, breast side down, in a broiler pan. Lower the heat and set pan 5 inches from the source of heat. Cook slowly for 5 minutes. Turn, and cook for 5 minutes longer. Turn, brush with oil, and cook for 5 minutes more. Turn again, brush with oil, and cook for 5 minutes. Turn, and this time brush with melted butter. Cook for 5 minutes, turn, brush with melted butter again, cook for 5 minutes longer, and serve immediately. Spoon the butter over top. Good with Ziti with Broccoli (page 74) which takes about 20 minutes to prepare, so when placing the chicken in the broiler, start cooking the ziti. Serves 4.

Pollo alla Diavola

(deviled chicken)

1 fresh spring chicken (3½ to 4 pounds) 6 tablespoons olive oil ¼ cup butter	1 large garlic clove, mashed Salt and pepper ½ cup dry white wine Juice of 1 lemon

Split the chicken into halves and pound it flat with a mallet or the flat side of a cleaver. Place a heavy skillet over moderate heat and add the olive oil. Heat it and add butter and garlic. Add the chicken halves, breast down. Increase the heat and brown the chicken on each side for 10 minutes (20 minutes in all). Season with salt and pepper. Lower the heat and add the wine and lemon juice. Cover and cook for 30 minutes. Uncover. Cook for 10 minutes longer. Baste well and check for cooking. Serve a fresh vegetable and a green salad with this. Serves 4.

Fried Chicken

2 fresh spring chickens (2½ pounds each)
¼ cup sifted all-purpose flour
½ cup milk
2 eggs, beaten
¼ cup butter
5 tablespoons olive oil

1 ounce salt pork, diced
2 teaspoons minced fresh rosemary
½ teaspoon salt
½ teaspoon freshly ground black pepper
Juice of 2 lemons

Cut each chicken into 4 pieces. Pound them lightly between 2 sheets of wax paper. Sprinkle the flattened pieces with flour, then dip them into the milk, then into the flour again. Shake off any excess flour and dip into beaten eggs. Place butter, olive oil and salt pork in a large heavy skillet; heat. Add chicken pieces and brown each side slowly for 15 minutes. Sprinkle with rosemary, salt and pepper. Cover and cook slowly for about 15 minutes. Test for doneness and add more salt if needed. Sprinkle lemon juice over the hot chicken. Serve with mashed potatoes on the same plate and spoon drippings over both chicken and potatoes. Serves 4.

Breaded Chicken Sauté

2 fresh spring chickens (2½ pounds each)
½ cup all-purpose flour
6 tablespoons olive oil
2 eggs, separated
Salt and pepper

1 cup sifted bread crumbs
6 tablespoons butter
8 fresh parsley sprigs, leaves only, chopped
Juice of 2 lemons
2 tablespoons brandy

Cut the chickens into serving pieces but do not remove the skin. Discard the bony ends of the wings and the backs. Place the pieces between 2 sheets of wax paper and flatten slightly with the flat side of a cleaver. Dip each piece into flour, shake off any excess, and then use about 2 tablespoons of the olive oil to pat over all the pieces. Beat egg yolks slightly and then beat the whites until frothy. Dip chicken pieces into egg yolks, then into egg whites. Sprinkle with salt and pepper. Next coat with bread crumbs. Combine remaining oil and ¼ cup of the butter in a skillet; heat. Add chicken to the skillet and sauté on each side for 10 minutes. Cover and cook over medium heat for 20 minutes. Add the parsley and squeeze the lemon juice over the chicken. Cover again and cook for 10 minutes. Remove chicken from skillet and keep warm.

Add remaining butter and the brandy to the pan and mix with the drippings. Heat for ½ minute, stirring well. Spoon over chicken. Serve with a salad of Belgian endive with lemon and olive-oil dressing. Serves 4.

Chicken Cacciatora

George M. Cohan occasionally came to Mother's for spaghetti with meat sauce and chicken cacciatora. On Mother's thirty-second anniversary, he came to her party and sang and danced "Give My Regards to Broadway," with our own Sir Owen Jones accompanying him at the piano.

2 fresh spring chickens (2¼ pounds each)
¼ cup olive oil
2 ounces salt pork, diced
¼ cup butter
½ pound onions, peeled and diced
2 chicken livers and 2 gizzards, chopped fine
2 garlic cloves, mashed
1 teaspoon fresh rosemary
10 fresh parsley sprigs, leaves only
½ teaspoon freshly ground black pepper
¼ teaspoon salt
4 medium-sized ripe tomatoes or 2 cups canned peeled plum tomatoes, chopped
1 tablespoon tomato paste

Cut each chicken into 4 pieces. Combine oil, salt pork and butter in a good-sized pot; heat. Add onions and brown slowly. Add the chicken pieces and chopped livers and gizzards and brown for 10 minutes. Chop garlic, rosemary and parsley together and add to the chicken along with the pepper and salt; stir well. Cook for 5 minutes. Add tomatoes and tomato paste and cook slowly for about 30 minutes, or until done. Check for cooking and salt. Do not overcook. This chicken is delicious with freshly cooked spaghettini on the same plate, with sauce spooned over all. Serves 4.

Pollo del Padrone

(the boss's chicken)

2 fresh spring chickens (2½ pounds each)
½ ounce dried Italian mushrooms
½ cup lukewarm water
2 tablespoons tomato paste
3 ounces salt pork, diced
¼ cup olive oil
¼ cup butter
½ pound onions, peeled and diced

2 chicken livers and 2 gizzards, chopped fine
2 garlic cloves, mashed
1 teaspoon fresh rosemary
1½ bay leaves, crumbled
½ teaspoon freshly ground black pepper
¾ cup dry white wine
2 medium-sized fresh tomatoes, chopped fine
2 tablespoons good dry brandy

Cut each chicken into 6 pieces. Soak the dried mushrooms in the lukewarm water for 15 minutes. Drain, saving the water, and chop the mushrooms. Stir the tomato paste into the mushroom water. Place salt pork, olive oil and butter in a large skillet or pot. Do not crowd the chicken; allow plenty of space for cooking. Add onions and cook to medium brown. Add chicken and brown for 10 minutes, but do not burn. Add chopped giblets, stir, and brown for 5 minutes. Chop garlic and rosemary together and add along with bay leaves and pepper. Do not add salt. Stir and cook for 5 minutes. Add wine, cover, and simmer slowly for 5 minutes. Add tomatoes, mushrooms, and mushroom water with tomato paste. Cook for 15 minutes, uncovered. Stir the brandy into the sauce. Taste for salt and cooking. Never overcook chicken. Serve on the same plate with ravioli. Mix a little chicken sauce with ravioli sauce and spoon over chicken and ravioli. Serve immediately. Serves 6.

Chicken alla Romana

1 fresh spring chicken (3½ pounds)
2 chicken livers
3 tablespoons olive oil
¼ cup fresh creamery butter
2 ounces salt pork, diced
½ pound onions, peeled and diced
1 bay leaf, crumbled

1 teaspoon fresh rosemary
2 large garlic cloves, mashed
¼ cup dry white wine
Pinch of freshly ground black pepper
Pinch of crushed red pepper
½ cup boiling water
Pinch of salt

Cut the chicken into 6 pieces. Chop the liver, heart and gizzard of the bird along with the extra livers into very small pieces. Combine oil, butter, and salt pork in a heavy skillet; heat. Add onions and sauté them slowly to medium brown. Add the chicken pieces and brown slowly for 15 minutes. Add all the chopped giblets and the bay leaf, stir, and cook for 5 minutes. Chop rosemary and garlic together and add to the pan. Cook for 5 minutes and stir. Add wine and black and red pepper, cover, and cook for 10 minutes. Uncover, add the boiling water, stir, and cook quickly over high heat for about 15 minutes. Test for doneness and add salt if necessary. Serve Fettucini al'Alfredo (page 75) on the same plate, spooning gravy over chicken and fettucini. A green salad and a cold bottle of white Frascati add a nice touch. Serves 2 to 4.

Chicken alla Fiorentina

2 fresh spring chickens (2¼ pounds each)
3 tablespoons olive oil
2 tablespoons fresh sweet butter
2 ounces salt pork, diced
6 tablespoons pickled onions

2 sweet (not hot) pickled peppers
1 garlic clove, mashed
Pinch each of salt and pepper
1 bay leaf, crumbled
½ cup dry white wine
12 small black olives, pitted

Cut the chickens into serving pieces and chop all the giblets into small pieces. Combine oil, butter and salt pork in a skillet; heat. Slice the pickled onions and peppers into thin slices and add with the garlic. Cook for 4 minutes. Stir, add chopped giblets, chicken pieces, salt, pepper and bay leaf. Cover and cook slowly for 15 minutes. Add wine and olives, cover, and cook for 15 minutes longer. Simmer, uncovered, for another 10 minutes. Test for doneness. If sauce is too thick, add a little boiling water and simmer for 2 minutes longer. Add a leafy green salad with a ripe Camembert or Brie cheese, a bottle of Valpolicella, and a loaf of fresh Italian bread. Serves 4.

Chicken and Eggplant

1 frying chicken (about 3 pounds), with liver	1 cup sifted bread crumbs
1 medium-sized eggplant	¼ cup butter, melted
3 eggs	1 ounce salt pork, diced
2 tablespoons cold water	All-purpose flour
1 teaspoon finely crumbled dried orégano	¼ cup olive oil
1 teaspoon finely chopped dried rosemary	¼ cup heavy cream
	Juice of 1 lemon
	¼ cup grated Parmesan cheese

Cut the chicken into serving pieces and chop the liver. Peel the eggplant and cut it into cubes. Beat the eggs well with the cold water. Mix the orégano and the rosemary with the bread crumbs. Preheat oven to hot (400° F.). Put the melted butter and the salt pork in a skillet and add the chopped chicken liver. Simmer for 2 minutes on top of the stove. Sprinkle the chicken pieces lightly with flour, dip them into the eggs, and dredge with bread crumbs.

Coat the bottom and sides of a baking pan with oil and leave remaining oil in the bottom of the pan. Arrange chicken pieces in the pan. Sprinkle a little flour over the eggplant cubes, then stir eggplant into remaining eggs, and dredge with remaining bread crumbs. Ring the chicken with eggplant, filling in all the empty spaces around chicken pieces. Add the cream to butter-liver mixture and spoon the sauce over the chicken and eggplant. Sprinkle lemon juice and cheese over the top. Place in the oven for 30 minutes, then reduce heat to moderate (350° F.) and bake for another 30 minutes, or until done. Serves 4.

Breast of Chicken Oreganato

4 chicken breasts (use 3-pound chickens)
6 tablespoons butter, melted
¼ cup all-purpose flour
2 tablespoons olive oil
1 ounce salt pork, diced
¼ pound onions, peeled and sliced
1 bay leaf, crumbled
1 garlic clove, mashed
Pinch of salt
Pinch of freshly ground black pepper
¼ cup dry red wine (Valpolicella)
1 tablespoon dried orégano

Brush chicken breasts with butter and dip into the flour, shaking off any excess. Combine remaining butter, the oil and salt pork in a skillet; heat. Add onions, bay leaf and garlic; sauté slowly for 5 minutes. Add chicken and cook over medium heat for 20 minutes. Add salt, pepper, and wine, cover, and cook for 10 minutes. Add orégano and cook, uncovered, for 10 minutes longer, or until done. Taste for salt and add more if necessary. Place chicken on a warm platter and spoon sauce over top. Serve with a salad of raw spinach on the same plate. Drink the rest of the wine with the dinner. (Remember, so-called "cooking wine" will not add the same flavor to the dish.) Serves 4.

Petto di Pollo al Champagne

(breast of chicken in Champagne)

4 chicken breasts (use 2½- to 3-pound chickens)
All-purpose flour
3½ to 4 ounces white Italian truffles
½ ounce sliced dried Italian or French mushrooms
½ cup fresh sweet butter
2 ounces salt pork, diced
2 chicken livers, chopped fine
½ teaspoon salt
1 teaspoon freshly ground black pepper
2 thin slices of prosciutto, diced
½ cup heavy cream
½ cup good Champagne

Remove bones from chicken breasts, but leave skin on for better flavor. Pound lightly with a mallet or the flat side of a cleaver. Sprinkle lightly with flour, shaking off any excess. Drain the juice from the truffles into a small bowl and soak the dried mushrooms in this until ready to use.

Place butter and salt pork in a large skillet and heat. Add chicken breasts and chopped livers. Cook slowly to medium brown, turn, and cook to medium brown on the other side. Add salt and pepper, mushrooms with soaking liquid, prosciutto, and cream. Stir, cover, and cook slowly for 5 minutes. Add the Champagne. (Remember, the better the Champagne, the better the flavor of the dish. Use the rest of the bottle to drink with the meal.) Stir, cover, and cook for 10 minutes. Uncover and simmer for 3 minutes. Shake skillet and check to see if the chicken is done.

Arrange 1 whole boned breast on each individual hot plate with a portion of spaghettini on the same plate. Spoon sauce over breasts and spaghettini and shave some truffles over each serving. A loaf of toasted fresh Italian bread, a salad of Belgian endive or Bibb lettuce, the Champagne, and for dessert a delicious Zabaglione Luisa (page 227) will complete a sumptuous meal. (In my opinion, this, in a minor way, is how the Romans lived.) Serves 4.

Petto di Pollo al Cognac alla Fiamma

(breast of chicken with Cognac)

4 chicken breasts (use 2¾-pound chickens)	2 tablespoons olive oil
	1 ounce salt pork, diced
3 tablespoons all-purpose flour	1 garlic clove, mashed well
2 tablespoons sifted bread crumbs	Salt and pepper
2 tablespoons heavy cream	¼ cup dry white wine
2 egg yolks, beaten	6 tablespoons Cognac
¼ cup fresh creamery butter	

Bone the chicken breasts except for the wing bones. Leave the wing attached. Sprinkle the chicken lightly with flour, shaking off any excess. Place between 2 sheets of wax paper and pound, but not too thin. Mix remaining flour and the bread crumbs. Dip breasts into cream, then into bread-crumb mixture, and then into the beaten egg yolks. Do this twice. Set aside.

Combine butter, oil, salt pork and garlic in a bowl. Warm slightly to melt butter and salt pork; stir well. Dip breasts into the warm butter mixture. Oil a broiler pan. Arrange breasts, skin side down, in the pan and pour remaining butter mixture and what is left of the egg and the bread crumbs over the top. Sprinkle lightly with salt and pepper. Place in preheated hot broiler for 5 minutes, then lower the heat slightly and broil for 10 minutes. Turn breasts and spoon drippings over top. Broil for another 15 minutes. Add the wine, cover with aluminum foil, and broil for 5 minutes more. Uncover and baste well. Have a warm ovenproof platter ready and arrange chicken on it. Mix 2 tablespoons of the Cognac with the drippings, stir well, and spoon over the top. Place back under the broiler for ½ minute.

For the grand entrance really required for this dish, warm the remaining Cognac, pour it over the chicken, ignite it, and bring the dish flaming to the table. Serve with Fettucini al'Alfredo (page 75), a green salad, and a good bottle of Pouilly-Fuissé. Serves 4.

Chicken Tetrazzini

8 ounces thin noodles or fettucini
1 garlic clove, mashed
6 fresh parsley sprigs, leaves only
2 tablespoons olive oil
½ pound fresh mushrooms, sliced
1 bay leaf, crumbled
½ teaspoon salt
¼ teaspoon black pepper
6 tablespoons fresh sweet butter

2 tablespoons all-purpose flour
1 cup hot chicken broth
½ cup light cream, warmed
¼ cup dry white wine
1 cup diced cooked chicken (from wings, legs, etc.)
8 thin slices of breast (from poached chicken or capon)
¼ cup grated Parmesan cheese

Cook the noodles in boiling salted water for 10 minutes, and drain. Chop garlic and parsley together. Place the oil in a skillet, heat, and add mushrooms, bay leaf, garlic and parsley, salt and pepper. Cook slowly for 4 minutes; stir. Place the butter in another saucepan, melt, and add the flour; blend. Add hot chicken broth, stirring constantly until mixture thickens. Remove from the heat. Add cream and wine and stir well. Place drained noodles in a buttered oven casserole, spoon mushroom mixture over the noodles, and arrange chicken over mushrooms. Pour the cream sauce over all and sprinkle the cheese on top. Bake in preheated moderate oven (350° F.) for about 15 minutes. Serve with a green salad, a ripe pear, a slice of Fontina cheese, and a glass of dry Orvieto. Serves 4.

Note: This can be cooked under the broiler. Cover casserole with foil and place on lowest shelf of a preheated broiler. Cook for 10 minutes and remove foil. Keeping a close watch, broil until a light brown crust appears.

Chicken Livers en Brochette

6 slices of bacon, each cut into 4 pieces
20 fresh chicken livers
2 bay leaves, broken into halves

1 large green pepper, cut into cubes
2 tablespoons warm butter
Salt, black pepper and crushed red pepper

Thread on a skewer 2 or 3 pieces of bacon, 5 livers, a piece of bay leaf and several cubes of green pepper. Put more bacon pieces at each end. Brush with butter. Broil for about 15 minutes, turning several times. Brush again with butter and lightly sprinkle with salt and peppers just before removing from the broiler. Serve with Broiled Tomatoes (page 219) and *fidellini al burro* (a pasta thinner than spaghettini, mixed with butter and cheese). Serves 4.

Chicken Livers with Green Peppers

25 fresh chicken livers
3 medium-sized green or red peppers
3 garlic cloves
5 slices of Italian bread
1/4 cup olive oil
1 ounce salt pork, diced
1/4 pound onions, peeled and diced
1 bay leaf, crumbled

Pinch of ground allspice
1/2 teaspoon salt
1/2 teaspoon freshly ground black pepper
Pinch of crushed red pepper
1/4 cup butter
6 tablespoons dry white wine
8 fresh parsley sprigs, leaves only, chopped
2 tablespoons hot water

Wash the livers and dry thoroughly. Halve the peppers, discard cores and seeds, wash, and cut into thin strips. Cut 1 of the garlic cloves and rub it over the bread slices. Toast the bread in the oven until golden brown and crisp. Mash remaining garlic. Combine olive oil and salt pork in a heavy-bottomed skillet and heat. Add the onions and cook to medium brown. Add mashed garlic and green peppers and sauté slowly; do not burn. Cook for 10 minutes. Add chicken livers, bay leaf, allspice, salt, black and red pepper. Stir, and cook slowly for 15 minutes. Add butter, wine, and parsley, cover, and cook for 2 minutes. Add hot water, stir, cover, and let simmer for about 5 minutes. Taste and add more salt if necessary.

Place a slice of toast on each warm plate and arrange 5 livers on each slice. Spoon the sauce over the livers. Serve with a salad of watercress or dandelion or field salad. Enjoy a nice bottle of Richebourg Burgundy. Serves 5.

Sautéed Chicken Livers with Thin Noodles

1 pound fresh or frozen chicken livers
4 heaping tablespoons fresh sweet butter
1 ounce salt pork, diced
1/4 cup olive oil
1/4 pound onions, peeled and sliced thin
1 garlic clove, mashed
Tiny pinch of ground allspice
1 bay leaf, crumbled
1/8 teaspoon freshly ground black pepper
1/8 teaspoon salt
2/3 cup dry white wine
Juice of 1 lemon
6 fresh parsley sprigs, leaves only, chopped fine
1 pound thin noodles

Wash the chicken livers and dry gently. Combine butter, salt pork, and olive oil in a skillet; heat. Add the onions and garlic and sauté until light brown. Add chicken livers and cook slowly for 4 minutes. Add allspice, bay leaf, pepper and salt, stir, and cook for 1 minute. Add the wine, stir, and cover. Cook slowly for 5 minutes. Add the lemon juice and parsley and simmer over medium heat for about 5 minutes. Taste for cooking and add more salt if necessary.

Cook the noodles to your taste and drain. Add a little butter and cheese to noodles. Arrange livers over noodles on individual plates and spoon the sauce over top. Serve a salad of Bibb or Boston lettuce with Italian Salad Dressing (page 49) and a chilled bottle of white Beaujolais. Serves 4.

Roast Stuffed Capon

Prepare a fresh capon (7 to 8 pounds) for cooking just as you would prepare a turkey. Make a stuffing; use any stuffing in this chapter, adjusting the amount of ingredients in proportion to the size of the bird. Stuff the bird and roast it, allowing about 12 minutes per pound. Baste well during the cooking and check carefully to avoid overcooking. When preparing the gravy add 2 tablespoons brandy for added flavor.

Serve with an immense platter of Shoestring Potatoes (page 216), a loaf of well-crusted Italian bread, and a good French Chablis or California white wine. Serves 8.

Stuffed Capon and Capon Soup

1 fresh capon (8 pounds)	1 good-sized potato, peeled
1½ pounds chicken feet, approximately	2 celery stalks with leaves, halved
	2 garlic cloves, mashed
2 pounds chicken necks, backs and wings	1 teaspoon salt
	¼ teaspoon black pepper
5 quarts cold water, or more	¾ pound vermicelli

Wash the capon and dry well. Set the giblets aside for the stuffing. Be sure to ask your butcher for extra chicken livers and giblets to add to the stuffing. Take the fat off the bird and dice enough to measure ¼ cup for the stuffing. Soak the feet of the capon and the chicken feet in boiling water for 15 minutes, then peel off the skin with a knife. (Chicken feet are of real value in a soup; your butcher will be able to supply these.) Wash the feet well and pound or mash with a mallet or the flat side of a cleaver. Wash all the necks, backs, and wings, and mash them too. Place them in a large kettle. Make the stuffing (page 142). Stuff the capon and sew up both ends of the bird. Truss the bird.

Place the trussed stuffed capon, breast up, in the kettle. Add the water; be sure there is enough to cover the bird. Add potato, celery, garlic, salt and pepper, and bring to a boil. Lower the heat and simmer for 40 minutes. Test capon for doneness; do not overcook. Turn capon breast down and cook for 20 minutes longer. Check cooking again—a capon cooks much faster than a fowl. When done to your taste, remove the bird from the soup and sprinkle it lightly with salt. Keep warm.

Cook the soup slowly for about 40 minutes longer. Remove from the heat and strain the broth. Force all cooked ingredients possible through a sieve, and discard the bones and whatever remains unsieved. Place soup back in the pot.

If you do not require all the soup at this time, pour some into a bowl and cool it. When cold, refrigerate, and you will have a delicious jellied soup for another occasion.

Bring the hot soup to a boil again and add the vermicelli. Cook for 6 minutes. Serve the broth and pasta in soup bowls. For the main course, carve the capon as you would a turkey. For each serving present some of the meat and some of the stuffing, and a leafy green salad on the same plate. A cold bottle of dry Orvieto will go nicely with this. The soup will serve 10 to 12, the capon will serve 6 to 8, with enough left over to make a salad for the next day (page 143).

GIBLET STUFFING

4 slices of bread	Capon giblets, chopped fine
½ cup milk	1 small garlic clove, mashed
2 tablespoons olive oil	1 bay leaf, crumbled
1 ounce salt pork, diced	Salt and pepper
¼ cup diced capon fat	2 eggs, lightly beaten
½ pound onions, peeled and diced	½ cup grated Parmesan cheese
2 chicken livers, chopped fine	½ bunch of fresh parsley, chopped
2 chicken gizzards, chopped fine	

Soak the bread in the milk, then squeeze out the moisture and shred the bread. Combine the olive oil, salt pork, and capon fat in a skillet; heat. Add the onions and brown them. Add all the chopped giblets, the garlic, and the bay leaf. Sauté for 20 minutes, then re-

move from the heat and cool for 10 minutes. Now add the shredded
bread, salt and pepper to taste, the eggs, cheese and parsley. Mix
well; taste, and correct seasoning if necessary.

Capon Salad

2 cups diced cooked capon, ap-   1½ cups Mayonnaise (page 50)
  proximately   or ready-made
1 can (5 ounces) pimientos   Salt and freshly ground black
2 cups diced celery   pepper

Pick over the poached stuffed capon and dice all the trimmings and
any meat from wings, drumsticks, or carcass. Drain the pimientos
and dice them. Mix capon, celery, pimientos and mayonnaise and
season with salt and pepper to taste. Serves 4 to 6.

Roast Turkey with Chestnut Stuffing

6 tablespoons butter   5 thin slices of salt pork
2 tablespoons olive oil   1 tablespoon fresh rosemary
1 turkey (16 to 18 pounds)   Salt and pepper
Chestnut Stuffing (page 144)   2 cups boiling water

Combine 2 tablespoons of the butter and the oil and rub the
turkey inside and outside with the mixture. Stuff the bird and sew
both openings closed. Preheat oven to hot (400° F.). Oil a roasting
pan with olive oil and place turkey in it, breast side down. Brown
for 5 minutes. Turn over and brown for 5 minutes longer. Add slices
of pork to top of breast and legs. Sprinkle rosemary, salt and pepper
over the turkey. Reduce heat to moderate (350° F.). Baste frequently.
Allow 25 minutes per pound. Check for doneness. When turkey is
cooked, remove from the pan and keep warm.

Make gravy. Pour off the grease from roasting pan. Place pan on
top of stove. Add remaining butter and the boiling water. Bring to
a boil. Simmer for 7 or 8 minutes, or until gravy thickens. Do not
use flour to thicken. Strain and serve. Serve with whole cranberry
sauce. Serves 10 to 12.

CHESTNUT STUFFING

Turkey liver and gizzard
½ pound sweet sausage
1½ cups uncooked rice
1½ pounds chestnuts
6 slices of bread
Milk
2 tablespoons olive oil
2 tablespoons butter
1 ounce salt pork, diced
⅓ pound onions, peeled and diced

2 tops of celery stalks (leaves), chopped fine
⅓ bunch of parsley (about 20 sprigs), chopped fine
2 fresh eggs, beaten lightly
¼ cup freshly grated Parmesan cheese
Salt and pepper

Chop turkey livers and gizzard into very fine pieces. Remove casing from the sausage and cut the meat into small pieces. Boil the rice for 10 minutes and drain. Roast the chestnuts and remove the shells. Peel them and cut each nut into quarters. Moisten the bread slices lightly with milk, then shred the bread.

Combine oil, butter, and salt pork in a skillet; heat. Add onions and cook to golden brown. Add chopped liver and gizzard, sausage pieces, and celery leaves. Cook slowly for 15 minutes. Remove from the heat. Add drained rice, quartered chestnuts, shredded bread, chopped parsley, beaten eggs and the cheese. Season with salt and pepper to taste. Mix well.

Breast of Turkey with Truffles and Champagne alla Leone

8 generous slices of cooked turkey breast
All-purpose flour
½ garlic clove, mashed
4 parsley sprigs, leaves only
¼ cup sweet butter, melted
2 egg yolks, beaten
¼ cup finely sifted bread crumbs
¼ cup olive oil

Black pepper
¼ cup freshly grated Parmesan cheese
Salt
1 can (2 ounces) white Italian truffles
4 thin slices of prosciutto, halved
¼ cup dry Champagne

Cut the turkey slices from a freshly roasted turkey. A 10-pound turkey will provide slices of the right size. For roasting, follow directions for Roast Turkey with Chestnut Stuffing (page 143). Use the rest of the bird for creamed turkey or in a turkey salad with celery and mayonnaise, and make a soup with the carcass and any remaining bits of meat.

Sprinkle the slices lightly with flour and set aside. Chop garlic and parsley together. Put the butter in a small bowl and stir in the garlic-parsley mixture. Dip the floured turkey slices into beaten egg yolks, then into bread crumbs. Heat the olive oil in a skillet over low heat. Add the breaded turkey slices and cook to a golden brown, about 3 minutes on each side; do not burn. Remove skillet from the heat. Sprinkle pepper over the slices and spoon half of the garlic-parsley-butter mixture over all. Add all the cheese and season very lightly with salt.

Open the truffles and save any juice. (If you want to splurge, use more than 2 ounces of truffles.) Using about half of the truffles, shave 2 thin slices onto each piece of turkey. Arrange a half-slice of prosciutto on top. Spoon remaining butter mixture over all and put back over low heat to cook for 1 minute. Baste, then pour in the Champagne. (Use a Champagne as good as you would to drink or the delicious flavor of this dish will not be achieved.) Add any truffle juice. Shake the skillet, cover, and cook for 3 minutes. Remove cover and while simmering for another 2 minutes, shave remaining truffles over the top and baste well. Serve Fettucini al'Alfredo (page 75) on same plate, spooning sauce and drippings over all. Serves 4.

Broiled Baby Turkey

1 baby turkey (6 pounds)	4 fresh parsley sprigs, leaves only,
½ cup butter	minced
Salt and pepper	

Split the turkey into 2 pieces. Preheat broiler. Melt half of the butter and brush some on all sides of the bird. Place the pieces, breast side down, in a broiler pan and sprinkle with salt and pepper. Broil for 10 minutes; turn turkey halves and broil for 10 minutes more. Turn breast down again, baste well with more of the melted butter, and broil for 15 minutes. Turn again and cook slowly for 30 minutes, or until done. Cut into 8 pieces. Put into a hot serving dish.

Make parsley butter by adding the parsley to the remaining butter, softened. Do not cook the parsley butter, but mix well and spoon it over the hot turkey. Serve with Fettucini al'Alfredo (page 75). Wines suggested, Soave, a dry Orvieto, or, if you are putting on a big splash, Romanée-Conti. Serves 4 to 6.

Roast Baby Turkey

1 baby turkey (5 to 6 pounds)	1 teaspoon minced fresh rosemary
Stuffing	1 cup boiling water
2 tablespoons olive oil, approximately	1/4 cup butter
6 thin slices of salt pork	

Stuff the turkey if you wish; use Sausage Stuffing (page 147) or the stuffing for Roast Stuffed Chicken (page 128). If you prefer, the bird can be roasted without stuffing; in that case, cooking time will be less.

Preheat oven to hot (400° F.). Rub the bottom of a baking pan with a little olive oil and brush the turkey with olive oil. Place turkey, breast side down, in the pan. Cook for 15 minutes. Turn turkey breast up and place the salt-pork slices over top. Sprinkle the rosemary over the bird. Reduce heat to slow (300° F.) and roast for 20 minutes. Baste with pan drippings and cook for 20 minutes more. Baste again, turn breast down, and cook for another 20 minutes. Baste once more and turn bird breast up. Check carefully for cooking. When turkey is done, remove from oven and keep warm until gravy is ready.

To make gravy, drain off grease from roasting pan, leaving drippings. Add the boiling water and the butter to drippings. Simmer slowly, stirring bottom of pan constantly, for about 10 minutes, or until the mixture is reduced to a medium-thick gravy. Strain and serve hot with the turkey. Serves 6.

Note: If you are cooking a larger bird, of course you will need to prepare proportionately more stuffing, and allow 18 minutes per pound cooking time.

Sausage Stuffing

½ pound sweet Italian sausage
2 tablespoons olive oil
½ cup chopped onion
½ cup chopped celery leaves
20 fresh parsley sprigs, leaves only, chopped
Pinch each of salt and black pepper

Pinch each of ground sage, thyme, and marjoram
Pinch of grated nutmeg
Turkey giblets, chopped fine
1 loaf of rye bread
Chicken broth or milk
2 eggs, beaten
2 tablespoons brandy

Remove casing from the sausage and cut the meat into 1-inch pieces. Put olive oil in a skillet, add the onion, and sauté until golden brown. Add celery, parsley, seasonings, and chopped giblets. Cook for 5 minutes. Break the bread into small pieces in a large bowl. Moisten with chicken broth or milk. Add cooked onion mixture, the eggs, sausage pieces, and the brandy. Mix well. This makes enough to stuff a 7- to 8-pound turkey.

Roast Duck

2 ducks (5 to 6 pounds each)
2 garlic cloves, mashed
½ cup butter, melted
Pinch of salt

Pinch of freshly ground black pepper
1 tablespoon minced fresh rosemary

Preheat oven to hot (400° F.). Wash ducks and dry well. Combine garlic, butter, salt and pepper. Rub ducks inside and outside with some of the mixture. Place ducks, breast side down, in a lightly greased roasting pan. Spoon remainder of butter mixture over ducks and sprinkle with the rosemary. Bake for 10 minutes. Baste, and reduce heat to moderate (350° F.). Cook for about 2 hours, basting several times. Test for doneness. Make pan gravy (see Roast Stuffed Chicken, page 128). Cut ducks into quarters and spoon gravy over top. Add a green salad and a Saint-Julien (claret). Serves 4.

Roast Ducklings with Madeira Sauce

2 Long Island ducklings (6 pounds each)	1/3 teaspoon freshly ground black pepper
1/4 pound onions, peeled and diced	1/2 teaspoon ground allspice
3 tablespoons olive oil	Pinch of grated nutmeg
2 duck livers, chopped fine	1 large garlic clove, mashed
1/4 cup fresh sweet butter	3/4 cup Madeira
	2 tablespoons Grand Marnier

Wash the ducklings and dry well. Save the livers for the sauce. Roast the birds for 1 hour and 10 minutes, following the method in the recipe for Roast Duck (page 147), but keep the ducklings slightly underdone. Remove the birds from the oven and cool for 10 minutes. Cut all the meat from the bones and slice into even pieces.

Sauté the onions in the oil until golden brown. Add chopped livers and cook for 4 minutes. Set aside. Finish cooking in a chafing dish, or a skillet, large enough to hold all the duck. Place the butter in the pan, heat it, and add the cooked onions and livers. Add sliced duck, the pepper, allspice, nutmeg, and garlic. Stir and cook slowly for 15 minutes. Add the wine, cover, and simmer for 15 minutes more. Uncover and pour the Grand Marnier over top. Cover for 1 minute and shake the pan. Serve with a salad of Bibb lettuce with Italian Salad Dressing (page 49). A white Bordeaux like Château Latour will be a perfect accompaniment. Serves 4.

Broiled Ducklings

2 ducklings (5 to 6 pounds each)	1/4 cup butter, melted
2 large garlic cloves, mashed	Salt
Pinch of freshly ground black pepper	

Wash the ducklings, dry well, and split each into halves. Preheat broiler. Add mashed garlic and black pepper to the butter and mix together well. Rub some of this mixture on both sides of the duck pieces. Sprinkle ducks lightly with salt. Arrange the ducks, breast side down, in a broiling pan. Spoon a little of the butter over top.

Place the broiling pan 8 inches from source of heat. Reduce heat to medium and cook ducks slowly for 20 minutes. Do not burn. Turn, and cook slowly for 10 minutes. Spoon remaining butter mixture over top and cook for 45 minutes longer. Baste with drippings. Check for doneness. When cooked to your taste, remove to a serving platter, spoon drippings over the birds, and serve immediately. Serve with French Fries (page 217), a leafy green salad, and a bottle of Soave. Serves 4.

Roast Stuffed Pheasant

2 pheasants (3½ to 4½ pounds each)
¾ pound Italian sweet sausage
½ cup uncooked wild rice
2 slices of bread
¼ cup milk
¼ cup olive oil
7 tablespoons butter, melted
1 ounce salt pork, diced
¼ pound onions, peeled and diced
1 bay leaf, crumbled
1 small garlic clove, mashed
½ cup dry white wine
2 eggs, lightly beaten
½ cup chopped fresh parsley
¼ cup freshly grated Parmesan cheese
3 thin slices of salt pork
¼ teaspoon minced fresh rosemary
Salt and pepper
¼ cup hot chicken broth or water

Be sure your birds have been hanging or aging long enough; 3 days usually is sufficient. Be sure birds are well cleaned. Save the livers and gizzards and chop them into small pieces to use in the stuffing. Remove casing from sausage and cut the meat into 1-inch pieces. Soak the rice in lukewarm water for 15 minutes, then drain, and cook in lightly salted water for about 20 minutes, or until just tender but not at all mushy; drain. Soak the bread in the milk, squeeze out the liquid, and shred the bread.

Combine 3 tablespoons of the oil, 4 tablespoons of the butter and the salt pork in a skillet; heat. Add onions and sauté to medium brown. Add sausage pieces, chopped giblets, the bay leaf and garlic. Cook for 20 minutes. Add wine, cover, and cook for 3 minutes. Remove mixture from the heat and cool for 10 minutes. Take the ingredients from the skillet and chop very fine; do not lose juices. Place all back in the skillet, add the shredded bread, beaten eggs, the parsley, cheese, and drained rice. Mix well. Fill the birds with the stuffing.

Preheat oven to hot (450° F.). Oil a roasting pan. Truss the birds and place them, breast side down, in the pan. Roast for 10 minutes. Turn birds and cover breasts with the salt pork. Sprinkle the rosemary and salt and pepper over the birds and pat remaining olive oil on the parts not covered with salt pork. Reduce heat to slow (300° F.) and cook for 45 minutes, basting occasionally. The whole cooking time should not be longer than 1 hour, perhaps less. Check carefully during roasting. When the birds are done to your taste, remove from the oven and keep warm.

Discard grease from the roasting pan. Add remaining butter and the hot broth or water to the drippings in the pan and simmer for 10 minutes, until mixture is reduced to a gravy. Strain. Spoon gravy over birds and serve immediately. Serve with souffléed potatoes or Shoestring Potatoes (page 216) and a salad of Belgian endives. For a special occasion serve a good Champagne or a German white wine like Forster Jesuitengarten Auslese. Serves 6.

Roast Stuffed Squab

Jimmy Walker, our oldest daughter Luisa's godfather, came for dinner at the restaurant every Thursday. Mother always prepared his favorite dish, whole roast stuffed fresh squab, with homemade noodles with butter.

6 well-breasted fresh jumbo squabs	3 tablespoons olive oil
	Salt and pepper
Rice and Giblet Stuffing (page 151)	12 thin slices of salt pork
	1 teaspoon minced fresh rosemary

Wash the squabs well and dry thoroughly. Put aside the giblets (hearts, livers, and gizzards) for the stuffing (page 151). Make the stuffing and stuff the birds. Oil a large roasting pan with 1 tablespoon of the olive oil and arrange the birds, breast side up, in the pan. Brush 1 teaspoon of the oil over each bird. Sprinkle lightly with salt and pepper. Lay 2 slices of salt pork over each breast and sprinkle rosemary over the top. Place birds in a preheated moderate oven (375° F.). After 10 minutes reduce the temperature to slow (300° F.). After 20 minutes turn birds breast down, baste well, and cook for about 30 minutes longer. Test for doneness. Do not overcook. Serve with buttered noodles or Polenta (page 89) or Shoestring Potatoes (page 216), and a leafy green salad. Serves 6.

Note: If you have room in your roasting pan and your oven, cook 2 or more extra birds at the same time and freeze them for a rainy day.

RICE AND GIBLET STUFFING

¼ cup uncooked rice	2 bay leaves, crumbled
1 ounce salt pork, diced	20 fresh parsley sprigs, leaves only, chopped
2 tablespoons olive oil	2 eggs, beaten
2 tablespoons butter, melted	6 heaping tablespoons grated Parmesan cheese
¼ pound onions, peeled and diced	Salt and pepper
Squab giblets, chopped fine	

Soak the rice in lukewarm water for 30 minutes. Cook in lightly salted boiling water for 15 minutes and drain. Combine salt pork, olive oil and butter in a skillet; heat. Add onions and cook until medium brown. Add chopped giblets and bay leaves, stir, and cook for 10 minutes. Remove from the stove and cool for 10 minutes. Add parsley, eggs, cheese and drained rice; mix well. Taste and add salt and pepper according to your preference.

Small Game Birds

Use this method for quail, doves, grouse or baby pheasants.

8 to 12 small game birds	Salt
16 to 24 small thin slices of salt pork	¼ cup butter
3 to 4 tablespoons olive oil	¼ cup hot chicken broth or water
1 teaspoon minced fresh rosemary	2 tablespoons brandy
¼ teaspoon freshly ground black pepper	

Clean the birds (or have your butcher do this for you) and wash and dry well. Preheat oven to moderate (375° F.). Place the birds in a roasting pan. Cover each bird with 2 slices of salt pork. Spoon 1 teaspoon of olive oil over each, and sprinkle the rosemary and black pepper over all. Use salt sparingly. Cook in the oven for 10 minutes and then reduce heat to slow (300° F.). Cook for about 20 minutes, according to the size and age of the birds, but do not overcook. In fact, game birds should be *sanguante,* that is, still slightly pink, rare, and juicy. Remove birds to a warm platter.

Make gravy in the roasting pan. Pour off pork fat and grease from the pan and add the butter, chicken broth or water, and the brandy. Place pan on top of stove and simmer and stir the mixture until the liquid is reduced to a smooth gravy.

Serve with toasted Italian bread spread with chive butter, and a chilled bottle of Orvieto or a good Champagne. A true sportsman's repast. Allow 1 to 1½ birds for each serving, depending on the size of the bird. Quail and doves are rather small, but 1 grouse or baby pheasant is ample for a serving.

Coniglio alla Caccia

(wild hare or domestic rabbit)

1 rabbit or hare (2½ to 3 pounds), with liver
3 tablespoons olive oil
2 tablespoons butter, melted
2 ounces salt pork, diced
⅓ pound onions, peeled and diced
2 garlic cloves, mashed

2 bay leaves, crumbled
¼ teaspoon black pepper
6 tablespoons dry red wine
1 large ripe tomato or ½ cup canned peeled plum tomatoes, chopped
¾ cup hot water
Salt

Cut the rabbit or hare into 6 pieces. Wash and dry well. Chop the liver into very small pieces. Combine olive oil, butter and salt pork in a saucepan; heat. Add onions and cook to medium brown. Add rabbit pieces and brown for 10 minutes. Add garlic, bay leaves, black pepper and chopped liver. Stir and cook for 10 minutes. Add wine, stir, cover, and cook for 5 minutes. Uncover. Add the tomato and the hot water, stir, and cook slowly for about 1 hour. Test for doneness; do not overcook. Carefully taste for salt and if needed add just a little at this point. When rabbit is cooked, cover and keep warm until serving time. This dish goes well with any pasta. Spoon the sauce over both rabbit and pasta. Serves 4.

8 🌿

Meats

THE BEEF available to American cooks is in a class by itself—tender, flavorful, plentiful. Our grading system, too, is of great value. Choice meats are readily available. For that special occasion, you can usually find prime beef, truly outstanding in quality.

General Dwight D. Eisenhower is known among his many friends for his interest in the culinary arts. During his Presidency I was indeed fortunate to be included in a small informal dinner party at the White House. The President supervised the dinner, as Mrs. Eisenhower was away. The President raised his own beef at Gettysburg, and he served some of it on this memorable occasion; it was a superb, delicious dinner.

I recall the thirty-fifth reunion of the West Point Class of 1915. It was on June 4, 1950, at our farm. The farm was transformed into an outdoor Italian Art Gallery and the courses were typical Leone. After the manicotti, Generals Eisenhower, Bradley and Swing and I went over to the open charcoal grills to inspect the steaks. General Eisenhower suggested to the cooks that we fix the steaks his way. Needless to say the cooks and I were speechless. I thought, surely this is the end of my wonderful hand-picked steaks—but they were delicious. Here is his recipe. Cut a two-inch-thick prime sirloin steak, cover it well with freshly ground black pepper on all sides, and sprinkle with garlic salt. In the meantime prepare your wood charcoal fire. Level off your fire well and toss your steaks into the fire—right on the coals. Cook for eight minutes and turn, salt lightly, and cook for eight minutes more. Serve on warm plates, with melted butter and a tiny bit of chopped parsley over the top. Thereafter I prepared all our double steaks over the hot coals at the restaurant.

BEEF

Black-Peppered Double Beefsteak

2 double sirloin steaks (1½ to 2
  inches thick)
Olive oil
¼ cup butter
½ garlic clove, mashed

4 fresh parsley sprigs, leaves only
3 tablespoons black peppercorns,
  pounded, or crushed in a mor-
  tar
Salt

Rub the steaks on all sides with olive oil. Place the butter in a small bowl. Chop garlic and parsley together and add to the butter; stir, and set aside. Pat the crushed pepper onto all sides of the steaks. Place the steaks over a very hot charcoal fire, or in a preheated broiler. Cook for 6 minutes and turn. Do not prick the meat with a fork when turning. Cook for 5 minutes longer and sprinkle with salt. This should be rare, but cook to your own taste.

Place steaks on a warm ovenproof platter. Slice each steak into 6 slices. Spoon butter-parsley mixture over the steaks and slide the platter under the broiler for 30 to 60 seconds. Serve on individual plates, spooning butter over steaks. Try with this a heaping platter of Shoe-string Potatoes (page 216) and a green salad, and to drink, a red Beaujolais. Serves 4 or 5.

Broiled Sirloin Steak

4 steaks (1 pound each)
Tiny, tiny bit of garlic
4 fresh parsley sprigs, leaves only

2 tablespoons butter, melted
Salt and pepper

Choose prime beef if available, otherwise choice. Chop garlic and parsley together and mix with the melted butter. Get ready a nice platter of French Fries (page 217). Throw the steaks onto a very hot charcoal fire or under a hot broiler. Cook on one side for 4 minutes. Turn, sprinkle with salt and pepper, and broil for 3 minutes longer.

This is medium rare. If you like your steak rare, cook for less time and check carefully. Turn the steaks once only.

Place steaks on a hot platter and spoon butter, garlic, and parsley over them. Place the platter under the broiler for a few seconds. Serve with the French fries and a salad of sliced sweet onions and tomatoes with oil and vinegar dressing. With this dish you should enjoy a loaf of fresh Italian bread and a bottle of Barolo or red Burgundy. Serves 4.

Broiled Minute Steak

Select 2 prime sirloin steaks (12 ounces each), or if prime is not available use choice. Preheat broiler. Place steaks about 6 inches from the source of heat. Cook for 3 minutes. Turn, and sprinkle with salt and pepper. Broil for 2 minutes longer. Serve immediately on a hot platter, and drink a bottle of Valpolicella. Serves 2.

Pimientos and Steak

2 flank steaks (1 pound each)	2 garlic cloves, mashed
3 tablespoons olive oil	8 fresh parsley sprigs, leaves only
1 ounce salt pork, diced	1/2 teaspoon black pepper
2 tablespoons sweet butter, melted	1/3 teaspoon salt
	1/4 cup dry red wine
1/4 pound onions, peeled and diced	1 large can (8 ounces) pimientos
	1 loaf of Italian bread

Cut each steak into 4 pieces. Place between 2 pieces of wax paper and pound with a mallet or the flat side of a cleaver until very thin. Cut into 1-inch strips. Combine olive oil, salt pork and butter in a large skillet; heat. Add onions and cook until medium brown. Add the beef strips; cook for 10 minutes. Chop garlic and parsley together and add to the beef with the pepper and salt. Cook for 3 minutes. Add the wine, cover, and cook for 2 minutes longer. Drain the pimientos and cut them into wide strips. Uncover the skillet, stir, and add pimientos. Cook slowly for 10 minutes, or until meat is done. Taste for salt. Slice the bread and toast the slices in an oven or broiler. Arrange 2 slices of toast on each plate. Arrange steak and pimientos over toast. Spoon sauce over top. This dish calls for a hearty red wine, nothing fancy. Serves 4.

Peppered Butterfly Steak

Split 2 minute steaks (12 ounces each) down the center, without cutting apart. Pound well to make a butterfly shape. Brush with melted butter. Sprinkle lightly with salt and generously with freshly ground black pepper on both sides. Place the steak in the middle of a double-handed grill and close. Or cook over a hot charcoal fire. Or place on a hot broiler pan under a preheated broiler and broil for 2 to 3 minutes on each side. Serve immediately with lots of Shoestring Potatoes (page 216) or au gratin potatoes. Serves 2.

Beefsteak Pizzaiola

2½ pounds sirloin or tenderloin steak	8 fresh parsley sprigs, leaves only
1 ounce salt pork, diced	1 teaspoon dried orégano
¼ cup butter, melted	Salt and freshly ground black pepper
2 tablespoons olive oil	½ cup canned peeled plum tomatoes or 2 good-sized ripe tomatoes, chopped
2 medium-sized green peppers	
2 medium-sized garlic cloves, mashed	

Steak pizzaiola is usually cut from ends of the sirloin, or tenderloin, or from other tender cuts of beefsteak. Allow 3 slices per person and have them cut about ⅜ inch thick. Combine salt pork, butter and olive oil in a saucepan; heat. Cut the green peppers into thin strips, discarding all cores and seeds. Chop garlic and parsley together. Add green peppers, garlic-parsley, orégano and black pepper to the saucepan. Cover and cook for 10 minutes. Add tomatoes and bring to a boil. Cover and simmer slowly for 20 minutes. Taste for salt and add a pinch if necessary. Keep warm.

Preheat broiler before putting in the steaks. It will take about 3 minutes to broil each side. When steaks are broiled to your taste, sprinkle lightly with salt and pepper and place on warm individual serving plates. Spoon sauce abundantly over them. Serve with a bottle of red Chianti. Serves 4.

Beefsteak Tartare

2 pounds fresh raw prime sirloin steak or filet mignon
4 fresh eggs
½ teaspoon salt
½ teaspoon freshly ground black pepper
1 garlic clove, mashed
2 tablespoons virgin olive oil
Juice of 1 fresh lemon
1 tablespoon wine vinegar

1 teaspoon capers
4 whole fresh green scallions, chopped fine
12 fresh parsley sprigs, leaves only, chopped fine
1 tablespoon Worcestershire sauce
1 teaspoon prepared mustard
8 anchovy fillets, chopped, or mashed with a fork

Chop the meat by hand or put through a food grinder until very fine. Make 4 flat patties of the steak and place each patty on a cold plate. Boil the eggs for 2 minutes, remove saucepan from the heat, and leave the eggs in the hot water for 1 minute. Remove the yolks and set aside the egg whites for dressing. Make a hole in center of each steak patty and place 1 egg yolk in each hole. Sprinkle lightly with salt and pepper.

Make a dressing. Stir garlic into the olive oil. Chop or sieve the egg whites. Combine olive oil, chopped egg whites, lemon juice and vinegar in a bowl. Beat well with a wire whisk or fork; discard bits of garlic. Add capers, scallions, parsley, Worcestershire sauce, mustard, and anchovies; beat well. Taste carefully for salt and add some if needed, but only a pinch at a time because anchovies are salty. Spoon dressing over the raw meat. Enjoy with a loaf of oven-toasted Italian bread and a chilled bottle of dry Orvieto. Serves 4.

Broiled Filet Mignon

3½ pounds beef fillet
2 thin slices of garlic (not even ½ clove)
4 fresh parsley sprigs, leaves only

3 tablespoons sweet butter, melted
Pepper and salt
Truffles (optional)

Trim the beef fillet of the tough skin and sinews and cut it into 4 *filets mignons.* Chop garlic and parsley together and stir them into the butter; set aside. Sprinkle the meat well with pepper. Place the steaks over a hot charcoal fire or in a broiler, 6 inches from the source of heat. Cook on each side for 4 minutes. Season with salt. At this point they are rare; cook a little longer for medium rare, but do not cook until well done. As soon as they are done to your taste, remove from the heat immediately and place on warm plates. Shave truffles over the meat if you are splurging. Spoon the warm seasoned butter over them. Serve *ravioli al burro* with it and a good red Burgundy. Serves 4.

Sliced Filet Mignon in Red Wine

1 ounce salt pork, chopped fine
1 large garlic clove, mashed
¼ cup sweet butter
2 thick *filets mignons,* sliced into halves

Salt and pepper
3 tablespoons Barolo or red Burgundy
8 fresh parsley sprigs, leaves only, chopped fine

Combine salt pork, garlic and butter in a skillet; heat. Add the steaks and cook on each side for 4 minutes. Add salt and pepper to taste. Add wine, cover, and cook for 2 minutes. Add parsley and shake the skillet. Place 2 half *filets* on each warm plate and strain the sauce over them. Serve Bibb lettuce with Italian Salad Dressing (page 49), a loaf of fresh Italian bread, and caffè espresso. Serves 2.

Sliced Beef and Green Peppers with Anchovy Sauce

1½ pounds chuck steak
1 large garlic clove, mashed
8 fresh parsley sprigs, leaves only
2 tablespoons butter, melted
4 anchovy fillets, chopped, or mashed with a fork
⅓ teaspoon freshly ground black pepper

Pinch of crushed red pepper
¼ cup olive oil
1 ounce salt pork, diced
3 medium-sized green peppers
1 medium-sized ripe tomato
Italian bread

Cut the steak into 8 pieces and pound them thin. Chop garlic and parsley together. Combine the butter, anchovies, black and red pepper, garlic and parsley in a small bowl. Mix and set aside. Combine olive oil and salt pork in a large skillet and heat. Cut green peppers and the tomato into thin sices. Add them to the skillet, cover, and cook slowly for 5 minutes. Add the steaks and cook over high heat for 15 minutes. Stir, cover again, and cook for 10 minutes longer. Uncover, stir again, and add the butter mixture. Stir for 1 minute and remove from the heat. Serve over slices of toasted Italian bread. This calls for a good bottle of red California wine. Serves 4 or 5.

Roulade of Beef

1½ pounds flank steak	¼ cup butter, melted
8 fresh parsley sprigs, leaves only	Pinch of black pepper
1 small garlic clove, mashed	Pinch of crushed red pepper
4 slices of prosciutto, chopped fine	1½ ounces salt pork, diced
1 tablespoon sifted bread crumbs	3 tablespoons olive oil
1 heaping tablespoon grated Parmesan cheese	¼ cup dry red wine
	2 tablespoons warm water

Cut the flank steak into 4 pieces and pound them thin between sheets of wax paper. Chop parsley and garlic together. Place prosciutto, bread crumbs, cheese, parsley and garlic, half of the butter, black and red pepper and one third of the salt pork in a bowl. Mix well. Add salt if necessary. Spoon the mixture evenly onto the flattened slices of beef. Roll up the meat evenly. Fasten both ends with skewers or food picks.

Combine olive oil, remaining salt pork and remaining butter in a saucepan; heat. Add the beef roulades and brown for about 10 minutes. Add wine and water mixed together, cover, and cook slowly over low heat for about 30 minutes. Uncover and simmer for about 5 minutes more. Serve with mashed potatoes. Spoon gravy over meat and potatoes. Serves 4.

Roast Beef

Prime (or choice) ribs of beef, ready to cook
Olive oil
Salt and freshly ground black pepper

Crumbled dried rosemary
Broth or water, boiling
Butter

Select a piece of beef large enough for your needs, allowing 1 pound for 2 or 3 servings. Take the beef out of the refrigerator at least 1 hour before roasting. Preheat oven to very hot (500° F.). Place beef, fat side up, in a roasting pan and brush well with olive oil. Season with salt and pepper and sprinkle with rosemary. Place in the oven and roast for 5 minutes. Reduce heat to moderate (350° F.). If the meat seems to be cooking too fast, reduce to slow (300° F.). Roast for about 20 minutes to the pound. Baste well and often.

When roast is cooked to your taste, remove it from pan. Pour out grease, leaving drippings at bottom of pan. Place pan on top of stove and add about 1 cup of boiling water or broth and about 2 table-spoons butter. Simmer, stirring and scraping the bottom of pan. When the liquid is reduced to a nice gravy, strain and keep warm until ready to serve. Serve the beef with baked potatoes and the gravy in a sauceboat.

Short Ribs al Diavolo

3½ to 4 pounds beef short ribs
¼ cup butter, melted
2 garlic cloves, mashed
1 ounce salt pork, diced
12 fresh parsley sprigs, leaves only, chopped fine
½ cup sifted all-purpose flour
2 eggs, beaten
½ cup sifted bread crumbs

1 teaspoon salt
⅓ teaspoon freshly ground black pepper
⅓ teaspoon crushed red pepper
Olive oil
Juice of 1 fresh lemon
3 tablespoons prepared French mustard

Cut the short ribs into serving pieces and trim off all fat and skin. Or have the butcher do this for you. Preheat oven to moderate (350° F.). Make a mixture of butter, garlic, salt pork and parsley;

set aside. Arrange the ribs in a broiler pan. Cook in the oven for 15 minutes. Turn the ribs and cook for 15 minutes longer. Lift out ribs and discard fat.

Dust ribs with the flour, shaking off any excess. Dip them into beaten eggs, then into bread crumbs. Sprinkle with salt, black pepper and crushed red pepper. Place the ribs in a roasting pan and spoon olive oil over the ribs, turning them so they are coated with oil. Then spoon the butter mixture over the top. Bake for 40 minutes. Combine lemon juice and mustard and spoon this mixture over the ribs. Cover the pan and cook for about 5 minutes more, or until meat is tender. Arrange ribs on a warm platter and spoon drippings and gravy over top. Serve with French-Fried Onions (page 215) and ravioli with butter and cheese. Try a bottle of Barolo with this. Serves 4 or 5.

Filetto di Manzo Duca di Piemonte

(beef fillet in crust)

1 beef fillet (about 4 pounds)	12 ounces *pâté de foie gras,* approximately (see note)
2 tablespoons olive oil	
2 cups sifted all-purpose flour	1 can (4 ounces) white Italian truffles
⅓ teaspoon salt	
6 tablespoons butter	1 ounce salt pork
¼ cup shortening	1 garlic clove, mashed
1 tablespoon freshly ground black pepper	2 tablespoons dry red wine

Use prime beef for this dish. The fillet will be lean, but trim away any fat and any skin or sinews. Place the beef in a large heavy skillet and brush well with olive oil. Brown on all sides.

Make a crust. Mix the flour, salt, half the butter and the shortening together. Slowly add about 5 tablespoons cold water, kneading until the dough sticks together. Put the dough on a floured board and roll it out into a rectangle large enough to enclose the beef. Place the meat in the center of the dough. Sprinkle with pepper. Cover the entire fillet with a generous coating of *pâté.* Shave just a few slices of the truffles over top. Bring the dough up around the meat and seal it carefully so that flavor and juices cannot escape. Preheat oven to very hot (500° F.)

Lightly oil a baking pan with olive oil and arrange the beef in the dough on it. Bake for 5 minutes. Reduce heat to moderate (375° F.) and bake for 30 minutes. Remove from the oven to a hot platter.

For each person serve 2 slices on a warm heatproof plate. Make the following sauce: Put remaining butter, the salt pork, chopped fine, and garlic in the pan, heat and add the wine. Shave the remainder of the truffles over the meat and spoon the sauce generously over the truffles. Serve with a salad of Belgian endives with lemon and olive-oil dressing. This important dish calls for nothing less than a Romanée-Conti or a La Tâche. Serves 4 or 5.

Note: Instead of using imported *pâté de foie gras,* you can make your own pâté using chicken livers. It will be delicious and much less expensive. See Pâté of Fresh Chicken Livers alla Leone (page 29).

Mother's Beef Pot Roast

Victor Herbert, one of Mother's closest friends, loved her beef pot roast, which I have never been able to cook as well as she.

5 pounds top or bottom round, rump or brisket of beef	8 fresh parsley sprigs, leaves only
Strips of salt pork	1 teaspoon crumbled dried rosemary
2 tablespoons olive oil	½ cup dry red wine
2 ounces salt pork, diced	2 tablespoons grated carrot
½ teaspoon salt	½ celery stalk, minced
1 teaspoon freshly ground black pepper	2 medium-sized ripe tomatoes, chopped
⅛ pound onions, peeled and diced	1 cup boiling water
2 garlic cloves, mashed	¼ cup butter, melted

Choose the cut of beef you prefer and with a skewer insert lengthwise through the meat 2 strips of salt pork ¼ inch wide. Or ask your butcher to lard it. Place olive oil and diced salt pork in a casserole and heat. Add the beef and brown slowly on all sides. Do not let it scorch. Add salt, pepper and onions and cook slowly for 10 minutes. Chop garlic and parsley together and add. Sprinkle rosemary all over the meat. Cook for 5 minutes. Add the wine, cover, and simmer for 10 minutes. Add carrot, celery, tomatoes and boiling water. Simmer slowly for about 3 hours, or until tender. Turn, stir, and baste occasionally. Add butter. Taste for salt. Serve mashed potatoes with the pot roast, and spoon the gravy over meat and potatoes. Serves 6 to 8.

Beef Stew

2½ pounds boneless lean beef (brisket, chuck, flank or round)
3 carrots
4 medium-sized potatoes, peeled
3 tablespoons olive oil
¼ cup butter
2 ounces salt pork, diced
¾ pound onions, peeled and diced
2 bay leaves, crumbled
1 teaspoon freshly ground black pepper
1 teaspoon crumbled dried rosemary

1 tablespoon all-purpose flour
2 large garlic cloves, mashed
10 fresh parsley sprigs, leaves only
½ cup dry white wine
1 celery stalk with leaves, diced
1 large green pepper, diced
2 cups hot water or broth
1½ pounds ripe tomatoes, chopped, or 3 cups canned peeled plum tomatoes, sieved
1 loaf Italian bread
1 garlic clove, split

Cut the beef into 1½-inch cubes. Trim ends from carrots, but do not peel or scrape. Wash them well and cut into ½-inch pieces. Cut each potato into 8 pieces. Set the vegetables aside. Combine olive oil, butter and salt pork in a heavy saucepan; heat. Add onions and bay leaves and brown slowly for 10 minutes. Add meat cubes, black pepper and rosemary and brown for about 10 minutes. Shake the flour through a sifter and sprinkle the meat lightly. Chop garlic and parsley together and add to meat. Stir, and cook for 4 minutes. Add the wine, stir, cover, and simmer for 10 minutes. Add celery, green pepper, carrots and potatoes. Stir, cover, and cook slowly for 20 minutes. Add hot water or broth and the tomatoes. Stir well and cook slowly, uncovered, for 40 minutes. Taste for cooking and salt. Slice Italian bread, rub slices with garlic on both sides, and toast in the oven. Pour the stew into a good-sized bowl and serve. Dunk your toast into the gravy and enjoy a bottle of Valpolicella with the stew. Serves 6.

Ragout of Beef, Pigs' Knuckles and Cabbage

1 pound lean top or bottom round or chuck of beef

1½ pounds fresh or frozen pigs' knuckles

1 ounce salt pork, diced

2 garlic cloves, mashed

1 hot cherry pepper

¼ ounce dried Italian or French mushrooms

2 cups warm water

2 pounds fresh cabbage

1 tablespoon olive oil

2 tablespoons butter

¼ pound onions, peeled and chopped

2 tablespoons finely diced prosciutto

1 ounce fresh chicken livers, diced

1 ounce fresh chicken gizzards, diced

1 large ripe tomato or ½ cup canned peeled plum tomatoes, chopped

Pinch of salt

Pinch of freshly ground black pepper

3 cups hot water

Cut the beef into ½-inch cubes. Crack the pigs' knuckles, or have your butcher do this. Chop the salt pork and garlic together. Split the cherry pepper and remove the core and seeds. Wash well and dice. Soak the mushrooms in the warm water for 15 minutes. Remove from the water (do not discard it), chop the mushrooms, and return the pieces to the water. Discard core of cabbage and cut leaves into shreds about 1 inch wide. Place the pigs' knuckles in a large soup pot and cover with hot water. Cover the pot and boil slowly for 30 minutes. Remove from the heat, take knuckles out of the pot and set aside, and discard the water.

Combine olive oil, butter, salt pork with garlic, and onions in the soup pot. Cook slowly for 5 minutes. Add the parboiled pigs' knuckles, the prosciutto, diced cherry pepper and the beef cubes. Stir, and cook slowly for 10 minutes. Add all the chicken giblets and cook for 5 minutes. Add mushrooms with mushroom water, the tomato, salt and pepper. Stir, and bring to a slow boil. Add the shredded cabbage and the hot water and stir. Place a layer of aluminum foil over the cabbage and press down tightly. Then cover the pot and cook slowly for 1 hour. Uncover and check; if the meat isn't tender, continue to cook slowly. When just cooked, remove from the heat and let the stew stand for 10 minutes. Serve in individual soup bowls or plates. Add a green salad and a loaf of Italian bread. For wine, a bottle of well-aged Chianti. Serves 4 to 6.

Broiled Hamburger Steak

1½ pounds beef chuck, shank, round or flank
12 leaves of fresh chives, chopped fine, or 1 tablespoon dried chives
3 tablespoons butter, melted
2 slices of bread
2 tablespoons grated onion
¼ teaspoon freshly ground black pepper
Salt

Remove all fat and skin from the beef and have it ground twice. Stir the chives into 2 tablespoons of the butter and keep it warm. Soak the bread in a little milk, squeeze out the liquid, and shred the bread. Place the ground meat, grated onion, pepper and bread in a bowl. Add salt to taste. Mix lightly with a fork and shape into 4 patties about ¾ inch thick. Pat and brush with remaining butter.

Preheat broiler. Place the patties in a greased broiler pan or on top of a greased grill about 8 inches from the source of heat. Cook for 4 minutes, turn, and cook for another 5 minutes. When cooked, spoon butter and chives mixture over top and put under broiler for ½ minute more. Drink a plain red Bordeaux, not an expensive château variety. Serves 4.

Hamburger Casalinga

2 pounds top round of beef
1 tablespoon dried chives or 15 leaves of fresh chives, chopped fine
¼ cup butter, melted
2 tablespoons olive oil
1 ounce salt pork, diced
¼ pound onions, peeled and diced
⅓ teaspoon salt
½ teaspoon freshly ground black pepper
3 teaspoons tomato paste
½ cup dry white wine

Have butcher trim fat and skin from the beef and put it through meat grinder three times. Divide meat into 4 or 5 parts, and mold them lightly into patties. Stir chives into melted butter and mix well. Place olive oil, salt pork, and one third of the butter and chives in a skillet; heat. Add onions and sauté slowly until medium brown. Add patties and cook on each side for 5 minutes. Sprinkle with salt and pepper and shake the skillet. Spoon remainder of butter and chives mixture over the patties, cover, and cook slowly for 10 minutes. Stir tomato paste into the wine and blend well. Add to the skillet, shake the skillet, and baste the patties with the sauce. Cover and cook for about 20 minutes longer. Uncover, baste, and simmer to thicken the sauce. Place hamburgers on a warm platter and spoon sauce over the top. Serve with mashed potatoes and Italian bread, Provolone cheese and apples for dessert. For wine, a good bottle of Bardolino. Serves 4 or 5.

Meat Balls

2 pounds meat, ground
1 slice of bread
2 eggs, beaten
8 fresh parsley sprigs, leaves only, chopped fine
12 leaves of chives, chopped fine
2 tablespoons butter
6 tablespoons freshly grated Parmesan cheese
Pinch of salt

Pinch of freshly ground black pepper
1 ounce salt pork
¼ cup olive oil
⅓ pound onions, peeled and diced
1 small garlic clove, chopped fine
2 cups Marinara Sauce (page 94), hot

For these, you may use all beef, or 1 pound beef, ½ pound veal, and ½ pound pork. If using the combination, grind together so the mixture is well blended. Soak the bread in a little milk, then squeeze out the moisture and shred the bread. Place the meat, eggs, bread, parsley, chives, butter, half of the cheese, and the salt and pepper in a bowl. Mix well. Make meat balls about 1½ inches in size.

Combine salt pork and olive oil in a skillet and heat. Add onions and garlic and cook until brown. Add meat balls and brown. Cover, and simmer slowly for 45 minutes. Add the marinara sauce and bring to a boil. Sprinkle remaining cheese on top and serve. Serve extra marinara sauce if you wish. For wine, Nebbiolo Spumante. Serves 6.

Smoked Beef Tongue

Place 1 smoked beef tongue (3½ pounds) in a soup kettle, cover with cold water, and bring to a boil. Lower the heat, cover, and cook slowly for 45 minutes. Remove tongue from the kettle and discard the water. Put tongue back in the kettle and immediately cover with fresh boiling water. Cover and cook slowly for about 2½ hours. Check for doneness. When cooked, remove from the kettle and allow to cool for 10 minutes. Trim off outer skin, fat, and any little bones and gristle. Serve with boiled spinach and buttered parsleyed potatoes.

Oxtail Stew

2 tablespoons olive oil
2 tablespoons butter
1 ounce salt pork, diced
¼ pound onions, peeled and diced
2½ pounds oxtail, disjointed
2 garlic cloves, mashed
1 teaspoon fresh rosemary
1 bay leaf, crumbled
⅓ teaspoon salt
⅛ teaspoon freshly ground black pepper
Pinch of crushed red pepper
6 tablespoons dry red wine
½ celery stalk, minced
1 medium-sized carrot, diced
1 large green pepper, diced
2 medium-sized ripe tomatoes or ½ cup canned peeled plum tomatoes, chopped
2 cups beef broth or hot water

Combine olive oil, butter and salt pork in a large skillet; heat. Add onions and cook to medium brown. Add oxtail pieces and brown on all sides. Chop garlic and rosemary together and add to skillet with bay leaf, salt and black and red pepper. Stir, and cook for 2 minutes. Add wine, stir, cover, and cook for 3 minutes. Add celery, carrot, green pepper and tomatoes; stir and cook for 5 minutes. Add broth or hot water, stir, cover, and cook slowly for 1½ hours, or until meat is tender. Stir, and taste for seasoning. Serve with Polenta (page 89) or with a heavy pasta like ziti. Add a ripe pear with Bel Paese cheese and a bottle of Valpolicella to complete the meal. Serves 4.

VEAL

Veal Cutlet Parmigiana

This was one of our most popular dishes. On a busy night we would serve as many as 2,500 portions.

2 pounds veal cut from the leg	2 cups Marinara Sauce (page 94),
4 heaping tablespoons all-purpose	hot
flour	4 slices of prosciutto
1 large egg, beaten	4 slices of Fontina or mozzarella
¾ cup sifted bread crumbs	cheese
¼ cup olive oil	Pinch of salt
¼ cup butter, melted	¼ tablespoon pepper
10 leaves of chives or 2 whole	4 heaping tablespoons freshly
fresh green scallions, chopped	grated Parmesan cheese

Cut the veal into 4 slices 3 by 5 inches. Pound them thin. Dip the cutlets into the flour, then into the egg, and then press into the bread crumbs, coating both sides. Do this twice. Place olive oil and half of the butter in a skillet and heat. Add the cutlets and sauté on each side for about 6 minutes. Meanwhile stir the chopped chives or scallions into the remaining butter and keep warm. Preheat oven to moderate (375° F.).

Pour a thin layer of marinara sauce on the bottom of a baking pan or casserole. Lay cutlets on top and spoon a little marinara sauce over them. Cover each cutlet with a slice of prosciutto and spoon the chive butter over the prosciutto. Now place the sliced cheese on top and sprinkle lightly with salt and pepper. Spoon more marinara sauce over all, covering the meat entirely. Sprinkle the top with the grated cheese. Bake for 20 minutes, then serve immediately. Wine, Valpolicella. Serves 4.

Breaded Veal Cutlet alla Milanese

2 pounds veal cut from the leg
2 tablespoons all-purpose flour
2 eggs, beaten
½ cup sifted bread crumbs
¼ cup olive oil
6 tablespoons butter, melted
Pinch of salt

Pinch of freshly ground black
  pepper
8 leaves of chives or 2 whole fresh
  green scallions, chopped
1 cup Meatless Tomato Sauce
  (page 96), hot

Cut the veal into 4 slices and pound slightly. Lightly sprinkle with flour and shake off any excess. Dip cutlets into beaten eggs and then press into the bread crumbs, coating on both sides. Do this twice. Combine oil and 4 tablespoons of the butter in a skillet and heat. Add veal cutlets and sauté on each side for 5 minutes over low heat. Add salt and pepper and cook slowly for about 15 minutes. Place cutlets on warm plates.

Stir chopped chives or scallions into the remaining butter. Spoon the mixture over the cutlets and then spoon 2 tablespoons of the tomato sauce onto each side of each cutlet. Serve with a salad of watercress or dandelion with a simple dressing, all on the same plate, as they do in Italy and France. Add toasted garlic bread and a cold bottle of California white wine. For dessert serve sliced Bel Paese cheese with slices of fresh pear. Serves 4.

Veal Scaloppine Piccata

1½ to 2 pounds veal cut from the
  leg or the fillet
¼ cup all-purpose flour
6 tablespoons fresh creamery butter
½ teaspoon salt

¼ teaspoon freshly ground black
  pepper
Juice of 1½ fresh lemons
10 fresh parsley sprigs, leaves
  only, chopped fine

Cut the veal into ½-inch slices and pound very thin. Dip the slices into the flour, shaking off any excess. Place the butter in a large skillet and heat. Add the veal and brown on both sides over high heat. Add salt and pepper and cook for about 5 minutes. Shake the skillet. Add lemon juice and parsley and cook for 1 minute. Stir well. Arrange on hot plates and spoon the sauce over the veal. This dish goes well with mashed potatoes. Serves 4.

Veal Scaloppine alla Marsala

2 to 2½ pounds veal, cut from the top round of the leg
All-purpose flour
6 tablespoons sweet butter
2 tablespoons olive oil
4 slices of prosciutto, diced
1 garlic clove, mashed
1 teaspoon crumbled dried rosemary
⅓ teaspoon salt
⅓ teaspoon freshly ground black pepper
6 tablespoons Marsala or sherry
2 cups (one 1-pound can) tiny French peas
8 fresh parsley sprigs, leaves only, chopped fine

Slice the veal into cutlets, pound them thin, and sprinkle with flour on both sides. Shake off any excess flour. Place butter and olive oil in a large skillet and heat. Add the veal slices and the prosciutto. Sauté for 3 minutes, then turn and add garlic, rosemary, salt and pepper. Cook for 2 minutes. Add the wine, cover, and sauté for 3 minutes. Discard bits of garlic. Warm the peas, but do not boil, and drain well just before adding to the skillet. Uncover the skillet, add drained peas and the parsley, and cook slowly for 6 minutes longer. Taste for salt and cooking. Serve a green salad with Brie or Camembert cheese. For dessert make Zabaglione (page 226) with Marsala. Serves 4.

Veal Scaloppine with Chianti

2 pounds veal cutlets
All-purpose flour
2 tablespoons olive oil
2 tablespoons diced salt pork
½ cup sweet butter
¼ pound onions, peeled and diced
⅓ teaspoon salt
⅓ teaspoon freshly ground black pepper
¼ cup red Chianti
½ pound fresh mushrooms
2 medium-sized green peppers
2 large ripe tomatoes, sliced thin
1 good-sized garlic clove, mashed
8 parsley sprigs, leaves only

Pound the cutlets thin and sprinkle them with flour on both sides, shaking off any excess. Place olive oil, salt pork and butter in a skillet; heat. Add onions and sauté until medium brown. Add the veal and brown slowly for 3 minutes. Turn over, and cook for 2 minutes longer. Add salt, pepper and wine, cover, and simmer for 5 minutes. Separate stems and caps of mushrooms. Chop the stems fine and cut the caps into thin slices. Discard cores and seeds from peppers and cut them into very thin slices. Add mushrooms, green peppers and tomatoes to the veal, cover, and cook for 5 minutes. Chop garlic and parsley together and stir the mixture into the sauce. Simmer, uncovered, for 10 minutes, or until done. Taste for salt. Drink Chianti with this. Serves 4.

Veal Rollatine with Polenta

2 pounds veal cut from the leg or shoulder
All-purpose flour
6 tablespoons butter
1 large garlic clove, mashed
6 fresh parsley sprigs, leaves only
Pinch of salt
Pinch of freshly ground black pepper
3 slices of prosciutto, minced
6 tablespoons freshly grated Parmesan cheese
2 tablespoons olive oil
1 medium-sized ripe tomato or ¼ cup canned peeled plum tomatoes, chopped
4 good-sized portions of Polenta (page 89)

Cut the veal into 8 slices. Place them between sheets of wax paper and pound thin. Sprinkle lightly with flour, shaking off any excess. Spread the floured slices on a working surface. Brush one side with about one third of the butter. Chop garlic and parsley together. Put the salt, pepper, garlic and parsley, prosciutto, half of the cheese, and 2 tablespoons of the butter in a bowl and mix well. Spread 1 teaspoon of the mixture down the center of each veal slice. Roll up each piece of veal and pin with a food pick. Heat olive oil and remaining butter in a skillet. Add the veal rolls and brown well on all sides. Add the tomato, cover, and cook slowly for about 25 minutes. Serve 2 veal rolls with each serving of polenta. Sprinkle remaining grated cheese over the top and then all remaining sauce over all. Serves 4.

Peppered Veal Paillard

1¼ pounds veal fillet
Black peppercorns
Salt

¼ cup fresh creamery butter, melted

Cut the veal into 2 slices. Place them between sheets of wax paper and pound lightly. Preheat broiler. Grind the peppercorns generously over the veal slices on both sides and pat the pepper into the surface so that it sticks to the meat. Place the veal in the broiler 6 inches from the source of heat. Broil under high heat for 3 minutes. Turn over, sprinkle with salt, and cook for 2 minutes. When cooked to your taste, place on a warm platter and brush with butter. Enjoy with a cold bottle of Chiaretto del Garda. Serves 2.

Veal Fillet alla del Sarto

1½ pounds veal fillet
All-purpose flour
¼ cup fresh creamery butter
1 garlic clove, mashed
3 thin slices of prosciutto, diced
10 fresh parsley sprigs, leaves only, chopped fine
½ teaspoon freshly ground black pepper
Pinch of salt

¼ cup dry white wine
¼ cup heavy cream
1 cup (one 8-ounce can or jar) roasted red peppers or pimientos
1 teaspoon capers
2 tablespoons hot water
12 canned or cooked frozen artichoke hearts, drained

Cut the veal into 8 pieces. Place them between sheets of wax paper and pound lightly; do not make them too thin. Sprinkle lightly with flour, shaking off any excess. Melt the butter in a skillet and add the garlic and veal slices. Sauté on each side for 2 minutes. Add prosciutto, parsley, pepper and salt. Shake the skillet, and cook for 1 minute. Mix the wine and cream together and pour over the veal. Cover, and cook for 2 minutes. Discard bits of garlic. Drain the peppers or pimientos and cut them into ½-inch strips. Add to the veal along with capers, hot water and artichokes. Shake the skillet, stir gently, cover, and cook for 5 minutes longer. Then check to see if everything is cooked and has enough salt. Serve with a salad of Bibb or Boston lettuce with Italian Salad Dressing (page 49). Serves 4.

Filetti di Vitello di Firenze

(veal fillets Florentine style)

2 pounds veal fillet
1/3 ounce dried Italian or French mushrooms
1/4 cup lukewarm water
1 can (3½ to 4 ounces) white Italian truffles
1/4 cup sweet butter
1 garlic clove, mashed well
1 tablespoon olive oil
1/2 teaspoon salt

1/3 teaspoon freshly ground black pepper
5 fresh parsley sprigs, leaves only, chopped fine
4 thin slices of prosciutto, diced
3 tablespoons dry white wine
3 tablespoons good brandy (optional)
1 tablespoon Grand Marnier (optional)

Cut the veal into 4 slices. Put them between sheets of wax paper and pound lightly. Soak the mushrooms in the water for 15 minutes. Drain, discarding the water, and chop the mushrooms. Open the truffles and drain off and measure the juice. There should be 2 tablespoons; set aside. Put butter, garlic and olive oil in a skillet; heat. Add the veal and cook for 3 minutes. Turn over, sprinkle with salt and pepper, and cook slowly for 3 minutes. Discard bits of garlic. Add chopped mushrooms, truffle juice, and parsley and simmer for 3 minutes. Add prosciutto and shake the skillet. Mix the wine with the brandy and liqueur; add the mixture to the skillet, cover, and simmer for 2 minutes. Uncover and cook for 2 minutes longer. Check carefully for salt.

Arrange the veal slices on warm plates and shave all of the truffles over the top. Serve Shoestring Potatoes (page 216) on the same plate and spoon the sauce over veal and potatoes. Serve a salad of Bibb or Boston lettuce or field salad, with a slice of ripe Gorgonzola cheese and a loaf of fresh Italian bread. Drink a bottle of white Frascati. Serves 4.

Saltimbocca alla Romana

W. C. Fields and James Montgomery Flagg were great friends and spent practically every evening at Leone's, enjoying our antipasto and spaghetti. Fields liked *saltimbocca alla Romana;* Flagg liked *scaloppine alla Marsala.*

2 to 2½ pounds veal fillet
All-purpose flour
⅔ cup fresh creamery butter, melted
Salt and pepper
4 very thin slices of Fontina cheese
8 thin slices of prosciutto
2 fresh sage leaves or ½ teaspoon dried leaf sage (see note)

A very tiny bit of garlic
4 fresh parsley sprigs, leaves only
2 tablespoons shaved white Italian truffles, or more
½ cup white Frascati or another good dry white wine
2 cups (one 1-pound can) small peas

Cut the veal into 8 slices. Place the slices between sheets of wax paper and pound thin. Sprinkle with flour on one side only. Place half of the slices, floured sides down, on a working board. Spoon some of the butter (about 2 tablespoons) over the slices and sprinkle lightly with salt and pepper. Place 1 slice of cheese and 1 slice of prosciutto over each veal slice and again spoon some butter lightly over them. Add half a leaf of the sage. Chop garlic and parsley together and divide the mixture among the 4 veal slices. Arrange the shaved truffles on top. (Use more truffles if you wish.) Add the remaining veal slices, floured sides up. Press the edges together with a knife handle. Spoon more of the butter over.

Reserve 1 tablespoon of the butter; place the rest in a skillet and heat. Add the little bundles and sauté for 5 minutes, until brown. Turn, cook for 3 minutes longer, and baste. Pour the wine over the veal, shake the skillet, baste again, cover, and cook for 5 minutes.

Dice the remaining slices of prosciutto. Place peas in a small pan and heat. Drain. Add diced prosciutto and the reserved tablespoon of butter. Season with salt and pepper to taste. Heat for a few minutes. Arrange saltimbocca on warm plates, spoon all of the sauce over, and serve with the peas. Drink the rest of the Frascati. Serves 4.

Note: If using dried sage, soak it in warm water for a few minutes and press dry before using. For this dish do not use ground sage.

Veal alla Maria

1 pound veal fillet, sliced into 2 cutlets
All-purpose flour
6 slices or pieces of dried mushrooms
3 tablespoons warm water
2 slices of prosciutto, diced
5 parsley sprigs, leaves only, chopped
Pinch of black pepper
3 heaping tablespoons butter
2 tablespoons virgin olive oil
3 tablespoons good dry vermouth
2 slices of Fontina or mozzarella cheese

Pound the cutlets thin and sprinkle lightly with flour. (Other cuts of veal may be used, but they may need to be cooked a little longer.) Soak the mushrooms in the water for 10 minutes. Drain mushrooms, saving the water, and chop coarsely. Mix prosciutto, parsley, mushrooms, and black pepper together. Place butter and olive oil in a skillet and heat. Add the veal and cook for 2 minutes; turn over. Add parsley mixture and cook for 4 minutes. Add vermouth and mushroom water, cover, and cook for 2 minutes. Shake the skillet and place the cheese on the cutlets. Cover and cook slowly for 2 minutes longer. Shake pan well and serve immediately. Make a salad of Bibb lettuce with a dressing of lemon juice, wine vinegar and olive oil. Serves 2.

Broiled Veal Chops

Take chops out of refrigerator 30 minutes before cooking. Brush 4 chops, 1 inch thick, with melted butter, and season with salt and pepper on both sides. Preheat broiler. Put chops on broiler pan 6 inches from the source of heat and broil on each side for 3 minutes, or longer if you prefer. Do not overcook or burn. Spoon a little butter over top of chops. Serve with fettucini or *spaghettini al burro,* a bottle of Barolo, a slice of Provolone and some well-crusted Italian bread. Serves 2.

Osso Buco

3½ to 4 pounds veal shin or knuckle
¼ cup all-purpose flour
2 tablespoons olive oil
2 ounces salt pork, diced
¼ cup butter, melted
½ pound onions, peeled and diced
1 large garlic clove, mashed
2 bay leaves, crumbled
1 teaspoon crumbled dried rosemary
1 teaspoon salt
1 teaspoon freshly ground pepper
¾ cup dry white wine
2 tablespoons grated or minced carrot
½ celery stalk with leaves, minced
8 to 10 fresh parsley sprigs, leaves only, chopped fine
2 large ripe tomatoes or 1 cup canned peeled plum tomatoes, chopped
1 heaping tablespoon tomato paste
½ cup warm water

Have the butcher saw the shins into 3-inch pieces. Sprinkle them lightly with flour and shake off any excess. Heat the olive oil, salt pork and butter in a heavy-bottomed skillet. Add the onions and brown. Add the pieces of veal shin and the garlic and brown on all sides for about 8 minutes. Add bay leaves, rosemary, salt and pepper. Stir and brown for about 10 minutes longer. Add the wine, cover, and simmer for 5 minutes. Discard bits of garlic. Add carrot, celery, parsley, and tomatoes. Stir tomato paste with the water until well blended and then add that to the mixture. Stir and cook for about 40 minutes, or until done to your taste.

Osso buco is often served with *risotto,* but I prefer *ravioli al burro.* Cook 8 ravioli per person, drain, and place in a warm bowl with butter and cheese. Serve 1 or 2 pieces of veal shin per person. Add ravioli on the same plate and spoon the meat gravy over all. Serve immediately. If you have some left over, serve cold the next day for lunch. With this tasty dish you can serve an imported Barbera or red Burgundy, or either type of wine produced in California. Serves 4 to 6.

Roast Veal

1 rolled veal roast (5 pounds)
3 tablespoons olive oil
1 ounce salt pork, diced
1/4 cup butter
1/4 pound onions, peeled and diced
1/3 teaspoon freshly ground black pepper
2 garlic cloves, mashed
2 bay leaves, crumbled
8 parsley sprigs, leaves only, chopped

4 thin slices of salt pork
1 teaspoon dried rosemary
6 tablespoons dry white wine
1/2 celery stalk, minced
1 heaping tablespoon grated carrot
1 heaping tablespoon tomato paste
1 cup hot broth or water

Preheat oven to hot (400° F.). Brush the roast with olive oil. Heat diced salt pork, remaining olive oil and the butter in an oven pan on top of the stove. Add the roast, and brown slowly on all sides. Add onions, pepper, garlic, bay leaves and parsley. Cook for 3 minutes. Remove from the heat. Cover the roast with the slices of salt pork and sprinkle rosemary over the top. Place in the oven and bake for 15 minutes. Add the wine and cook for 5 minutes. Add celery and carrot. Stir tomato paste into the hot water or broth and blend well. Pour over the roast and stir. Lower heat to moderate (350° F.) and bake for about 1 hour, basting several times. Check gravy for seasoning. Arrange the roast on a serving platter and slice. Strain gravy over and serve with Roasted Potatoes (page 216). Serves 4 or 5.

Veal Stew

1 pound onions, peeled
2 tablespoons olive oil
2 tablespoons butter
1 ounce salt pork, diced
1 garlic clove, mashed
1/2 carrot, diced
1/2 celery stalk, minced
1 1/2 bay leaves, crumbled
1 pound veal, cut into 1-inch cubes

Salt and pepper
1/2 cup dry white wine
1/2 tablespoon tomato paste
3/4 cup warm water
2 cups (one 1-pound can) peas, drained
5 parsley sprigs, leaves only, chopped

Cut half of the onions into quarters, the other half chop fine. Combine olive oil, butter and salt pork in a saucepan; heat. Add chopped onions only and cook until brown. Add garlic, carrot, celery, and the quartered onions. Stir and cook slowly for 6 minutes. Add bay leaves, veal cubes, and salt and pepper to taste. Stir and cook for 5 minutes. Add the wine, cover, and cook for 3 minutes. Stir tomato paste into the water until well blended. Uncover the saucepan, stir, and add tomato paste and water. Cook slowly for about 15 minutes. Add the drained peas and the parsley. Cook for 3 minutes longer. Taste and adjust seasoning. Serves 3 or 4.

Broiled Sweetbreads

2 pairs of fresh veal sweetbreads	Salt and pepper
1 lemon	6 tablespoons butter, melted
½ teaspoon salt	6 fresh parsley sprigs, leaves only,
2 bay leaves, crumbled	chopped fine
1 egg, beaten	4 slices of Italian bread, toasted
4 heaping tablespoons sifted	
bread crumbs	

Soak the sweetbreads in cold water for about 1 hour. Change the water several times during the hour; drain. Place sweetbreads in a saucepan and cover with fresh cold water. Add the juice of the lemon and drop the squeezed peel into the water. Add salt and bay leaves, bring to a boil, and simmer slowly for 25 minutes. Drain the sweetbreads and place them under cold running water. Remove tough membranes and tubes. Dry well.

Preheat broiler. Dip sweetbreads into beaten egg, then dredge with bread crumbs and shake off any excess. Season lightly with salt and pepper. Place in a broiling pan, brush with some of the butter, and broil under medium heat for 10 minutes. Turn, brush with butter again, and broil for another 10 minutes. Stir the chopped parsley into remaining melted butter and spoon some of the mixture over the toast. As soon as sweetbreads are cooked, place them on the buttered toast and spoon any remaining parsley butter over them. Serve immediately.

Sweetbreads spoil easily. Prepare them as soon as possible after purchase and enjoy them fresh. Serve with Camembert cheese, additional toast, and a Rhine, Liefraumilch or Bernkastel Moselle wine. Serves 4.

Sweetbreads with Olives

1 pair of fresh veal sweetbreads (about 1¼ pounds)	¼ cup fresh creamery butter
2 tablespoons wine vinegar	1 garlic clove, mashed
Juice of ½ fresh lemon	10 medium-sized black olives, pitted
All-purpose flour	¼ cup dry white wine
2 egg yolks, beaten	1 small firm tomato, sliced very thin
3 tablespoons sifted bread crumbs	Salt and pepper
2 tablespoons olive oil	
1 ounce salt pork, diced	

Soak the sweetbreads in slightly salted cold water for 1 hour. Drain, and place them in a saucepan. Cover with fresh cold water with the vinegar and lemon juice added. Bring to a boil and simmer for 7 minutes. Drain, and plunge sweetbreads into ice water. Leave for 2 or 3 minutes, then remove cartilage, tubes, and membranes. Dry well. Sprinkle lightly with flour, shaking off excess. Then dip into egg yolks and then into crumbs. Use more crumbs if necessary to coat evenly. Set aside.

Combine olive oil, salt pork, butter and garlic in a skillet and stir well. Heat, then discard bits of garlic. Add sweetbreads and olives. Stir and shake skillet. Cook for 5 minutes, turn, and cook for another 5 minutes. Add wine, cover, and cook for 3 minutes. Add tomato, season lightly with salt and pepper, stir, and cook slowly for about 15 minutes. Serve with *spaghettini al burro* on the same plate and spoon the sauce over both. Serve with Italian bread and a bottle of Valpolicella. Serves 2.

Sweetbreads with Tomato

2 pairs of fresh veal sweetbreads (about 2 pounds)	1 garlic clove, mashed
¼ cup vinegar	Pinch of freshly ground black pepper
Juice of 2 lemons	Tiny pinch of crushed red pepper
1 orange, sliced	
1 tablespoon olive oil	Pinch of salt
2 tablespoons sweet butter	Pinch of dried rosemary
1 ounce salt pork, diced	1 large ripe tomato, sliced thin

Soak the sweetbreads in cold water for about 1 hour. Change the water several times during the hour; drain. Place drained sweetbreads in a saucepan and cover with fresh cold water. Add vinegar, juice of 1 lemon, and the orange slices. Bring to a boil and cook for 5 minutes. Remove from the heat and place under cold running water. Remove membranes and tubes. Drain and set aside.

Combine olive oil, butter, salt pork and garlic in a skillet; heat. Add sweetbreads, cover, and cook slowly on one side for 5 minutes. Turn, add black and red pepper and salt, and shake the skillet. Add rosemary, cover, and cook for 5 minutes longer. Add the tomato, cover, and cook slowly for 20 minutes. Simmer, uncovered, for 3 minutes more. Transfer to a serving platter. While still hot, pour remaining lemon juice over, then spoon on the tomato sauce. Serve with Bibb lettuce with lemon and olive-oil dressing. If there is any left over, it is good served cold as an antipasto the next day. Serves 4.

Broiled Calf's Liver

1 pound fresh calf's liver, cut into 2 slices	Pinch of salt
1 tablespoon olive oil	⅓ teaspoon freshly ground black pepper

Preheat broiler. Brush liver well with olive oil. Place liver on broiler pan 5 inches from the source of heat. Broil under high heat for 3 minutes. Turn over, sprinkle with salt and pepper, and cook for about 2 minutes longer, or to taste. Place on a hot serving plate.

Broiled liver may be served in a variety of ways. It may be served just as cooked, above, on the same plate with a salad of various lettuces or field salad, and with a fruit salad of persimmon and avocado (see page 48) on a separate plate.

Another nice way to serve it is with a pungent butter. To make this, remove core and seeds from ½ hot cherry pepper, wash and dry, then chop very fine. At the same time chop 16 leaves of fresh chives. Stir both into 2 tablespoons melted sweet butter. When the liver is cooked, spoon this butter sauce over the slices. Serve with potatoes au gratin and a bottle of Bardolino. Serves 2.

Sautéed Calf's Liver

1 tablespoon olive oil
3 tablespoons butter
1 ounce salt pork, diced
½ hot cherry pepper (optional)
1 medium-sized onion, sliced very
    thin
1 garlic clove, mashed
2 chicken livers, chopped fine
1 pound fresh calf's liver, cut into
    2 slices

Pinch of salt
Pinch of freshly ground black
    pepper
Tiny, tiny pinch of ground all-
    spice
¼ cup dry white wine
7 fresh parsley sprigs, leaves only,
    chopped fine
Juice of 1 fresh lemon

Combine olive oil, butter and salt pork in a skillet; heat. Cut the cherry pepper into 3 pieces and discard the core and seeds. Add onion, garlic and cherry pepper to skillet and cook slowly for 3 minutes. Add chicken livers, stir, and cook for 2 minutes. Add slices of calf's liver and cook slowly for 3 minutes. Turn over, and cook for 3 minutes more. Add salt, pepper and allspice and shake skillet. Add the wine, baste, cover, and cook slowly for 5 minutes. Add parsley and lemon juice, shake skillet, and baste. Cook slowly, uncovered, for 3 minutes more. Baste again and simmer for 2 minutes. Serve wide noodles, mixed with butter and grated cheese, on the same plate and spoon the sauce over liver and noodles. Drink a good red Burgundy. Serves 2.

Calf's Liver alla Leone

4 slices of fresh calf's liver ½ inch
    thick (about 2 pounds)
1 egg, beaten
½ cup sifted bread crumbs
½ pound green peppers
2 tablespoons olive oil
¼ cup butter
½ pound onions, peeled and
    sliced thin

1 large garlic clove, mashed
1 bay leaf, crumbled
¼ cup dry red wine
½ teaspoon salt
⅓ teaspoon freshly ground black
    pepper
8 fresh parsley sprigs, leaves only,
    chopped fine

Dip liver slices into beaten egg, then into bread crumbs. Discard cores and seeds of green peppers and cut them into very thin slices. Let them drain in a strainer for 20 minutes. Combine olive oil and butter in a skillet and heat. Add onions and sauté to light brown. Add garlic, bay leaf and green-pepper slices; cook for 5 minutes. Stir, add liver slices, and cook quickly on each side for 2 minutes. Add wine, salt and pepper, cover, and sauté for 5 minutes. Check for doneness. Sprinkle parsley over top, shake skillet, and serve. Spoon strained sauce over top. Calf's liver is very tender, so do not overcook, and always serve immediately as soon as ready. Serves 4.

Calf's Liver alla Veneziana

1 pound fresh calf's liver	Pinch of salt
All-purpose flour	Pinch of freshly ground black pepper
6 tablespoons olive oil	
3 tablespoons fresh creamery butter	Tiny, tiny pinch of ground allspice
1 ounce salt pork, diced	2 tablespoons tomato paste
¼ pound onions, peeled and diced	¼ cup dry white wine
	1½ tablespoons wine vinegar
2 whole fresh green scallions, shredded	Juice of ½ lemon
	1 small garlic clove

Cut the calf's liver into 4 thin slices and sprinkle lightly with flour. Place half of the olive oil, the butter and salt pork in a skillet; heat. Add onions and scallions and cook slowly until medium brown. Add liver slices and cook for 2 minutes. Turn over and sprinkle with salt, pepper and allspice. Cook for 3 minutes, stir, and shake skillet. Stir tomato paste into the wine and mix thoroughly. Add to the skillet, stir well, cover, and cook for 4 minutes. Shake skillet, baste the liver, and arrange the slices on a serving plate.

Spoon some of the sauce over the liver, leaving a little in the skillet. Add to it the remaining olive oil, the wine vinegar, lemon juice and the garlic. Stir and heat for ½ minute. Discard garlic. Pour the hot sauce over a leafy green salad, add a little salt and pepper, and toss well. Serve on the same plate with the liver. Serves 2.

Broiled Veal Kidneys

4 fresh veal kidneys
Salt
2 lemons
¼ cup sweet butter, melted
Pinch of crushed red pepper

Pinch of black pepper
2 bay leaves, broken into pieces
8 fresh parsley sprigs, leaves only, chopped fine
1 teaspoon Worcestershire sauce

Split the kidneys lengthwise into halves. When trimming, leave a little of the veal fat attached to each kidney. Place in ice water and add a little salt. Squeeze one of the lemons into the water and drop in the peel as well. Soak for 2 hours. Wash well under cold running water and dry. Remove skin and cores.

Preheat broiler. Brush the kidneys with half of the melted butter and place them in a broiling pan. Sprinkle with the red pepper. Add black pepper and a little salt and place a piece of bay leaf over each kidney. Place about 6 inches from the source of heat and broil on each side for about 8 minutes. Baste with drippings several times.

Make a sauce by mixing the remaining melted butter, juice of the second lemon, the chopped parsley and Worcestershire sauce. Just before serving, place the sauce in the broiler for a few seconds to heat, then spoon it over the hot kidneys. Serve Pickled Eggplant with Jalapeño Peppers (page 42) with this. Serves 4.

Note: This method can also be used for fresh lamb kidneys.

Sautéed Veal Kidneys

4 or 5 veal kidneys
½ fresh lemon
10 slices of dried mushrooms
¼ cup lukewarm water
3 tablespoons olive oil
¼ cup fresh creamery butter, melted
2 ounces salt pork, diced
⅓ pound onions, peeled and sliced thin
1 bay leaf, crumbled

1 garlic clove, mashed
⅓ teaspoon freshly ground black pepper
Tiny pinch of ground allspice
½ cup dry white wine
1 large ripe tomato, sliced thin
6 fresh parsley sprigs, leaves only, chopped fine
Salt
Toasted slices of Italian bread

Cut the kidneys lengthwise into halves. Remove all fat, skin, and white membrane. Cut into ½-inch pieces. Place kidneys in cold salted water. Squeeze the lemon into the water and drop in the peel as well. Soak for 30 minutes. Wash under cold running water, drain, and dry. Soak the mushrooms in the lukewarm water for 20 minutes. Drain, saving the water, and chop the mushrooms coarsely.

Place olive oil, butter and salt pork in a skillet; heat. Add onions, bay leaf and garlic and sauté until medium brown. Add kidneys and cook slowly for 5 minutes. Add black pepper and allspice, stir, and cook for 1 minute. Add the wine, cover, and cook for 3 minutes. Uncover, add tomato, parsley, mushrooms and mushroom water; stir, and simmer for 6 minutes. Season lightly with salt. Test for doneness and add more salt if needed. Spoon over the toast and serve with a bottle of red Chianti. Serves 4 to 6.

Tripe Stew from Milano

Many people won't eat tripe, but it can be very good. I suggest you prepare it this way and serve it without telling your family what they are eating until they ask for seconds.

1½ pounds fresh veal tripe	2 garlic cloves, mashed
2 tablespoons olive oil	½ teaspoon freshly ground black pepper
2 tablespoons butter	
2 ounces salt pork, diced	1 hot cherry pepper, seeds and all, chopped fine
½ pound onions, peeled and diced	
¼ celery stalk, minced	12 Italian or other small black olives, pitted
½ medium-sized carrot, diced	1 cup dry red wine
12 fresh parsley sprigs, leaves only, chopped	Salt
	Risotto alla Milanese (page 86)
3 green peppers, sliced thin	8 slices of dried mushrooms

Wash the tripe well in cold water and cut it into 1½-inch squares. Place in a medium-sized saucepan and add 3 cups boiling water, or enough to cover the tripe. Cook very slowly for 40 minutes. Drain well.

Combine olive oil, butter and salt pork in a large saucepan or kettle; heat. Add the onions and cook slowly for 3 minutes. Add celery, carrot, parsley, green peppers and garlic; cook for 5 minutes. Add the drained tripe, stir, and cook for 5 minutes. Add black pepper, chopped cherry pepper, olives and wine. Stir, cover, and cook for 3 minutes. Add salt to taste. Uncover, stir, and add 2 quarts hot water. Cover and cook slowly for about 2 hours.

About 1 hour before the tripe is finished, assemble the ingredients for the risotto. Soak the mushrooms in the chicken broth for the risotto for 15 minutes. Lift them out of the broth and chop fine. Return to the broth. Prepare the risotto, adding the mushrooms at the same time as the broth. When tripe and risotto are ready, stir the risotto into the stew and serve at once. Serves about 6.

Boiled Veal Tongue

1 fresh veal tongue (about 2 pounds)	2 medium-sized potatoes, peeled
	Salt and pepper
4 medium-sized onions, unpeeled	Vinaigrette Dressing (page 51)
1 large garlic clove, mashed	2 whole fresh green scallions
2 celery stalks with leaves	4 leaves of chives
4 large carrots	8 parsley sprigs, leaves only

Place the tongue in a large soup pot, cover with boiling water, and add the vegetables. Add salt and pepper to taste. Cook for 1 hour. Lift out the vegetables and set aside. Cook the tongue for about 45 minutes longer. Meanwhile make the dressing. Omit the mustard and capers if you wish. Dice both green and white parts of the scallions, and chop the chives and parsley fine. Stir the herbs into the dressing. Lift out the tongue and replace vegetables in the pot to warm.

Remove the skin from the tongue. Remove the skin from the boiled onions, drain well, and cut into halves. Quarter the potatoes and the carrots. When all is ready, slice the tongue and arrange it on a serving platter with the onions, potatoes and carrots around. Spoon the dressing over all and serve with a bottle of Freisa Spumanti. Serves 4.

LAMB

Roast Spring Leg of Lamb

3 garlic cloves, halved
1 leg of spring lamb (about 6 pounds)
¼ cup olive oil

Salt and pepper
1 tablespoon dried rosemary
¼ cup butter
1½ cups boiling water

Preheat oven to hot (450° F.). Rub 1 garlic clove on the outside of the lamb. Place the rest under the skin, but do not pierce the meat. Brush lamb well with the olive oil and sprinkle with salt and pepper. Oil the pan with a little olive oil and place meat, fat side up, on a rack in the pan. Sprinkle rosemary over all. Roast for 10 minutes, then reduce heat to moderate (325° F.). Allow about 20 minutes per pound. Do not cover. Do not overcook.

Remove lamb to a hot platter. Pour off grease from the roasting pan, leaving the drippings. Place the pan on top of stove and add the butter and the boiling water. Simmer, stirring constantly, for about 10 minutes, until you have a brown gravy. Serve the meat with the gravy and with Fresh Broccoli (page 208) with Vinaigrette Dressing (page 51) and roasted potatoes. Serve a vintage Bordeaux like a Château Latour. Serves 8 to 10.

Braised Rack of Lamb

¼ cup olive oil
2 ounces salt pork, diced
¼ cup fresh creamery butter
1 rack of lamb (about 3 pounds)
2 garlic cloves
2 medium-sized onions, quartered
1 teaspoon crumbled dried rosemary

6 tablespoons dry red wine
2 tablespoons grated carrot
1 medium-sized firm tomato, sliced thin
¼ teaspoon salt
½ teaspoon freshly ground black pepper

Combine olive oil, salt pork and butter in a small saucepan, and heat until salt pork has rendered most of the fat, but not long enough to burn the mixture. Brush the roast well on both sides with this mixture. Slice 1 garlic clove into halves and mash the other. Pierce the skin of the meat and insert garlic halves. Place the meat in a large heavy saucepan on top of the stove over low heat. Pour the rest of the oil, butter and salt pork over the top. Add the onions, cover, and cook slowly for 15 minutes. Add mashed garlic and rosemary, stir, and cook slowly for 5 minutes. Add the wine, cover, and simmer for 5 minutes more. Add carrot, tomato, salt and pepper, cover, and cook slowly for about 45 minutes, or until done to your taste. Taste for salt and add more if needed. To serve, cut the meat into 5 or 6 pieces and spoon the strained sauce over them. Enjoy with a bottle of red Château Haut-Brion. Serves 5 or 6.

Note: This cut may be called a rib roast; it is one side of the rib chops before they are cut apart.

Roast Baby Lamb

1 baby lamb (16 to 18 pounds)	Pinch of crushed red pepper
4 ounces salt pork, diced	2 tablespoons crumbled dried
¾ cup butter	rosemary
½ cup olive oil	Salt
3 garlic cloves, mashed	Shoestring Potatoes (page 216)
1 teaspoon freshly ground black pepper	3 cups boiling water

Preheat oven to hot (400° F.). Cut the lamb into 6 pieces, the legs, the loins each with half of the rib chops, and the shoulders. Place the pieces in an oven pan large enough to contain them. Render the salt pork and combine the fat with ¼ cup of the butter, the olive oil, garlic and black pepper in a bowl; let stand for 30 minutes; stir. Brush all of the mixture over all surfaces, inside and outside, of the roast. Sprinkle red pepper and rosemary over the meat. Sprinkle lightly with salt. Place in the oven and cook for 15 minutes. Reduce oven to moderate (325° F.) and roast for 45 to 60 minutes longer, or until tender. Baste frequently and turn over the pieces when half roasted. Do not overcook.

Meanwhile prepare the potatoes, using 5 pounds of potatoes. Place cooked potatoes on brown paper spread over a large strainer or bowl, sprinkle with salt, and keep warm until ready to serve.

When lamb is cooked, remove it from the pan and place it on a large carving board. Discard grease from the pan, leaving the drippings. Add the boiling water and remaining butter. Simmer and stir for about 10 minutes, or until the mixture is reduced to a nice brown gravy. Carve the lamb into good-sized pieces and arrange them on a very large warm platter. Strain the gravy over the meat. Serve the potatoes, and for wine either Barolo or Valpolicella. Serves about 12.

Italian Spring Lamb Stew

4 pounds shoulder, shanks or ribs of lamb
3 tablespoons olive oil
1/4 cup sweet butter, melted
2 ounces salt pork, diced
1 pound yellow onions, peeled
1 pound fresh mushrooms or 1 ounce dried mushrooms
2 garlic cloves, mashed
10 fresh parsley sprigs, leaves only
2 bay leaves, crumbled
1/2 cup dry white wine
5 cups boiling water
1/2 pound carrots, scraped and diced

1/2 pound whole small white onions
5 celery stalks with leaves, minced
1 pound potatoes, peeled and diced
1/2 teaspoon salt
1/2 teaspoon freshly ground black pepper
1 loaf of Italian whole-wheat bread
1/4 cup butter, softened
12 leaves of chives, minced

Have the butcher trim the lamb, discard any surplus fat, and cut the meat into pieces for stewing. Place olive oil, melted butter and salt pork in a heavy saucepan; heat. Cut each yellow onion into 8 wedges and add to the saucepan. Cook slowly for 5 minutes. Add the meat and brown for 15 minutes.

Detach stems from mushrooms. Chop the stems and cut the caps into thin slices. If using dried mushrooms, soak them in 1/2 cup warm water for 15 minutes. Drain, saving the water, and chop the mushrooms. Chop garlic and parsley together. Add mushrooms to the stew, then the garlic and parsley and the bay leaves. Cook for 5 minutes. Add the wine, stir, cover, and cook for 5 minutes. Add the boiling water and the mushroom water, if any, and cook for 1 hour.

Stir the stew and add diced carrots, whole white onions, minced celery, diced potatoes, salt and pepper. Cover and cook slowly for 30 minutes. Uncover and simmer slowly until done. Check for cooking and taste for salt; add more salt if needed.

Meanwhile slice the bread almost to the bottom but do not detach the slices. Mix the softened butter and the chives and spread between the slices of bread. Wrap in foil and place in a moderate oven. (375° F.) for about 15 minutes. Serve the bread with the stew and have an aged bottle of Barolo or red Chianti. Serves 6 to 8.

Broiled Thick Lamb Chops

It was our good friend Joe Williams who brought Rocky Marciano in for lunch one day. Marciano was on his way to Grossinger's to train for a big fight. Joe Williams, a very light eater, had part of a small broiled hamburger, but Rocky had 12 thick lamb chops broiled over charcoal, a bowl of spaghetti, and a loaf of Italian bread.

4 double or triple prime rib or loin lamb chops
½ very tiny garlic clove

3 fresh parsley sprigs, leaves only
2 tablespoons butter, melted
Salt and pepper

Preheat broiler. Skin the chops and trim away most of the fat. Place chops on a broiler pan or oven grill 8 inches from the source of heat and cook for 10 minutes if double, 12 minutes if triple. Turn over and cook for 8 minutes more if double, 10 if triple. Chop garlic and parsley together and mix into the butter. Add salt and pepper to taste. Spoon the mixture over the chops when they are done to your taste. Heat under the broiler for ½ minute longer. Serve on warmed plates with Fried Zucchini (page 219). Serves 4.

Broiled Frenched Lamb Chops

Trim off all fat and skin from the rib bones of 6 lamb chops, each ½ inch thick. Place in a double-handed grill or on a broiler pan about 8 inches from the source of heat. Broil for 3 minutes, turn over, and broil for 4 minutes longer. Sprinkle with salt and pepper and serve immediately. Serves 2 or 3.

PORK

Roast Suckling Pig

A suckling pig should be 7 to 8 weeks old and should weigh 12 to 16 pounds when cleaned.

1 suckling pig	Stuffing (see below)
¾ cup olive oil	Salt
1 cup butter, melted	10 to 12 large baking potatoes
1 tablespoon black pepper	2 ounces salt pork, diced
2 large garlic cloves, mashed	2 cups boiling water
3 tablespoons crumbled dried rosemary	

Have the butcher prepare the pig for roasting. Save the liver and heart for the stuffing (page 191). Wash the pig well and pat dry. Combine ½ cup of the olive oil, ½ cup of the butter, the black pepper and garlic in a bowl. Mix well, and let stand for 30 minutes. Brush pig well inside and outside with the mixture, and sprinkle 2 tablespoons of the rosemary over all surfaces. Make the stuffing. Preheat oven to hot (450° F.).

When stuffing is ready, stuff the pig and sew up the vents. Place a small piece of wood in the mouth and cover ears and tail with foil. Oil a large oven pan. Arrange the pig in the pan, pulling the forelegs forward and bending the hind legs under. Sprinkle lightly with salt. Place roasting pan in the oven and bake for 15 minutes. Reduce heat to moderate (325° F.). Cook for about 2 hours, basting well every 20 minutes. Do not overcook or cook too fast. Check for doneness to avoid this.

While the pig is cooking, wash the potatoes, peel them, and cut into quarters. Oil a baking pan and place potatoes in it. Pour ¼ cup of the butter, ¼ cup of the olive oil and the salt pork over potatoes. Sprinkle with the remaining rosemary and a little salt and pepper.

Place in oven 45 minutes before the pig is ready. Stir and turn the potatoes when you baste the pig.

When the pig is cooked, place it on a large serving board, or a serving platter especially designed for a suckling pig. Drain grease from the pan, leaving the drippings. Add the remaining butter and the boiling water. Shake the pan and stir well so that the water mixes completely with the drippings. Stir constantly while simmering. Simmer for about 10 minutes, or until the mixture is reduced to a nice brown gravy.

Remove the foil from ears and tail of the pig. Take the piece of wood from the mouth and replace it with a shiny red apple. Bring to the table and carve there. Serve with the roasted potatoes and a salad of Belgian endives with Vinaigrette Dressing (page 51). This delicious dinner deserves a chilled Soave and a white Château Haut-Brion later. Serves 10 to 12.

RICE AND SAUSAGE STUFFING

1 pound Italian sweet sausage	2 bay leaves, crumbled
8 slices of bread, crusts removed	Liver and heart of pig, chopped
1 cup milk	1½ bunches of fresh parsley,
1 cup uncooked rice	leaves only, chopped
¼ cup olive oil	Salt and pepper
2 ounces salt pork, diced	2 eggs, beaten
1½ pounds onions, peeled and	6 tablespoons grated Parmesan
diced	cheese

Remove the casing from the sausage and cut the meat into pieces. Soak the bread in the milk. Soak the rice in lukewarm water for 10 minutes, then cook in boiling water for 6 minutes, and drain. Heat olive oil and salt pork in a large skillet. Add the onions and sauté to medium brown. Add bay leaves, sausage pieces, and chopped liver and heart; brown slowly for 20 minutes. Remove from the heat and cool for 10 minutes. Squeeze most of the liquid out of the bread and shred it. Add it to stuffing with the parsley and salt and pepper to taste. Stir and mix well, then put all through a food grinder or chop fine, carefully saving all the juices. Place solids and liquid all back in the skillet. Add drained rice, beaten eggs, and the cheese; mix well. Taste for salt, and add more if necessary.

Roasted and Broiled Loin of Pork

1 center-cut loin of pork (3½ pounds)
¼ cup melted butter
Pinch of dried rosemary
Pinch of salt
Pinch of freshly ground black pepper
Pinch of crushed red pepper (optional)
3 thin slices of salt pork

Preheat oven to hot (400° F.). First brush the pork with some of the melted butter, then sprinkle it with rosemary, salt, and black and red pepper. Place salt pork over top. Wrap the whole loin in aluminum foil and cook in the oven for 30 minutes. Remove from oven and unwrap. Cut into 4 thick chops and brush the sides with more of the butter. Place under the broiler and broil slowly for 10 minutes. Turn over, brush with remaining butter, and cook for 15 minutes longer, or until done. Serve with fried thin potato slices and a leafy green salad with Italian Salad Dressing (page 49). For wine, a dry red wine from California. Serves 4.

Pot-Roasted Crown of Pork

3 tablespoons olive oil
1 crown of pork (6 to 7 pounds)
Salt and pepper
½ teaspoon dried rosemary
8 fresh parsley sprigs, leaves only
1 very small garlic clove
¼ ounce dried mushrooms
¼ cup warm water
2 tablespoons butter
2 tablespoons heavy cream
4 whole fresh green scallions, minced
½ cup dry white wine
½ cup warm water
4 to 6 Belgian endives

Place 1 tablespoon of the olive oil in a large heavy saucepan and heat. Put the pork in the pan, sprinkle it with salt, pepper and rosemary, and brown on all sides. Lower the heat, cover, and cook slowly for 1 hour, basting occasionally. Chop parsley and garlic together and set aside. Soak the dried mushrooms in the warm water for 15 minutes. Drain, saving the water, and chop the mushrooms. Return the chopped pieces to the water and set aside. Remove the meat from the pan and discard grease. Put the meat back in the pan and add the butter, cream, scallions and remaining olive oil. Cover and cook slowly for 20 minutes. Add the wine, leave the saucepan uncovered, and cook for 5 minutes. Turn the meat and add the chopped parsley and garlic, chopped mushrooms and mushroom water, and the warm water. Stir, cover, and cook slowly for 30 minutes longer.

Trim the endives and cut lengthwise into quarters. Add them to the pork and cook for 15 to 20 minutes longer, until the pork is cooked and the endives just tender. (Do not overcook the endives or they will be mushy.) When everything is ready, slice the pork between the ribs and serve some of the pork and some of the endive on each plate, with the sauce spooned over both. Also serve ravioli or spaghettini. Serves 8 to 10.

Broiled Breaded Pork Chops

4 pork chops, each 1 inch thick
2 eggs, beaten
6 tablespoons sifted bread crumbs
Salt and black pepper
2 tablespoons olive oil
3 tablespoons butter, melted
Juice of 1 lemon

$\frac{1}{4}$ cup grated Parmesan cheese
1 tablespoon prepared mustard
1 garlic clove, split
$\frac{1}{2}$ teaspoon cayenne pepper
$\frac{1}{8}$ teaspoon crushed red pepper
or a dash of Tabasco

Dip chops into beaten eggs, then into bread crumbs; do this twice. Then sprinkle a little salt and black pepper over the chops. Preheat broiler. Place chops in a lightly greased broiler pan 8 inches from the source of heat. Broil slowly for 10 minutes. Mix all the other ingredients to make a basting sauce. When well blended, discard the garlic. Spoon half of the sauce over the chops. Cook slowly for 20 minutes longer. Turn chops over and spoon remaining sauce over them. Cook slowly for about 30 minutes more. Check for doneness. Serve with spaghettini with Marinara Sauce (page 94) on the same plate. Serves 4.

Pork Chops with Spaghetti

3 tablespoons olive oil
½ cup butter, melted
2 large garlic cloves, mashed
⅓ teaspoon freshly ground black pepper
Pinch of crushed red pepper (optional)
4 lean pork chops, 1 inch thick
1 teaspoon crumbled dried rosemary

½ teaspoon salt
4 medium-sized ripe tomatoes or 2 cups canned peeled plum tomatoes, chopped
10 fresh parsley sprigs, leaves only, chopped
¾ pound spaghetti
¼ cup grated Parmesan cheese

Combine olive oil and half of the butter in a large heavy-bottomed skillet and heat. Add garlic and black and red pepper and cook slowly for 2 minutes. Add pork chops, sprinkle with rosemary, and brown on each side for 5 minutes. Lower heat to medium and add salt, tomatoes and parsley. Cover and cook slowly for 20 minutes. Uncover and cook slowly for 20 minutes longer, or until done. Taste for salt.

Place spaghetti in a pot of boiling salted water. Cook for about 10 minutes. Taste 1 strand. If as desired, drain well. Place back in the pot in which it was cooked. Add remaining butter and mix well. Add the grated cheese and a little sauce and mix. Place spaghetti on a hot plate with the chops and pour sauce over both. Cut a head of romaine into 4 parts and serve with Italian Salad Dressing (page 49); for wine, a Bardolino. Serves 4.

Italian Sausage and Eggplant

1 pound Italian sweet sausage
1 eggplant (about 1 pound)
Salt and pepper
2 garlic cloves, mashed
8 fresh parsley sprigs, leaves only
2 hot cherry peppers (if you like hot dishes)
¼ cup olive oil
2 medium-sized green peppers, sliced thin

2 medium-sized firm tomatoes, sliced thin
1 teaspoon dried orégano
1 teaspoon dried rosemary
3 large shallots, minced
3 tablespoons chopped onion
¼ cup freshly grated Parmesan cheese
¼ cup sifted bread crumbs
¼ cup butter, melted

Use the thicker sausage for this dish. Cut it into 3-inch pieces. Peel the eggplant and cut it into 1-inch cubes. Sprinkle them lightly with salt and spread on brown paper to drain for 30 minutes. Chop garlic and parsley together. Halve the cherry peppers and discard the cores and all seeds. Cut the peppers into small pieces. Preheat oven to moderate (375° F.).

Oil an oven pan lightly with a little of the olive oil. Place drained eggplant cubes on the bottom of pan. Top with sausage pieces, green-pepper slices and tomato slices. Spoon oil over top and sprinkle with orégano and rosemary, salt and pepper, and shallots and onion. Bake for 20 minutes, then stir. Add garlic and parsley and cherry peppers if used. Bake for 20 minutes. Sprinkle cheese and bread crumbs over the dish and spoon butter over all. Bake for 10 minutes more, or until done. Serves 4 or 5.

Italian Sausage with Green Peppers

1 garlic clove, mashed
8 fresh parsley sprigs, leaves only
1 pound cabbage
2 pounds Italian sweet sausage
¼ cup olive oil
2 ounces salt pork, diced
⅓ pound onions, peeled and diced
6 medium-sized green or red peppers, quartered
2 large ripe tomatoes, sliced thin
1 teaspoon crumbled dried rosemary
Pinch of freshly ground black pepper
¼ pound prosciutto, diced

For this dish do not use the thin sausage. Chop the garlic and parsley together. Slice or shred the cabbage and steam it with a little boiling water until just tender. Drain, and keep warm. Cut the sausage into pieces. Combine olive oil and salt pork in a saucepan and heat. Add the onions and brown slowly. Add the sausage and cook slowly for 20 minutes. Add green peppers, tomatoes, rosemary, black pepper, and garlic and parsley. Cook for 10 minutes, or until done. Add diced prosciutto and cooked cabbage. Cover and cook slowly for 10 minutes to blend flavors. Serve with a loaf of Italian bread toasted in the oven and a bottle of California red wine. Serves 4 to 6.

9

Light Meals

IN our modern weight-watching world there are many occasions when a light, low-calorie meal is called for. There is no reason why these simple meals cannot be delicious and satisfying. The next time your appetite (or conscience) is not up to a steaming plate of lasagne or veal cutlet parmigiana, try one of the sandwiches or egg dishes that follow.

Fritto Misto

(a mixed fry)

This dish can be made up of an assortment of meats including breast of chicken, calf's liver, strips of veal, chicken livers, calf's brains, sweetbreads, etc., as well as vegetables such as carrots, green beans, eggplant, artichoke hearts, mushrooms, zucchini and cauliflowerets. Fish too may be used.

Make the batter (page 197) so it has time to stand. Select the meats or vegetables you plan to use and cut them into even-sized chunks. If you are using vegetables, parboil them. Dip the selected foods into the batter. Heat 1½ quarts light virgin olive oil and ½ cup fresh creamery butter in a deep heavy frying pan to 380° F. on a frying thermometer. Cook a few batter-dipped foods at a time. Do not crowd them in the pan. When golden brown, remove to a large warm platter and cover. When the cooking is finished, uncover, sprinkle lightly with salt, and serve with quartered lemons.

BATTER FOR MIXED FRY

1/4 cup melted butter	Pinch each of salt and pepper
1/2 cup heavy cream	3 large eggs, beaten well
1/2 cup milk	1 1/2 cups sifted all-purpose flour

Place the melted butter, cream, milk, salt and pepper in a large bowl. Add well-beaten eggs and stir in the flour. Let the batter stand for 1 1/2 to 2 hours before using.

Spinach and Rice Frittata

1 package (10 ounces) fresh spinach	2 ounces salt pork, diced
8 large fresh eggs	1 pound onions, peeled and sliced
1/2 teaspoon salt	1 garlic clove, mashed
1/2 teaspoon freshly ground black pepper	2 medium-sized ripe tomatoes, sliced thin
1/2 cup uncooked rice	1/3 cup freshly grated Parmesan cheese
1/4 cup olive oil	
6 tablespoons fresh creamery butter, melted	1/4 bunch of fresh parsley, leaves only, chopped fine

Preheat oven to moderate (350° F.). Wash the spinach and steam it for 2 minutes. Drain well and chop coarsely. Beat the eggs and add salt and pepper. Soak the rice in 1 1/2 cups water for 5 minutes, then boil for 10 minutes, and drain. Oil 2 pie plates each 10 inches in diameter.

Combine olive oil, 3 tablespoons of the butter and the salt pork in a skillet; heat. Add onions and cook until golden brown. Add garlic and tomatoes. Cook for 5 minutes. Remove from the heat and stir in chopped spinach, drained rice and then the eggs. Stir and add the cheese and parsley. Mix well. Spoon the whole mixture into one pie plate. Spoon the rest of the butter on top. Bake for 15 minutes. Then turn upside down into the other pie plate. Bake for 20 minutes longer, to form a crust on the other side. Serve hot as a main course or as an accompaniment to a meat dish. Or serve cold with Italian Salad Dressing (page 49). Serves 4.

Eggs for Dinner

3 tablespoons olive oil
3 tablespoons sweet butter
1 medium onion, diced
1 garlic clove, mashed
1 pound Italian sweet sausage
1 pound beef
1 medium-sized baking potato, peeled and diced
½ teaspoon crumbled dried rosemary

1 large ripe tomato, sliced thin
½ teaspoon freshly ground black pepper
⅓ teaspoon salt
1 hot cherry pepper
8 fresh parsley sprigs, leaves only, chopped
8 fresh eggs, beaten well

Combine olive oil and butter in a skillet and heat. Add onion and garlic and cook until medium brown. Remove the casing from sausage and cut the meat into small pieces. Put the beef twice through a food grinder. Add both sausage and beef to the onion. Add diced potato. Cover and cook slowly for 20 minutes. Add rosemary, stir, then add tomato, black pepper and salt and stir. Cut the cherry pepper into halves, remove cores and seeds, wash the pepper, and dice it. Add diced cherry pepper and parsley to the skillet. Cook for 15 minutes, then pour beaten eggs over the top. Cook to taste, for 2 to 3 minutes. Taste for salt and sprinkle a little more on if necessary. Serve with toasted slices of Italian bread and with a bottle of aged Chianti. Serves 4.

Spinach Omelet

1 package (10 ounces) prewashed spinach
2 tablespoons olive oil
¼ cup fresh creamery butter
1 medium-sized onion, minced
1 small garlic clove, mashed
Pinch of salt

Pinch of freshly ground black pepper
2 slices of Italian salami or prosciutto, diced
4 eggs, beaten
3 tablespoons grated Parmesan cheese

Wash the spinach again and drain well. Place olive oil and butter in a skillet and heat. Add onion and garlic and cook slowly until light brown. Add spinach, stir, cover, and cook for 15 minutes. Add salt, pepper and salami or prosciutto and cook for 2 minutes. Pour eggs into spinach and stir. Cook until done to taste. Sprinkle cheese on top. Serves 3.

Mushroom Omelet

6 fresh pullet eggs or 4 large fresh
 eggs
2 tablespoons heavy cream
Pinch of salt
Pinch of freshly ground black
 pepper
2 tablespoons olive oil
1/4 cup butter

1 large green or red pepper
1/2 hot cherry pepper (optional)
1/2 cup sliced fresh mushrooms
1 garlic clove, mashed
6 fresh parsley sprigs, leaves only
3 slices of Italian salami or prosciutto, diced
Grated Parmesan cheese

Beat the eggs in a bowl. Add the cream, salt and pepper. Combine olive oil and butter in a skillet and heat. Cut the green pepper into thin slices. If using the cherry pepper (for a little more zip), dice it. Add sliced green pepper and sliced mushrooms to the skillet. Sauté slowly for 10 minutes. Chop garlic and parsley together and add to the skillet with diced cherry pepper and diced salami. Lower the heat. Stir in the eggs. Lift edges of eggs with a pancake turner so eggs run smoothly over bottom of pan. When a light crust appears, turn the whole egg mixture over and cook on the other side to taste. Sprinkle some cheese on top. Serve with toasted Italian bread and a good caffè espresso. Serves 2.

Eggs with Tomatoes

2 tablespoons olive oil
2 tablespoons butter
1 medium-sized onion, diced
2 medium-sized ripe tomatoes,
 sliced thin

4 fresh eggs, beaten
2 tablespoons freshly grated Parmesan cheese
Salt and pepper

Place olive oil and butter in a skillet and heat. Add the onion and cook to medium brown. Add tomatoes and cook slowly for 10 minutes. Stir in eggs and cook for about 2 minutes. Sprinkle cheese over top. Add salt and pepper to taste. Serve over toasted Italian bread. Serves 2 or 3.

Eggs with Zucchini

1 medium-sized to small zucchini	4 fresh eggs, beaten
¼ cup olive oil	Salt and pepper
2 tablespoons sweet butter	2 tablespoons grated Parmesan
2 slices of mortadella, salami or prosciutto, diced	cheese

Wash and dry the zucchini. Scrape the skin slightly and cut the vegetable into thin slices. Place olive oil and butter in a skillet and heat. Add zucchini slices, cover, and cook for 5 minutes. Add mortadella, or whatever you are using, stir, and cook for 5 minutes. Add the eggs, cover, and cook for 2 minutes. Season with salt and pepper to taste. Sprinkle cheese over the top and cook, covered, for 1 minute. Serve Italian bread with this, and at breakfast caffè espresso with cream, at dinner black coffee. Serves 2.

Boiled Eggs and Spinach

8 eggs	3 slices of bacon, broiled and crumbled
1 package (10 ounces) prewashed fresh spinach	1 cup tomato sauce, warmed
2 tablespoons virgin olive oil	8 fresh parsley sprigs, leaves only, chopped fine
¼ cup sweet butter	Pinch of salt
1 garlic clove, mashed	Pinch of black pepper
1 small- to medium-sized onion, diced	

Boil the eggs for 5 minutes with a pinch of salt in the water to make peeling easier. When cooked, place under cold water. Peel, cut into halves, and set aside. Wash the spinach again and drain it well.

Combine olive oil and butter in a skillet and heat. Add garlic and onion and cook to medium brown. Add spinach and bacon. Stir, cover, and cook slowly for 15 minutes. Add the warmed tomato sauce, chopped parsley, salt and pepper. Stir. Cook for 2 minutes. Add egg halves, shake the skillet, and cook for 3 minutes longer. Serve 4 half-eggs to each person and spoon spinach and sauce over eggs. Serves 4.

Egg Sauce

4 whole fresh green scallions, diced, or 2 heaping table-spoons chopped sweet onion
8 fresh parsley sprigs, leaves only, chopped
1/4 cup virgin olive oil
1 tablespoon vinegar
Juice of 1 fresh lemon

2 tablespoons sweet butter, melted
1 teaspoon chopped fresh basil
1/3 teaspoon salt
1/3 teaspoon black pepper
8 hard-boiled eggs, mashed fine with a fork
1/4 cup mayonnaise

Place all ingredients except eggs and mayonnaise in a bowl and mix well. Then add eggs and mayonnaise and mix. Serve over leafy green salads and over cold meats such as chicken and turkey and with fish.

To serve as an antipasto sauce, place 2 heaping tablespoons of the egg sauce on an individual serving plate and arrange 2 sardines in olive oil over it. Serve with lemon juice and a few drops of the sardine oil over top.

Chicken and Eggs for Breakfast

4 fresh eggs, beaten
Salt and pepper
2 tablespoons light cream or milk
2 tablespoons olive oil
2 tablespoons sweet butter

1/2 cup sliced or diced cooked chicken
2 tablespoons freshly grated Parmesan cheese

This dish may be made with chicken left over from poaching, broiling, or roasting. Season the eggs with salt and pepper. Stir the cream into the eggs. Combine olive oil and butter in a skillet and heat. Add the chicken and heat for 2 minutes. Pour eggs and cream over the chicken, shake the skillet, and stir. Cook for 2 to 3 minutes, to your taste. Sprinkle cheese over the top, cook for 1 minute longer, and spoon over toasted slices of Italian bread. Serves 2.

Tongue and Eggs for Breakfast

Make this in the same way as Chicken and Eggs for Breakfast (page 201), but substitute ½ cup thin strips of cooked tongue, or more according to your taste, for the chicken.

Tongue Salad

Shred 1 head of Boston lettuce into a bowl. Add 2 hard-cooked eggs per person, chopped. Make a salad dressing with olive oil, wine vinegar, fresh lemon juice, and salt and pepper. Add to eggs and lettuce and toss well. Arrange sliced tongue around each serving of salad. Round out the meal with toasted Italian bread, a ripe fresh pear with a wedge of Camembert, Brie or Bel Paese cheese, and a glass of good red Chianti.

Prosciutto–Tomato–Egg Sandwich

2 tablespoons olive oil	4 large eggs
¼ cup diced onion	2 tablespoons light cream
1 medium-sized firm tomato, sliced very thin	Salt and pepper
4 thin slices of prosciutto, diced	4 slices of Italian bread, toasted

Place olive oil in a skillet and heat. Add the onion and cook for 3 minutes. Add tomato slices and cook for 3 minutes. Add diced prosciutto and cook for 2 minutes. Beat the eggs with the cream and pour the mixture over all. Mix lightly and cook to taste. Add pepper, and taste carefully for salt, because prosciutto is salty. Spoon over the bread and enjoy caffè espresso with it. Serves 2.

Note: This is called a sandwich, but it makes a good breakfast dish. If you prefer, you may use diced bacon instead of prosciutto.

Eggplant–Cheese–Salami Sandwich

2 slices of eggplant	4 slices of Italian bread
All-purpose flour	2 slices of mozzarella cheese
2 tablespoons olive oil	4 slices of mortadella or salami
1 tablespoon butter	Salt and pepper

Sprinkle eggplant lightly with flour. Put olive oil and butter in a skillet and sauté the eggplant in it on both sides. Arrange 1 slice of bread on each of 2 serving plates. Place one of the sautéed eggplant slices on each bread slice. Add slices of cheese and mortadella. Sprinkle with salt and pepper to taste. Spoon oil and butter drippings over top. Top with remaining bread slices. Press well together. Enjoy the sandwich with a cappucino or a double caffè espresso. Serves 2.

Hot Prosciutto–Camembert Sandwich

From a large loaf of Italian bread cut 2 pieces 8 inches long, and slice them horizontally. Preheat oven to moderate (350° F.). Butter one side of each pair of bread slices. Place slices of prosciutto or mortadella over the buttered sides. Cover the meat with Camembert cheese, then cover the cheese with more prosciutto or mortadella. Put the upper pieces of bread on top and press together. Place in casserole or ovenware dish and bake for 10 minutes. Do not burn. Remove from oven and arrange on warm plates. Tuck a large napkin under your chin. This is a sandwich for a real hero. Serves 2.

A Hero Sandwich

2 tablespoons olive oil	Salt and pepper
2 tablespoons sweet butter	4 slices of prosciutto, mortadella
3 fresh eggs, beaten lightly	or salami
4 good-sized slices of fresh Italian	2 slices of Gorgonzola, Roque-
bread	fort, or blue cheese

Combine olive oil and butter in a skillet and heat. Add the eggs and cook to your taste. Spoon the eggs and pan juices over 2 slices of bread. Add salt and pepper to taste. Cover eggs with slices of prosciutto, then with the cheese slices. Top with the other slices of bread. Press together. Serves 2.

Tongue Hero Sandwich

Use a loaf of Italian bread. Stuff it with lettuce, tomato, mayonnaise mixed with chopped fresh parsley leaves, sliced tongue, thin slices of Swiss cheese, and salt and pepper to taste. Try a schooner of half beer and half ale with it.

Steak Sandwich

Slice about 1½ pounds of ends of beef tenderloin or sirloin into 1½- to 2-inch slices. Place in hand-grill broiler to make easy handling. Cook to taste. Season with salt and pepper. Make an open sandwich with toasted Italian bread. Spoon butter over the steak, place under broiler, and allow a few seconds for the butter to melt and drip over toast. Serves 2.

Steak with Egg Sandwich

2 slices of beef sirloin or tenderloin	4 fresh eggs, beaten
2 tablespoons olive oil	Pinch of salt
2 tablespoons fresh creamery butter	Pinch of black pepper
	4 slices of Italian bread, toasted

Have butcher cut for you slices that weigh 2 ounces each, or more. Place each slice between 2 sheets of wax paper and pound lightly. Put olive oil and butter in a large skillet and heat. Add the steaks and cook on each side for 1 minute, or a little more if you prefer. Add eggs, salt and pepper, and cook as desired. Arrange 2 pieces of the toast on a serving plate. Place steaks on the toast and spoon eggs over steaks and any pan juices on top. Cover with remaining toast. Press together. If the sandwich is served at dinner, complete the meal with a good red wine and caffè espresso. At breakfast, no *vino,* just a double caffè espresso. Serves 2.

Welsh Rabbit

Italian bread	2 egg yolks
1 pound aged Cheddar cheese or store cheese	1 tablespoon Worcestershire sauce
1 garlic clove, mashed	½ teaspoon prepared mustard
2 tablespoons fresh creamery butter	½ teaspoon salt
½ cup beer and ½ cup ale, or 1 cup of either	½ teaspoon cayenne pepper

Prepare a small basket of toasted Italian bread, cut into cubes. Cover and keep warm. Cut the cheese into even dice. Rub the garlic around the inside of an earthenware crock or skillet. Put in the butter, heat slightly, and add the cheese. When cheese is melted, add beer and/or ale gradually. Beat in the egg yolks, stirring constantly. Add Worcestershire, mustard, salt and cayenne pepper; bring to a boil. Taste for salt and add more if needed. Pour into buttered hot individual earthenware crocks or deep dishes. Serve the rabbit immediately while it is bubbling. Pass toast around to dip into the rabbit. Try a good bottle of California white wine. Serves 4.

Fonduta con Tartufo Bianco

(melted cheese with white truffles)

Italian bread
1 garlic clove, mashed
1 pound Fontina (a Piedmont cheese), diced
1 tablespoon butter
1 cup dry white wine

1 cup kirsch
1 tablespoon all-purpose flour
Pinch of freshly grated nutmeg
1 to 4 ounces white Italian truffles

Prepare a small basket of toasted Italian bread, cut into 1-inch cubes. Cover and keep warm. Rub the garlic around the inside of an earthenware crock or skillet. Place cheese and butter in the vessel, place it over low heat, and stir. When the cheese melts, add the wine and stir until mixture thickens and begins to cook. Add kirsch and stir well. Add the flour, cook for a few minutes, and add nutmeg. When boiling, pour into buttered individual earthenware crocks. Bring to the table immediately. Shave the truffles over the top of the *fonduta* (the more truffles your pocketbook can afford, the more delicious it will be). Dip the bread cubes into the *fonduta*. Enjoy with a bottle of Château d'Yquem. Serves 4.

10

Vegetables

WE, in this fertile America, can enjoy garden-fresh vegetables practically the year around—and that's when vegetables are best—right out of the ground. Of course, if fresh vegetables are not available, frozen or canned are acceptable.

Italian cookery makes wonderful use of a wide variety of vegetables too often ignored in many American homes. As a welcome change from peas, French fries, canned corn, etc., try some of the recipes that follow using artichokes, zucchini, eggplant, mushrooms, broccoli, etc. They can add real zest and palate-pleasing variety.

Baked Artichokes

6 fresh artichokes
1 garlic clove, mashed
8 fresh parsley sprigs, leaves only
1 teaspoon fresh or dried mint
1 slice of bread, without crust

7 tablespoons olive oil
3 tablespoons butter, melted
1/2 teaspoon salt
1/2 teaspoon black pepper

Trim off outer leaves of artichokes and cook artichokes in boiling water for about 40 minutes, or until leaves pull off easily. Lift artichokes from the water and drain.

While artichokes are cooking, chop together garlic, parsley, mint and bread. Add 6 tablespoons of the olive oil, the butter, salt and pepper. Mix well. Open the artichokes by spreading out leaves. Spoon dressing into and over artichokes. Place them in a small roasting pan with 1 inch of water on the bottom. Pour the remaining olive oil over artichokes and cover the pan with a piece of wet unwaxed white paper. Add another sheet of wet paper over the first layer. Now cover tightly with aluminum foil.

Preheat oven to moderate (350° F.). Put the pan on top of the stove and bring to a boil. Lower the heat and cook slowly for about 20 minutes. Place the pan in the oven and bake for 40 minutes. Remove from oven and remove foil and papers. Spoon the juices in the pan over artichokes. Cool. Serve with natural juices. Serve as an antipasto or a vegetable. Serves 6.

Fresh Asparagus

Wash 2 pounds fresh asparagus; this will allow about 6 stalks per serving. Cut off ends and scrape off scales. Tie each portion separately with string. Place in enough boiling salted water to cover the asparagus. Cook slowly for 10 to 12 minutes, or until just barely tender. Drain well immediately and place on a hot platter. Spoon melted butter and a sprinkle of grated Parmesan cheese over top. Place under broiler for 1 or 2 minutes. Serves 4 or 5.

The Italians also enjoy their asparagus with eggs fried in lots of fresh creamery butter as a main course. Place 2 eggs per serving in a well-buttered skillet. Cook to taste. Slide eggs and butter over a serving of hot asparagus and top with a heavy sprinkle of grated Parmesan cheese. Add a pinch each of salt and pepper. Place under a hot broiler for 1 minute. Serve with Italian garlic bread.

Asparagus is also good cold with Vinaigrette Dressing (page 51). This way it can be served as an antipasto, a vegetable, or a salad.

Fresh Green Beans

Wash 1 pound green beans, cut off ends, and slice lengthwise into halves. Cook slowly in boiling salted water for 15 to 20 minutes, or until tender. Drain. Place in a serving bowl and pour 1½ cups Marinara Sauce (page 94) over. Serve hot. Serves 4.

Green beans can also be served cold. Leave them whole after trimming. Cook in the usual way. While still warm after draining, pour Italian Salad Dressing (page 49) over them and add a chopped garlic clove and some fresh parsley. Cover for a few minutes, uncover, and allow to cool. Discard the garlic. Serve as an antipasto, a vegetable, or a salad.

Fresh Broccoli

Wash a bunch of fresh green broccoli (1½ to 2 pounds). Trim. Place, heads up, in 1 inch of boiling salted water in a saucepan. Water should just cover bottom of stems. Cover and cook for about 15 minutes, or until tender; do not overcook. Drain immediately, place on a warm platter, sprinkle with Parmesan cheese, and spoon hot melted butter over. Another way is to use a hot vinaigrette sauce with anchovies and garlic; or serve with a hollandaise sauce. Serves 4.

Broccoletti

1½ to 2 pounds broccoletti
   (tender young leaf broccoli)
¼ cup butter, melted
2 tablespoons olive oil

2 garlic cloves, mashed
1 teaspoon powdered mustard
Juice of 1 fresh lemon

Trim the broccoletti, wash it well, and cook it in boiling salted water for about 15 minutes. Drain.

Combine the butter, olive oil and garlic and stir well. Add mustard and lemon juice. Discard bits of garlic. Pour the sauce over warm broccoletti. Serves 4.

Brussels Sprouts

Soak 1 pound Brussels sprouts in cold water with a few drops of vinegar added for about 10 minutes. Trim stems and any wilted leaves. Cook, uncovered, in boiling salted water with the juice of ½ lemon added for 12 to 15 minutes. Do not overcook. Drain. Dress with melted butter blended with chopped parsley. Serves 4.

Savoy Cabbage

1 head of Savoy cabbage (1 to 1½
   pounds)
1 medium-sized onion, chopped
   fine
½ cup butter

6 thin slices of cooked or Genoa
   salami, chopped fine
Pinch each of salt and pepper
Pinch of grated nutmeg

Cut the head of cabbage into halves, remove the hard core, and trim. Cook in boiling salted water for 30 to 40 minutes, or until tender. Drain well and chop coarsely. Sauté the onion in the butter until medium brown. Add salami, salt, and pepper and nutmeg. Mix well and pour over chopped cabbage. Serve hot. Serves 4 or 5.

Baked Carrots

6 good-sized carrots
2 tablespoons olive oil
1/4 cup fresh creamery butter
2 teaspoons caraway seeds

1 teaspoon salt
1/2 teaspoon freshly ground black pepper
2 tablespoons chopped parsley

Preheat oven to hot (400° F.). Cut off ends and tops of carrots. Wash well but do not scrape or peel (to save the vitamins). Cut lengthwise into halves and then into cubes. Oil a baking dish with a little of the olive oil. Arrange carrots in the dish and add all other ingredients except parsley. Cover. Bake for 30 minutes. Uncover and bake for about 20 minutes more. Remove from oven and sprinkle the parsley over top. Serves 4 to 6.

Carrots au Gratin

6 good-sized carrots
3 tablespoons butter
1½ tablespoons all-purpose flour
1/2 cup hot milk

1 teaspoon dried orégano
Pinch each of salt and pepper
1/4 cup grated Parmesan cheese

Scrub the carrots well, but do not scrape or peel. Cut them into thin slices. Cook in boiling salted water for 15 minutes. Drain. Place in a shallow oven or broiler pan.

Melt the butter in a saucepan over low heat. Add flour, stirring constantly. Cook for 2 minutes. Remove from the heat and stir in the hot milk. Place back on heat and bring slowly to a boil, stirring. When smooth and thickened, add orégano and salt and pepper. Pour over carrots. Sprinkle cheese over top. Place under preheated broiler and cook for about 15 minutes, or until done. Serves 4.

Fresh Cauliflower

Wash 1 medium-sized head of cauliflower. Cut off the bottom of the stem, but leave some of the tender leaves attached. Put a small amount of liquid, half milk and half water, in a saucepan and add salt to taste. Bring to a boil and add the cauliflower. Cook the whole head, covered, for 15 to 20 minutes. Drain. Serve with melted butter and grated cheese. Serves 4.

Cauliflower is also good cold. Cook it and drain it. Add ½ teaspoon powdered mustard and the juice of 1 lemon to ½ cup Italian Salad Dressing (page 49). Mix well and spoon over the still warm drained cauliflower. Serve as an antipasto, a vegetable, or salad.

Breaded Cauliflower

1 medium-sized head of cauliflower	¼ cup milk
	¼ cup heavy cream
2 eggs, well beaten	2 tablespoons melted butter
½ cup sifted all-purpose flour	Olive oil for frying
Salt and pepper	Grated Parmesan cheese

Wash and trim the cauliflower. Break it into flowerets. Place eggs, flour, and salt and pepper to taste in a bowl. Combine milk, cream and butter and add to flour mixture to make a batter. Dip flowerets into batter. Fry the breaded flowerets, a few at a time, in the hot olive oil. Serve hot with a sprinkle of freshly grated Parmesan cheese. Serves 4.

Buttered Celery Root

1 pound celery root (celeriac)	Juice of 1 lemon
¼ cup melted butter	1 teaspoon prepared mustard
1 garlic clove, mashed	

Peel or scrape the root and cook in boiling salted water for about 20 minutes. Do not overcook. Drain well. Cut into ¼-inch strips. Put the butter in a bowl and stir in the garlic. Add lemon juice and mustard and mix well. Discard bits of garlic. Spoon mixture over warm celery root. Serves 4.

Fried Eggplant

1 medium-sized eggplant
Juice of 1 fresh lemon
½ cup seasoned bread crumbs
3 tablespoons olive oil
3 tablespoons butter

1 medium-sized onion, minced
1 medium-sized green or red pepper
Salt and black pepper

Peel the eggplant and cut it into cubes. Place cubes in a bowl, pour the lemon juice over, and mix well. Then sprinkle bread crumbs over eggplant and stir well to coat all cubes. Place olive oil and butter in a skillet and heat. Add the minced onion and cook until medium brown. Wash the pepper, discard cores and seeds, and cut it into thin strips. Add eggplant cubes and green-pepper strips to the skillet, cover, and cook slowly for 20 minutes. Uncover, season with salt and pepper to taste, and stir. Cook, uncovered, for 2 minutes longer. Serves 4.

Eggplant Parmigiana

2 medium-sized eggplants
½ cup sifted all-purpose flour
2 eggs, well beaten
½ cup sifted bread crumbs
1 teaspoon crumbled dried
    orégano
6 tablespoons olive oil
¼ cup butter, melted
1 teaspoon salt

1 teaspoon freshly ground black pepper
3 cups Marinara Sauce (page 94), warmed
½ cup freshly grated Parmesan cheese
Thin slices of mozzarella or Swiss cheese

Wash and dry the eggplants but do not peel them. Cut into ½-inch slices. Sprinkle slices lightly with salt, place them on brown paper, and let them drain for 30 minutes. Pat dry and sprinkle lightly with flour. Dip into beaten eggs. Mix bread crumbs with orégano, then dip eggplant slices into bread crumbs. Combine olive oil and butter in a skillet and heat. Add eggplant slices and sprinkle lightly with the salt and pepper. Sauté to a medium brown, about 5 minutes on each side.

Preheat oven to moderate (325° F.). Oil a baking pan and cover the bottom with a thin layer of the marinara sauce. Arrange browned eggplant slices on top of the sauce, and sprinkle them lightly with Parmesan cheese. Place a small slice of mozzarella or Swiss cheese on each eggplant slice. Spoon another thin layer of marinara sauce over all. Bake for 20 to 25 minutes. This dish is substantial enough to serve as an entrée. Serves 6.

Eggplant Livornese

1 eggplant (1½ pounds)
6 tablespoons olive oil
¼ cup sweet butter
2 ounces salt pork, diced
1 teaspoon minced fresh rosemary
1 teaspoon salt
½ teaspoon freshly ground black pepper

¼ pound Italian salami
½ pound mozzarella cheese
1 cup Marinara Sauce (page 94), hot
6 tablespoons freshly grated Parmesan cheese

Wash and peel the eggplant and cut it into ½-inch cubes. Preheat oven to moderate (375° F.). Combine olive oil and butter in an oven pan. Add eggplant cubes and sprinkle salt pork, rosemary, salt and pepper over top. Place in the oven, lower heat to slow (275° F.), and cook for 20 minutes. Remove casing from salami and cut it into very thin strips. Dice the mozzarella. Stir the eggplant, and add the salami, mozzarella and marinara sauce. Cook for 10 minutes longer. Before serving, sprinkle the Parmesan cheese over top. You may also serve this dish with poached eggs. Serves 4 or 5.

Belgian Endives au Gratin

1½ pounds Belgian endives
½ cup sweet butter
¼ cup all-purpose flour
Pinch each of salt and pepper
1 cup milk, warmed

2 tablespoons heavy cream
6 tablespoons sifted bread crumbs
6 tablespoons grated Parmesan cheese

Wash the endives, trim bottoms slightly, and cut lengthwise into halves. Cook in boiling salted water, just enough to cover, for 10 minutes. Drain well. Place in an oiled baking pan.

Preheat broiler. Melt the butter and add the flour, salt and pepper. Stir well, and add the milk and cream. Stir and cook until mixture thickens. Spoon over the endives. Sprinkle bread crumbs and cheese on top. Place under the broiler and cook slowly for about 10 minutes, or until a light-brown crust forms. Serves 4.

Finocchio au Gratin

2 good-sized finocchio (fennel)	¼ cup milk, warmed
2 medium-sized onions, peeled	2 tablespoons heavy cream
5 tablespoons butter	2 tablespoons sifted bread crumbs
2 tablespoons all-purpose flour	2 tablespoons grated Parmesan
Pinch each of salt and pepper	cheese

Trim the heads of finocchio, leaving about 2 inches of the stalk above the bulb. Cut into quarters. Cut the onions into quarters. Drop finocchio and onions into boiling salted water and cook for about 15 minutes, or until tender. Drain thoroughly. Place in an oven dish or casserole.

Preheat broiler. Melt the butter and add the flour, salt and pepper. Blend well. Add warmed milk and the cream and cook and stir until the sauce thickens. Pour sauce over the vegetables and sprinkle bread crumbs and cheese on top. Place under broiler for a few minutes, until a crust forms. Serves 4.

Jerusalem Artichokes

These artichokes are no relation to the real artichoke. This one is a very bland vegetable and therefore must have a dressing for flavor.

Wash 1½ pounds Jerusalem artichokes and cook in boiling salted water for 15 to 20 minutes. Test for doneness; do not cook them until they are too soft. Peel and slice thin. Place in a bowl 1 cup Italian Salad Dressing (page 49), 1 teaspoon minced shallots, chives or green onions, and salt to taste. Mix well, and spoon over artichokes. Serves 4.

Baked Mushrooms

12 medium-sized to large mushrooms
1 large garlic clove, mashed
6 fresh parsley sprigs, leaves only
2 chicken livers, chopped fine
2 tablespoons sifted seasoned
bread crumbs
½ medium-sized onion, chopped
fine

4 slices of prosciutto, chopped
fine
4 heaping tablespoons sour cream
¼ cup fresh creamery butter
Salt and pepper
3 tablespoons olive oil

Preheat oven to slow (300° F.). Wash the mushrooms and dry
thoroughly. Cut the stems completely out of the caps and chop the
stems fine. Chop garlic and parsley together and mix with the chicken
livers, bread crumbs, onion, prosciutto, and chopped mushroom
stems. Add sour cream and butter. Taste and correct the seasoning
if necessary. Stuff the mushroom caps with the mixture. Place caps,
stuffed side up, in an oiled baking dish. Sprinkle a few drops of olive
oil on top of each mushroom. Bake for about 45 minutes. Check for
cooking. Serve warm as an antipasto, spooning a little Italian Salad
Dressing (page 49) over top. Or serve hot with meat dishes, or as a
separate vegetable, or as a main course by itself. Serves 3 or 4.

Mushrooms Trifolati

¼ ounce dried Italian or French
mushrooms
1 pound medium-sized fresh
mushrooms
¼ cup olive oil
2 tablespoons fresh creamery
butter

1 large garlic clove, mashed
8 fresh parsley sprigs, leaves only
Pinch of freshly ground pepper
Pinch of salt
4 anchovy fillets, mashed with a
fork

Soak the dried mushrooms in lukewarm water to cover for 15
minutes. Drain and chop fine. Cut the fresh mushrooms into thin
slices. Place olive oil and butter in a skillet and heat. Add fresh and
dried mushrooms. Stir and cook for 3 minutes. Chop garlic and

parsley together and add to mushrooms with pepper and salt. Stir, cover, and cook slowly for 20 minutes. Remove from the heat and add mashed anchovies. Serve with veal scaloppine or sautéed sliced beef or a steak or filet mignon. These go very well in an omelet, too, and of course as a vegetable. Serves 4 to 6.

French-Fried Onions

Cut 2 large sweet onions into crosswise slices about ¼ inch thick. Soak the slices in about 2 cups milk for 30 minutes. Drain on brown paper. Dip into Fritter Batter (page 218). Heat deep fat to 360° F. on a frying thermometer. Fry the onions, a few slices at a time, until golden brown. Serves 4.

Fresh Garden Peas

¼ cup fresh creamery butter, melted
4 thin slices of prosciutto, minced
6 fresh parsley sprigs, leaves only, chopped fine

2 shallots or 2 whole fresh green scallions, diced
Pinch each of salt and freshly ground black pepper
2 pounds fresh peas in the pods

Combine in a skillet the butter, prosciutto, parsley, shallots, and salt and pepper; heat. Hull and wash the peas and place them in a saucepan. Add enough boiling salted water to cover. Add about half of the pods, well washed, to give more flavor. Cook for 15 to 20 minutes, until tender. Drain, and discard pods. Add the peas to butter-ham mixture. Cook slowly for 5 minutes, and serve. Fresh garden peas go exceptionally well with veal dishes. You may use frozen or canned peas if fresh are not available, of course. Serves 4.

Baked Potatoes with Sour Cream

2 large Idaho baking potatoes
¼ cup butter
½ cup sour cream
Pinch of freshly ground black pepper

Pinch of salt
12 leaves of fresh chives, minced, or 1 teaspoon dried chives
2 tablespoons freshly grated Parmesan cheese

Preheat oven to hot (400° F.). Wash the potatoes and wrap in foil. Bake potatoes for about 1 hour. When done, cut lengthwise into halves and scoop out the pulp without breaking the skins. Mash the pulp, add butter, sour cream, pepper, salt and chives, and mix well. Add more salt if necessary. Place mixture back in skins and sprinkle cheese over top. Return to oven until light brown. Serve immediately, very hot. Serves 4.

Roasted Potatoes

When preparing a roast in the oven, fix these too. About 1 hour before roast is done, wash and peel 1 or 2 potatoes per person. Cut into quarters. Place ¼ cup olive oil and 1 ounce salt pork, diced, in an oven dish. Heat, and add potatoes, 1 teaspoon minced fresh rosemary, and salt and pepper to taste. Put in oven and stir occasionally during baking. Serve with slices of the roast on the same plate. These are good with veal.

Mashed Potatoes alla Norma

5 large potatoes, peeled	4 slices of Italian salami, diced
1 garlic clove, split	¼ pound mozzarella cheese, diced
2 egg yolks	diced
Freshly ground black pepper	2 tablespoons heavy cream
½ cup butter	2 tablespoons grated pecorino or
1 cup hot milk	Parmesan cheese

Cover potatoes with boiling salted water. Add garlic to water. When potatoes are cooked, drain well and discard garlic. Preheat broiler. Beat the egg yolks with a sprinkle of black pepper. Mash potatoes with butter and milk and beat in egg yolks. Place in a buttered oven dish. Stir in diced salami and diced cheese. Spoon cream over top and sprinkle with the grated cheese. Place in the broiler 8 inches from the source of heat. Cook slowly until a light-brown crust appears. Serves 4.

Shoestring Potatoes

Peel 6 good-sized baking potatoes and place in ice water. When ready to cook, drain and dry well. Slice into thin strips. My first choice for deep frying is olive oil; second, fresh rendered veal suet; third, vegetable oil. Place 1½ quarts of oil or suet in a deep heavy-duty kettle. To get good frying results, do not skimp on oil. Preheat slowly to 370° F. on a frying thermometer. Drop 1 little piece of potato or bread into the hot oil to see if oil is hot enough to use; a 1-inch cube of bread should brown in 1 minute. When ready, lower potato slivers into hot oil. For best results, do not crowd. Cook them for 2 minutes. Remove, drain well, and place on brown paper to cool. When ready to serve, place potatoes back in hot oil and cook until golden brown. Again drain, and place on a hot platter. Sprinkle lightly with salt and freshly ground black pepper. Cover with a napkin. Serve immediately. Serves 6.

Note: Strain the cooking oil, cool it, and refrigerate for future use.

French Fries

Use the same procedure as for Shoestring Potatoes (see above), but cut the potatoes into slices 2 inches long and ¼ inch thick. Browning will take a little longer. Keep oil very hot and occasionally skim off burned potato scraps or any burnt slices.

Pumpkin Flowers

Use fresh male flowers of the pumpkin, green squash, zucchini, or any other of the squash family. Of course, it's nice if you live in the country and have your own vegetable garden. If not, your Italian vegetable dealer has them for sale. In choosing from your own garden, the male flowers can be determined by the longer stem. Leave the female to bear pumpkins. Pumpkin flowers are a delicacy usually enjoyed by the Italians and the French and not often known elsewhere. This is how we cook them.

Wash and dry 24 pumpkin flowers. Make Fritter Batter (page 218). Place 6 tablespoons olive oil in a skillet and heat it, but do not burn it. Dip flowers into the batter, then place them in the hot oil. Do not crowd flowers in the skillet. Cook over medium heat. When cooked, sprinkle a little salt over them, and serve them while they are still hot. Serve as an antipasto or vegetable. Serves 4 to 6.

FRITTER BATTER

¾ cup sifted all-purpose flour
½ cup milk
¼ cup heavy cream
2 eggs, well beaten

Pinch each of salt and pepper
1 teaspoon baking powder
1 teaspoon olive oil

Blend flour into milk. Add cream, eggs, salt, pepper, baking powder and olive oil. Mix well.

Steamed Spinach

Wash 1½ pounds fresh spinach very well several times to get all sand out of it. (As this is quite a chore, you can buy the packages of already washed spinach in your supermarket. Rinse that once.) Drain well. Steam the spinach, covered, in very little water for about 15 minutes. Drain well, squeeze dry, and chop fine. Place in a bowl or on a platter and spoon 3 tablespoons melted creamery butter over top and mix. Or spoon over the spinach a mixture of olive oil, lemon juice, mashed garlic, and salt and pepper to taste. Serves 4.

Spinach Sauté

1 pound fresh spinach
2 tablespoons olive oil
¼ cup fresh creamery butter

1 medium-sized onion, diced
Pinch each of salt and freshly
ground black pepper

Wash the spinach thoroughly several times to make sure the sand is out of it; or buy prewashed spinach at the supermarket, and rinse it again. Drain thoroughly. Place olive oil and butter in a large skillet. Add onion and sauté for 3 minutes. Add spinach, salt and pepper; stir and cover. Cook for about 15 minutes, or until just tender. Serves 3.

Baked Acorn Squash

2 acorn squashes
¼ cup butter

2 teaspoons olive oil
Salt and pepper

Preheat oven to moderate (325° F.). Wash and dry the squashes and cut them lengthwise into halves. Scoop out the seeds. Mix butter, olive oil, and salt and pepper to taste. Rub some of the mixture over the cut surfaces of the squash halves and put some of the remainder in each squash hollow. Place the halves in a baking pan and add about 1 inch of water to bottom of pan. Bake for about 1 hour, or until done. Serves 4.

Note: You can cook pumpkin in the same way. Cut it into large squares and spread the butter mixture over all surfaces.

Baked Tomatoes

8 large ripe tomatoes
1/4 cup butter, melted
1 teaspoon dried orégano

1/4 cup bread crumbs
Salt and pepper

Cut off the tops of tomatoes and scoop a little out of the centers, making a well. Mix butter, orégano, bread crumbs, and salt and pepper to taste. Place tomatoes in an oiled baking pan. Fill the well in each tomato with some of the butter mixture. Bake for about 12 minutes. Serves 8.

Broiled Tomatoes

4 good-sized ripe tomatoes
1/4 cup bread crumbs
2 tablespoons olive oil

Pinch each of salt and black
  pepper
1 teaspoon dried orégano

Cut the tomatoes into halves and scoop out a little from each cut side. Mix bread crumbs, olive oil, salt, pepper and orégano together. Spread over tomatoes and fill the little hollow with the crumb mixture. Arrange in an oiled broiler pan. Place under a broiler with low heat for 15 minutes. Serves 4.

Fried Zucchini

3 medium-sized zucchini
Salt and pepper
1/3 cup sifted all-purpose flour
1/2 cup olive oil

2 garlic cloves, mashed
1 tablespoon minced fresh sage
1/4 cup wine vinegar

Wash zucchini, cut lengthwise into halves, and then into ¼-inch slices. Mix salt and pepper into the flour and then dip each zucchini slice into the seasoned flour. Shake off any excess. Place olive oil and garlic in a skillet and heat. Do not burn either oil or garlic. Sauté some zucchini slices in the hot oil until brown. Place the browned slices on a warm platter until all are fried. Discard bits of garlic. Continue to fry the slices, a few at a time, until all are done. As each batch is finished, put it aside on the warm platter. When all are done, return them to the warm skillet and add sage and wine vinegar to oil drippings. Heat and spoon over the zucchini. Cover pan for a few minutes. Serve on a warm platter as an antipasto or vegetable. Serves 3 or 4.

Stuffed Zucchini

4 medium-sized zucchini	½ teaspoon freshly ground black
2 tablespoons olive oil	pepper
¼ cup butter	1 teaspoon crumbled dried rose-
2 medium-sized onions, minced	mary
1 tiny garlic clove, mashed	3 slices of bread
8 parsley sprigs, leaves only	½ cup milk
¼ pound Italian sweet sausage or	¼ cup grated Parmesan cheese
3 chicken livers	3 tablespoons Italian Salad Dress-
½ pound beef, chopped	ing (page 49)
½ teaspoon salt	

Buy zucchini that are about 1½ inches thick and 4 to 5 inches long. Do not buy them too big or they may be old and tough. Wash and dry them and cut off the stems. Parboil them whole in boiling salted water for about 8 minutes. Drain and cool enough to handle. Cut zucchini lengthwise into halves. Scoop out some of the pulp and set aside. Place olive oil and butter in a skillet and heat. Add minced onions. Chop garlic and parsley together and add to onions. Sauté for 3 minutes. If using the sausage, remove the casing and chop the meat; if using chicken livers, chop them fine. Add beef, sausage or chicken livers, salt, pepper and rosemary. Cook for 15 minutes. Remove from the heat.

Preheat oven to moderate (325° F.). Soak the bread in the milk until milk is all absorbed. Squeeze out the liquid and shred the bread. Add grated cheese, shredded bread, and reserved zucchini pulp to the skillet. Blend well. Stuff zucchini with the mixture. Oil a baking pan with a mixture of oil and butter. Arrange zucchini in the pan and sprinkle a few drops of olive oil over top. Bake for 20 to 25 minutes. When cooked, spoon about 1 teaspoon of the salad dressing over each warm zucchini half. Serve with the meat course, or as an antipasto. Serves 4.

11 🥀

Desserts—Fruits, Sweets, Pastries and Caffè Espresso

CHEESE tops off an Italian dinner beautifully. A nice soft Brie or Camembert, a Taleggio, Certosino, or Stracchino di Milano, served with crisp romaine lettuce, is a treat. With my big red or yellow apple, I like Gorgonzola or Roquefort, but with a ripe fresh pear Bel Paese is delightful. With a heel or two of Italian bread, a bit of Provolone, a Gruyère, aged Parmesan or Fontina, is delicious.

No meal is complete for me without a bowl of fresh fruits—a colorful fitting finale. Select the finest fruits in season and arrange them attractively.

In the pages that follow, you will find zabaglione, cheeescake, cannoli, zeppole and other justly famous Italian sweets. Many of them are fairly easy to make. Try a few.

Baked Apples in Burgundy

4 large red apples, cored	¼ cup red Burgundy
2 tablespoons butter, softened	1 cinnamon stick
4 teaspoons sugar	4 lemon slices

Place apples in a saucepan and cover with water. Cover the saucepan and boil the apples for 5 minutes. Preheat oven to moderate (375° F.). Transfer apples to a small oven dish, just large enough to hold the apples. Make a mixture of the butter, sugar and wine. Pour the mixture into the hollows and over the apples. Pour a few tablespoons hot water into the bottom of the dish. Break up the cinnamon stick and add it to the dish. Add lemon slices. Bake for about 40 minutes, basting several times during baking. Serves 4.

Fresh Strawberries or Raspberries with Ricotta

½ pound fresh ricotta
1 quart fresh strawberries or raspberries
2 tablespoons granulated raw sugar

1 banana, sliced thin
6 tablespoons banana cordial

Drain the ricotta for 15 minutes. Wash the strawberries or raspberries, clean and hull them, and drain until quite dry. Place ricotta on a deep serving plate. Add the berries, sugar (use regular sugar if raw is not available) and banana slices and mix gently. Spoon banana cordial over top. Serve with ladyfingers or Bugie (page 231). Serves 4.

Coffee Ice Cream

½ cup very strong caffè espresso
2 cups milk, scalded
2 egg yolks, well beaten
2 whole eggs, well beaten
3 tablespoons sugar

¼ cup sifted all-purpose flour
Pinch of salt
1 cup heavy cream, whipped
3 tablespoons coffee cordial

Make the coffee; it should be almost an essence of coffee. Add scalded milk to hot coffee. Mix egg yolks and whole eggs with the sugar, flour and salt. Stir well. Add coffee-milk gradually to eggs, stirring. Cook over hot water for 10 to 12 minutes, or until mixture thickens. Remove from the heat and cool. Then fold in the whipped cream and stir in the cordial. Freeze. Makes about 1½ quarts.

Orange and Lemon Ice

2 cups cold water
½ cup granulated sugar
1 teaspoon grated lemon rind
½ cup fresh lemon juice

1 cup fresh orange juice
6 tablespoons Grand Marnier, Cointreau or Triple Sec

Boil the water, sugar and lemon rind together for about 5 minutes. Cool. Add lemon and orange juice; mix well. Place in the freezer for about 1½ hours. Remove from freezer and beat in 2 tablespoons of the liqueur. Return to the freezer until ready to serve. When ready, spoon into wineglasses and float 1 tablespoon of the liqueur over each glass; float, do not mix. Serves 4.

Espresso Granita

(coffee ice)

4 cups extrastrong caffè espresso	3 tablespoons granulated raw sugar
Rind of ½ orange	
Rind of ½ lemon	½ cup imported apricot brandy

Make the coffee. Cut the rinds into very thin slivers. Pour the hot coffee over them, cover, and let steep for about 15 minutes. Add the sugar (use regular sugar if raw sugar is not available). Stir well. Freeze for about 1½ hours. Remove from freezer before the ice is solid and beat in ¼ cup of the apricot brandy. Return to freezer. When ready to serve, spoon into wineglasses and float 1 tablespoon of the apricot brandy over each serving; float, do not stir. Delicious! Serves 4.

Crème de Menthe Frappé

4 cups water	¾ cup green crème de menthe, approximately
1½ cups sugar	
1 cup fresh lemon juice	

Make a syrup by boiling the water and sugar together for about 5 minutes. Remove from the heat and cool. Add lemon juice and stir. Add 5 tablespoons of the crème de menthe and freeze for about 2 hours. Then stir well, and return to freezer. When ready to serve, spoon into small wineglasses or cocktail glasses and float 1 tablespoon (or more) crème de menthe on top. Makes about 1 quart.

Neapolitan Delight

4 good-sized fresh peaches	¼ cup lemon juice
2 cups sugar	¾ cup apricot brandy
4 cups orange juice	

Peel the fresh peaches, cut into halves, and remove pits. Then cut into small cubes. (Or use 8 canned-peach halves.) Add the sugar and stir well. Add orange and lemon juice, stir, then add 1/4 cup of the apricot brandy. Mix all ingredients well and freeze. Serve with 1 tablespoon of apricot brandy floated on top. (Or use more of the liqueur if you wish.) Serves 8.

Biscuit Tortoni

1/2 cup crushed macaroons	2 cups heavy cream
1/2 cup crushed toasted almonds	3 tablespoons dark rum
1/4 cup confectioners' sugar	3 or 4 maraschino cherries

Mix the macaroons, most of the almonds, the sugar and 1 cup of the cream together. Whip the remaining cream and fold it and the rum into the first mixture, stirring gently. Spoon the mixture into paper muffin cups and freeze. After about 2 hours sprinkle the tops with remaining crushed almonds. Place 1/2 cherry in the center of each cup for decoration. Return to freezer. Fills 6 to 8 paper cups.

Spumoni di Leone

4 egg yolks	1/4 cup diced mixed candied fruits
2 tablespoons cold water	1 cup heavy cream, whipped
1/4 cup granulated sugar	Chocolate Ice Cream (page 226)
1/2 cup Marsala	

Beat egg yolks well. Add the water, then the sugar, then the wine. Beat well. Place in the top part of a double boiler over hot water and cook over low heat, beating all the time, until mixture thickens. Remove from the heat and cool. When cool, stir in candied fruits and fold in the cream. Pour into freezer tray.

Make chocolate ice cream. When cool, spoon it over the first layer in the freezer tray. Freeze. When ready to serve, cut spumoni on a slant from one side of pan to the other, making triangular-shaped pieces. Serve each wedge of spumoni on a small paper doily. Serves 7 or 8.

CHOCOLATE ICE CREAM

¼ cup sugar
Pinch of salt
1 egg
1 teaspoon all-purpose flour

½ cup milk, scalded
1 ounce (1 square) unsweetened
   chocolate
1 cup heavy cream, whipped

Mix sugar, salt, egg and flour together. Slowly add hot milk. Stir well. Melt chocolate over hot water, add to mixture, and stir well. Cool the mixture. When cool, fold in whipped cream.

Zabaglione

8 large egg yolks
¼ cup granulated raw sugar
1 cup Marsala

2 tablespoons brandy
1 tablespoon chilled water

Place egg yolks and sugar in the top part of a double boiler. (Use regular sugar if raw sugar is not available.) Beat well with egg beater or wire whisk. Add wine and brandy and beat well. Add the water and beat well. Place the pan over hot water and beat or stir over hot water until mixture thickens; do not let it boil. Serve in wineglasses immediately. Serves 4.

ZABAGLIONE DELIGHT

For 4 servings, prepare Zabaglione (above), using ¾ cup Marsala and apricot brandy instead of brandy. Place a slice of panettone or good spongecake on a dessert plate. Douse with apricot brandy to your taste, and spoon the zabaglione over it. Serve warm.

COLD PEARS IN ZABAGLIONE

For 4 servings, prepare Zabaglione (above). Peel 4 medium pears. Place in a saucepan and cover with cold water. Add 2 lemon slices and 1 teaspoon sugar; cook until tender; do not overcook. Drain.

Place each pear in an individual serving dish and pour zabaglione over the pears. Cool and refrigerate until ready to serve.

ZUPPA INGLESE

Zabaglione (page 226)
½ cup heavy cream, whipped
4 thin slices of poundcake
2 tablespoons rum

2 tablespoons broken or shaved
   chocolate pieces
Apricot brandy

Prepare zabaglione using ¾ cup Marsala and 2 tablespoons apricot brandy instead of brandy. Fold in the whipped cream. Place a slice of poundcake on each individual serving dish. Sprinkle rum over the cake. Spoon zabaglione and cream over the cake. Scatter the chocolate on top. Refrigerate for 1 hour. When ready to serve, sprinkle with apricot brandy. Serves 4.

Zabaglione Luisa

4 fresh egg yolks
1 egg white
2 tablespoons granulated raw
   sugar
½ cup Marsala
2 tablespoons Campari Bitters

2 tablespoons brandy
1 tablespoon chilled water
Rind of ¼ orange (zest)
Rind of ¼ lemon (zest)
2 fresh peaches

Place egg yolks, egg white and sugar in the top part of a double boiler. (Use regular sugar if raw sugar is not available.) Beat well with an egg beater or wire whisk. Add wine, bitters and brandy and beat well. Add the water and beat well. Cut the orange and lemon rinds into thin slivers and add to the mixture. Place the pan over hot water and beat or stir over hot water until mixture thickens; do not let it boil. Peel and pit the peaches and cut into slices. (Or use well-thawed frozen sliced peaches.) Arrange the peach slices at the bottom of large wineglasses. Pour zabaglione over the peaches and serve immediately. Serves 2.

Crêpes Suzette

CRÊPES

1 cup water
1 cup milk
2 cups sifted all-purpose flour
4 egg yolks, beaten

¼ cup melted butter
2 tablespoons Grand Marnier
Pinch of salt
Butter and olive oil for frying

Mix first 7 ingredients well and refrigerate for at least 2 hours or overnight. When ready to cook, place a small amount of butter and olive oil in a 6-inch skillet. Roll and turn skillet until sides are covered lightly with oil. Spoon in enough batter to cover bottom of pan lightly. Cook until golden brown (do not burn), then turn and quickly cook the other side. When crêpe is cooked, place on a warm plate and cover. Continue until all crêpes are made.

SUZETTE SAUCE

24 sugar lumps
4 whole oranges
2 whole lemons
4 good-sized strips of orange rind
4 good-sized strips of lemon rind

¾ cup cold butter
5 tablespoons Grand Marnier
3 tablespoons yellow Chartreuse
6 tablespoons Cognac

Have everything ready before starting to prepare the sauce. Rub all sides of 12 lumps of sugar well over the skins of the oranges to absorb the orange oil. Rub the other 12 lumps of sugar over the lemons. Then cut the oranges into halves. Pound or mash the flavored sugar lumps on a board. Cut the strips of orange and lemon rind (zest) into very thin slivers. Place the cold butter, slivers of lemon and orange rind and the mashed sugar in the bottom pan of a chafing dish. Then take 1 orange half at a time in the left hand. Holding the orange over the pan, with the right hand use a fork to extract the orange juice; about ¾ cup will be squeezed from the oranges. Mix the juice well into the butter mixture. Add 2 tablespoons of the Grand Marnier.

Light the flame under the pan; let the pan warm and then place

4 crêpes in it. Turn and baste. Then fold each in half, baste again, and fold each into a triangle. Move the triangles to the edge of the pan. Heat the rest of the crêpes in the same way, as quickly as possible. Then shake pan and add the rest of the Grand Marnier, the Chartreuse and the Cognac. Be careful to shield your face from pan. Ignite the sauce, shake the pan, and baste the crêpes. Serve immediately, with all the sauce spooned over the crêpes. Enjoy a pony of Cognac or Grand Marnier or Chartreuse with your delicious crêpes Suzette. Serves 4 to 6.

Leone's Cheesecake

CRUST

10 tablespoons sifted all-purpose flour	3 tablespoons sugar
	6 tablespoons sweet butter
1 egg	

Preheat oven to slow (300° F.). Lightly oil the bottom of a 10-inch springform pan 3 inches high with a little olive oil. Mix flour, egg, sugar and butter to make a dough. Roll out on a floured board into a sheet 1/4 inch thick and shape into 10-inch circle. Bake the crust on the bottom of the pan for about 15 minutes. Cool.

FILLING

1 pound ricotta	2 whole eggs, very well beaten
1/2 pound cream cheese	4 egg whites
1/4 cup sifted all-purpose flour	3/4 cup sugar
1/2 teaspoon salt	3/4 cup crushed pineapple, drained
1/2 teaspoon vanilla extract	
Grated rind of 1/2 lemon	

While bottom crust is baking and cooling, make the filling. Drain the ricotta for 15 minutes. Place cheeses, flour, salt, vanilla, grated lemon rind and whole eggs in a mixer and mix well. Whip egg whites well with the sugar and fold into the cheese mixture.

Put the sides of the pan around the cooled bottom and crust and oil the sides. Spread the pineapple over the cooled crust and pour the cheese mixture over the pineapple. Set the cake pan in a pan of hot water and put in the oven, still at slow (300° F.). Bake for about 45 minutes. Allow to cool and refrigerate. Serves 8.

Italian Crêpes with Marsala

When you are making crêpes for Cannelloni (page 81), make some extra. Soak the crêpes in Marsala or brush well on both sides with the wine. Place 1 heaping tablespoon of jelly in the center of each crêpe and fold crêpe over twice. Preheat broiler. Use a shallow broiler pan. Arrange the rolled crêpes on the pan and sprinkle well with more Marsala. Broil under low heat for about 2 minutes. Remove from broiler and sprinkle with a few drops of Grand Marnier, Cointreau or Triple Sec. Serve immediately as dessert.

Cannoli

14 tablespoons sifted confectioners' sugar
2 tablespoons butter
1 egg
1 cup sifted all-purpose flour
3 tablespoons cream sherry
1 tablespoon wine vinegar
Fat for deep frying (half olive oil and half vegetable shortening)

1 pound ricotta
1/4 pound diced mixed candied fruits
1 teaspoon vanilla extract
1/2 teaspoon ground cinnamon
1 tablespoon heavy cream, or more

Mix together 2 tablespoons of the sugar, the butter, egg, flour, sherry and vinegar. If too stiff, add a little water. Let dough stand at room temperature for about 30 minutes. Cut dough into pieces about the size of a walnut. Roll out each piece to an oval shape. Wrap each around an oiled wooden stick about 1 inch in diameter and 6 inches long. Seal the edge with a drop of cold water. Heat the fat to 365° F. on a frying thermometer. Gently remove the stick and drop each rolled wafer into the fat. Fry until golden brown, lift out carefully, drain, and place on a cake rack to cool.

Drain the ricotta. Be sure it is cold and dry, but not iced. Mix it with the remaining confectioners' sugar, the candied fruits, vanilla, cinnamon and cream. If the mixture is too thick, add a little more cream. Mix well. Use to fill the cooled cannoli. Refrigerate until ready to serve. Serves 12.

Bugie

4 cups sifted all-purpose flour
1/4 cup granulated sugar
Pinch of salt
1 teaspoon baking powder
1 cup milk
7 egg yolks, beaten
1/2 teaspoon olive oil

3 tablespoons butter, melted
2 tablespoons Jamaica rum
2 tablespoons anisette
1 tablespoon vanilla extract
Fat for deep frying (half olive oil
    and half vegetable shortening)
Confectioners' sugar

Mix the first four ingredients. Combine milk, egg yolks, 1/2 teaspoon olive oil and the butter and mix into dry ingredients. Add rum, anisette and vanilla, mixing well. Let dough stand at room temperature for about 30 minutes. Roll out the dough on a floured board into a thin sheet. Cut into strips about 1 inch wide and 6 inches long. Tie each strip gently into a knot.

Fill a 2-quart saucepan about half full of the cooking oil and heat it. Lower the heat to keep oil at a steady temperature (365° to 370° F. on a frying thermometer). Lower several pastries at a time into the hot oil and cook until golden brown. Be sure not to burn them or to crowd too many in the pan. Lift from the oil, place on brown paper, and sprinkle with confectioners' sugar. Add more oil if necessary. When finished, strain oil through a fine wire sieve or cloth and set aside for further use. Serve bugie on a large platter. Makes about 8 dozen.

Zeppole di San Giuseppe

1 cup water
6 tablespoons vegetable shortening
2 tablespoons butter
3/4 cup sifted all-purpose flour
Pinch of salt
5 eggs
1 tablespoon sugar

1 heaping teaspoon grated orange
    rind
1 teaspoon orange liqueur
Fat for deep frying (half olive oil
    and half vegetable shortening)
Confectioners' sugar
Filling for Zeppole (page 232)

Put water, vegetable shortening and butter in a saucepan and heat until butter and shortening are melted. Add flour and salt all at once, stirring vigorously. Cook over low heat for about 10 minutes. Do not stop stirring until you remove mixture from the heat. Remove saucepan from the heat and add the eggs, one at a time, stirring constantly until mixture is smooth. Add sugar, grated rind and orange liqueur; mix well.

You will need a pastry bag about 12 inches long with a plain round tip. Fill the pastry bag with the dough. Cut a sheet of pastry paper or airmail letter paper to fit the top of the saucepan you are using to cook the pastries. Press out the dough onto the paper, making about 4 rings, each about 1½ inches in diameter.

Heat olive oil and shortening to 350° F. on a frying thermometer. Gently turn the paper upside down into the boiling oil. After ½ minute, lift out the paper. Cook zeppole until golden brown, turning occasionally. Place on brown paper to drain. Continue until all are cooked. Sprinkle a little confectioners' sugar on top. When ready to serve, fill centers with filling. Makes about 28. Serve 2 or 3 to each person.

FILLING FOR ZEPPOLE

1 cup ricotta	2 tablespoons broken chocolate
3 tablespoons sugar	bits
2½ tablespoons diced mixed candied fruits	2 tablespoons Jamaica rum
	1 cup heavy cream, whipped

Drain the cheese for 15 minutes, then mix well with the sugar. Add fruits and chocolate; mix. Add rum and fold in whipped cream. Refrigerate until ready to serve. Makes enough filling for 28 zeppole.

Caffè Espresso

This is made from a finely ground Italian roasted coffee, best prepared in a steam espresso machine, or failing that, according to instructions on the package of coffee. Serve it in a glass with a twist each of lemon and orange peel.

Caffè Romano Caldo

Fill the espresso coffee basket with ground coffee. For each serving pour 2 tablespoons of a good brandy over the ground coffee. Let it stand for 10 minutes. Then make the coffee.

Caffè Espresso Romano Frappé

Prepare caffè espresso for two. When it is ready, put ¼ cup brandy, a twist of each of lemon and orange peel, 2 lumps of sugar, and the coffee in a shaker full of ice. Shake it well. Serve in glasses.

Caffè Espresso Fiorentino

Fill the espresso coffee basket with ground coffee. For each serving pour 2 tablespoons anisette over the ground coffee. Let it stand for 10 minutes. Then make the coffee. Serve the finished coffee in tulip Champagne glasses with a dash of anisette over the top.

Cappucino

I have been told that this drink got its name from the coffee-colored habits of Italian monks. Cappucino is usually made in the regular espresso machine. However, it can be made by home methods. Prepare caffè espresso. Measure ½ cup milk for each serving and bring it to the boiling point. Blend into the coffee and add sugar to taste. Sprinkle a pinch of ground cinnamon and a pinch of grated chocolate over the top of each serving.

Caffè Espresso al Diavolo

Warm a good-sized silver bowl. Place 8 sugar cubes in the bowl and mash lightly. Cut the rinds of 1 orange and 1 lemon (zest) into thin slivers and add to the sugar. Cut the peeled orange and lemon into quarters and stick with about 24 whole cloves altogether. Add fruit pieces to sugar with 2 cinnamon sticks. Add ½ cup good brandy and ¼ cup Grand Marnier. Make caffè espresso for eight. Take some of the mashed sugar from the bowl in a ladle. Add a little of the liqueur to the sugar. Lower to near bottom of bowl and ignite the liqueur in the ladle. This will light the entire bowl. Keep stirring slowly with the ladle and slowly pour the caffè espresso into the bowl while the liqueurs are still burning. Ladle into fancy wineglasses and serve. Serves 8.

Irish Coffee with Caffè Espresso

The Irish and the Italians get together. This blend can be called a successful marriage, just like my own 39 years of happiness with a wonderful Irish girl named Mary Sullivan. Prepare caffè espresso. Pour the coffee into warm goblets. To each glass add 1 teaspoon granulated sugar, 2 tablespoons Irish whiskey, 1 tablespoon Italian brandy, and 1 tablespoon anisette. Top each goblet with a spoon of cold whipped cream.

Index